# THE AMERICAN POLITICS OF FRENCH THEORY

Derrida, Deleuze, Guattari, and Foucault in Translation

# The American Politics of French Theory

*Derrida, Deleuze, Guattari, and Foucault in Translation*

JASON DEMERS

UNIVERSITY OF TORONTO PRESS
Toronto Buffalo London

© University of Toronto Press 2018
Toronto Buffalo London
utorontopress.com


ISBN 978-1-4875-0448-9


Cultural Spaces

---

**Library and Archives Canada Cataloguing in Publication**

Demers, Jason, 1979–, author
The American politics of French theory : Derrida, Deleuze, Guattari, and Foucault
in translation / Jason Demers.

(Cultural spaces)
Includes bibliographical references and index.
ISBN 978-1-4875-0448-9 (hardcover)

1. Translating and interpreting – Political aspects – United States.   2. Translating
and interpreting – Philosophy.   I. Title.   II. Series: Cultural spaces

P306.97.P65D46 2019        418'.02        C2018-904202-8

---

This book has been published with the help of a grant from the Federation for
the Humanities and Social Sciences, through the Awards to Scholarly Publications
Program, using funds provided by the Social Sciences and Humanities Research
Council of Canada.

University of Toronto Press acknowledges the financial assistance to its publishing
program of the Canada Council for the Arts and the Ontario Arts Council, an agency
of the Government of Ontario.

Canada Council    Conseil des Arts
for the Arts      du Canada

ONTARIO ARTS COUNCIL
CONSEIL DES ARTS DE L'ONTARIO
an Ontario government agency
un organisme du gouvernement de l'Ontario

Funded by the    Financé par le
Government    gouvernement
of Canada    du Canada

# Contents

# Figures

# Acknowledgments

This project came together thanks to the assistance and support of a great number of people. Barbara Godard was a dear friend, and a careful early reader of this project when it was in its formative stages; every encounter with Barbara was an event. Conversations with Neil Smith were spirited; his excitement about this project kept me going at a difficult juncture. Although the passing of these two scholars is a tremendous loss for their respective fields, their impact will continue to be felt in the people and texts they inspire. A tremendous amount of thanks must go out to Darren Gobert, Art Redding, Marcus Boon, Gary Genosko, Garry Sherbert, Martin Breaugh, and Tom Loebel for being generous readers of various drafts as this project was coming together. I also received helpful feedback on working drafts at conferences of the Association of Canadian College and University Teachers of English, the Canadian Association of American Studies, the Canadian Comparative Literature Association, and the Cultural Studies Association. The enthusiasm and support of Vanessa Mathews, Troni Grande, Jean-Jacques Demers, and Patricia Demers was unwavering throughout. Mark Thompson, acquisitions editor at the University of Toronto Press, and his predecessor, Siobhan McMenemy, backed this project and were helpful guides throughout the editing process. Production editor Christine Robertson and freelance copy-editor Barbara Tessman also helped bring this project to fruition. Thanks to Denis Hollier, Fredric Jameson, Jean-Jacques Lebel, Sylvère Lotringer, and John Rajchman for discussing their participation in, and perceptions of, the transatlantic travels of theory.

The research for this project would not have been possible without funds from the Social Sciences and Humanities Research Council (SSHRC), the Pierre Elliott Trudeau Fellowship at York University, research and fieldwork cost funds from CUPE 3903, and a Humanities Research Institute Fellowship at the University of Regina. Together, these funds allowed me to consult the

William S. Burroughs collection at Ohio State University; the Allen Ginsberg collections at Columbia and Stanford Universities; the Downtown collection at New York University; the City Lights and Lawrence Ferlinghetti collections at University of California Berkeley; the Michel Foucault, Groupe d'information sur les prisons, and Félix Guattari collections at l'Institut Mémoires de L'Édition Contemporaine (IMEC); and La Contemporaine's political and social history archives at l'Université de Paris Nanterre. That the unpredictable twists and turns encountered in these archives felt at eve ry juncture seamless is testament to the patience and resourcefulness of the archivists and staff who facilitated my research. Special thanks to José Ruiz-Funes at IMEC for helping me make connections beyond the archives.

Portions of this book were first published, in different form, as "An American Excursion: Deleuze and Guattari from New York to Chicago," *Theory and Event*, vol. 14, no. 1, 2011; "Prison Liberation by Association: Michel Foucault and the George Jackson Atlantic," *Atlantic Studies*, vol. 13, no. 2, 2016; "The Radicle Semiotics of Semiotext(e)," *Semiotic Review of Books*, vol. 19, no. 2, 2010; and "Taking Deleuze in the Middle, or, Doing Intellectual History by the Letter," *Trans/acting Culture, Writing, and Memory: Essays in Honour of Barbara Godard*, edited by Eva C. Karpinski et al., Wilfrid Laurier University Press, 2013.

# Abbreviations

| | |
|---|---|
| APL | Agence de presse libération |
| BPP | Black Panther Party |
| BwO | Body without Organs |
| CORE | Congress on Racial Equality |
| DNC | Democratic National Convention |
| FSM | Free Speech Movement |
| GIP | Groupe d'information sur les prisons |
| GP | Gauche prolétarienne |
| IDA | Institute for Defense Analyses |
| LNS | Liberation News Service |
| PCF | Parti communiste français |
| SAS | Students' Afro-American Society |
| SDS | Students for a Democratic Society |
| SNCC | Student Non-violent Coordinating Committee |
| SRI | Secours rouge international |
| UAW/MF | Up Against the Wall Motherfucker |
| UPS | Underground Press Syndicate |
| WUO | Weather Underground Organization |
| YIPPIE | Youth International Party |

# THE AMERICAN POLITICS OF FRENCH THEORY

Derrida, Deleuze, Guattari, and Foucault in Translation

# Introduction: Margins, Rhizomes, Relays, and Conversation – Thinking Translation Associatively

This book considers what it looks like to think the translation of French theory associatively, as a set of multidirectional relations between French thinkers and cultural and political movements and icons across the Atlantic. Rather than understanding a set of French thinkers as "post-structuralism" or "French theory" *avant-la lettre*, I explore what it means to understand these thinkers within the context of the social movements that animate them, and that they help to animate in turn. What is a movement, after all, but a mass of associations between people, groups, places, ideas, and moments in time? Movements are translators that are always themselves in translation.

While the ability to speak a metalanguage demonstrates scholarly competency (each thinker, text, and concept has its place within one or several of the codes that scholars use to speak with one another in journals, at conferences, and in the hallway), scholarly inquiry itself operates by association. One text or topic leads to the next via the scanning of texts and bibliographies or by way of (code-driven) conversations with colleagues.[1] Sometimes the associative movement from one idea, text, or phenomenon to the next moves systematically, but often the movement itself (and not just our "best ideas") is generated by accident: the unexpected discovery of a course-changing book in the

---

1 I should also mention here the advantages or disadvantages afforded by affiliation with this or that school or centre, let alone the fact of official affiliation itself, where the contemporary phenomenon of widespread precarity often means a lack of access to the funds and time required to conduct and disseminate research. As I will explore in chapter 3, Michel Foucault's status as a Collège de France chaired professor provided him with the time and profile necessary not only to be a prolific writer, but also to be a particular type of public intellectual (an increasingly rare breed in the neoliberal era of audit culture).

vicinity of the one you are actually seeking out by call number in the library stacks, the resonance of an article you are reading with a story in the news, the fortuitous time or space of reading a particular text, or any other chance juxtaposition that sparks a neural firestorm. Put simply, ideas are not developed in the vacuum of a system; they are born of borders meeting and border crossings. This is the cumulative and ongoing process of translation.

So I begin by describing my own line of inquiry, complete with a series of chance encounters that ultimately led to my fascination with such encounters and to the writing of this book. I began my inquiry by focusing on two events: the Languages of Criticism and the Sciences of Man conference, which took place at Johns Hopkins University in 1966, and the 1975 Schizo-Culture conference organized by Sylvère Lotringer in New York. There was a stark contrast between these two events. The former brought Roland Barthes, Jacques Derrida, and Jacques Lacan, among other French thinkers, to Baltimore in order to introduce structuralism to an audience of 150 academics. This conference is often mentioned in narrative histories of French thought as the moment that inaugurated post-structualism: Derrida's performance of "Structure, Sign and Play in the Discourse of the Human Sciences," a paper that deconstructed structure by talking about its entry into philosophical discourse as an event (247) and that played chicken and egg with Claude Lévi-Strauss's distinction between the engineer and bricoleur (252–65). The Schizo-Culture conference, on the other hand, marked the arrival of Gilles Deleuze, Félix Guattari, and Michel Foucault, who spoke alongside William S. Burroughs, John Cage, Richard Foreman, and representatives from the anti-psychiatry, prison, gay, and women's liberation movements. While the former conference became *representative* of post-structuralism by the turn of the 1980s, the latter was *associative*, sparking a run of *Semiotext(e)* journals that juxtaposed French thinkers and American artists, writers, and activists without a running meta-commentary. While the proceedings for the Schizo-Culture conference were not printed until recently, the Johns Hopkins proceedings were printed in the early 1970s as *The Structuralist Controversy*, in the process eliding the effects of the late 1960s on the becoming of French thought.

When we return to the beginning of the 1970s in France, what we find is, of course, yet another event. The context for much of the thought that constituted post-structuralist philosophy was May '68. In the late 1960s, university students introduced social movements into the classroom and demanded that what was discussed in the classroom be relevant to the outside world. The inside of the university was folded out, and the outside was folded in, a relationship of reciprocal implication. One of the manifestations of such folding was that May '68 was a student-worker event.

And May '68 was also a French-American event. What I learned as I pursued May '68 was, first, that it was *much* longer than a month and, second, that it was part of a movement that far exceeded national bounds. It was only days before a research trip to consult the Allen Ginsberg and William Burroughs holdings at Columbia, and to talk with Sylvère Lotringer, John Rajchman, and Denis Hollier about Semiotext(e), that I ran into the fact that Columbia had its own '68. I picked up some books and read Joanne Grant's *Confrontation on Campus* on daily subway trips between Brooklyn and Morningside Heights.[2] In her book I read about how students at Columbia threw cobblestones in the spring of 1968, quoting students in Paris (122). Grant's 1969 book began with parallel quotes by Mark Rudd (leader of the Columbia revolt in New York) and Daniel Cohn-Bendit (leader of the March 22nd movement, which was a crucial motor for the events in Paris) (xiii–xiv). When I picked up Daniel and Gabriel Cohn-Bendit's *Obsolete Communism*, I found prominent references to Columbia and the mid-1960s Berkeley free speech movement (23–5, 32–3). There was a relationship of reciprocal implication between the movements taking place in Paris and New York (*and* Berlin *and* Berkeley *and* Strasbourg, and so on). As Kristin Ross makes clear in her indispensible tome *May '68 and Its Afterlives*, "May '68" is constituted of a complex set of associations that exceed the temporal and spatial bounds that the term implies; it is a metaphor that does not capture the enfolding, unfolding, and refolding of the events that it is employed to represent. The events of 1968 exceed metaphorical treatment.

So Paris and New York are folded into one another, but what about French theory? Shortly after I arrived in New York, I went to St. Mark's bookstore and found Jean-François Bizot's *Free Press* on a display table. Bizot's coffee table-style book of newspaper covers pointed me to the Underground Press Syndicate (UPS), an internationally networked group of newspapers in which the culture and politics of what was collectively called "the movement" was produced and

---

2 I also took a midday break from the microfiche reader to stand in solidarity with Columbia students protesting the Iraq War on the steps of Low Library, a location central to the Columbia protests of 1968. While it almost goes without saying that the moment was nowhere near as momentous as the events that transpired on those steps in '68, the juxtaposition of events, for me, was uncanny, with four decades passing in the time it took to walk down three flights of stairs, and this likely pales in comparison to the experiences of others for whom the protest was enlivened by other encounters or trajectories. In other words, moments do not have universal meanings, but are instead meaningful only because of their relations (relations that are, similarly, not universal). The clarion call for objectivity stifles entire networks of feeling (to adapt Raymond Williams's term [see Williams 128–35]).

distributed. Alongside shared advertising revenue, the syndicate kept its growing roster of member papers afloat by selling university libraries microfiche subscriptions. Columbia had the collection. With Columbia '68 fresh on my mind, I was drawn to *RAT Subterranean News*, a paper that was produced in New York's Lower East Side and played a significant role in the Columbia revolt. The Columbia-Lower East Side connection was one that I was already pursuing via Lotringer's Semiotext(e) project, which drew uptown and downtown together with the Schizo-Culture conference, and in the run of *Semiotext(e)* journals that followed. Although I did not find Deleuze and Guattari in *RAT*, I did find Jean-Jacques Lebel relating his experiences of the barricades in Paris (where he was *with* Guattari).

I had run into Lebel's name a few months prior in France. François Cusset's book *French Theory* had just been published (another bookstore find), and in it Cusset mentions an eye-catching road trip that Deleuze and Guattari took with Lebel, from New York to San Francisco, after the Schizo-Culture conference in 1975. The trip included encounters with Bob Dylan, Allen Ginsberg, Lawrence Ferlinghetti, and Patti Smith (Cusset 68). Alongside Burroughs and John Cage, whom Deleuze and Guattari encountered at the conference, the names of the American personalities they encountered are peppered through "Rhizome," originally published independently of *Mille plateaux* (*A Thousand Plateaus*) in 1976, and Deleuze and Parnet's *Pourparler (Dialogues II)*, which was published in 1977. *A Thousand Plateaus* is a book built of associations. As interesting and enlightening as it was to learn about some of the associations out of which it was made, why cut the book from the cloth? If *A Thousand Plateaus* is a rhizome and not a root book, where do its associations lead?

What does theory become when we think it according to its associations? It proliferates; it is taken away by a sea of movement(s). In such a space, tangents are not distractions or asides; they are the lines that take us in the middle, which, for Deleuze and Guattari, is a productive and multifarious space. *And* is how translation works. *And* in the middle is where an associative theory of translation awaits further elaboration. To return to the distinction that I made at the outset, to label and ultimately understand the work of thinkers such as Deleuze and Guattari, Derrida, or Foucault under the rubric of "poststructuralism" or "French theory" severs them from the associations that characterize their thought. This is a metaphorical approach to theory. It is driven by substitution: selecting a term that captures a mode of thinking, and that generally renders acts of thinking into systems of thought. While we understand that these metaphors are a kind of shorthand that cannot capture the complexity of philosophy, they nevertheless have an effect on the way that we understand and deploy thinkers and their concepts. To approach theory associatively, on the other hand, is to think metonymically. Rather than substituting a term for a system, associative or metonymic thinking is driven by contiguity, by considering the influences that border, inflect, and are inflected by, thought.

In discussing metaphor and metonymy, here, I am alluding to the work of Roman Jakobson. In order to describe two types of aphasia, or severe language disturbances, Jakobson distinguishes between the metaphoric and metonymic poles. His "Two Aspects of Language and Two Types of Disturbances" has been widely anthologized because it makes a distinction germane to literary criticism: while poetry, particularly of the Romantic and Symbolist variety, works metaphorically, emphasizing the axis of selection, prose, particularly that of the Realist bent, works metonymically, in digressions "from the plot to the atmosphere and from the characters to the setting in space and time" (255). At the end of his essay, Jakobson makes a striking point:

> Similarity in meaning connects the symbols of a metalanguage with the symbols of the language referred to. Similarity connects a metaphorical term with the term for which it is substituted. Consequently, when constructing a metalanguage to interpret tropes, the researcher possesses more homogeneous means to handle metaphor, whereas metonymy, based on a different principle, easily defies interpretation. (258)

What do we do when we use and discuss translated theory? For the most part, we use it as a metalanguage, or code, to interpret other texts, or we discuss the metalanguage itself, creating new metalanguages (as was done in the 1980s, 1990s, and first decade of the twenty-first century with post-structuralism, postmodernism, and French theory) that serve to explain broad sets of authors, texts, and terms. While this is not wrong, it is, as per Jakobson's blanket observation about a general tendency in criticism, a mode of doing theory that exhibits the traits of a contiguity disorder.[3] In his analysis of the work of Russian

---

3  In our dealings with theory, we have somewhat of a contiguity disorder: we tend to select and substitute rather than think about combination and contexture. Our use of theory is more poetic than prosaic. Rather than blaming ourselves entirely, however, this tendency towards systematization and selection corresponds to Saussure's privileging of the synchronic to the diachronic pole in the *Course in General Linguistics* that inspired the work of the so-called structuralists and their successors. This is to say that this tendency is built into many, though not all, of these texts, meaning that, as per Jakobson's observation about studies of poetry and prose, preference of a pole is also attributable to the object of study and not simply the aphasic tendencies of a reader.

novelist Gleb Ivanovic Uspenskij, who, Jakobson points out, had a similarity disorder, Anatolij Kamegulov makes note of Uspenskij's "penchant for metonymy," saying that "he carried it so far that 'the reader is crushed by the multiplicity of detail unloaded on him in a limited verbal space, and is physically unable to grasp the whole, so that the portrait is often lost'" (qtd. in Jakobson 257). When one considers such a scene from a novel, one might consider the correspondent scene of theory in the midst of the '68 tumult. Although the aim of criticism should not be to move from one pole to the other – from a contiguity disorder to a similarity disorder – one wonders what such critical praxis might look like.[4]

Fredric Jameson's early book-length assessment of French structuralism, *The Prison-House of Language*, proposes that we take a tempered approach when doing theory. In closing, the Marxist theorist laments the privileging of synchronic over diachronic and imagines a self-conscious hermeneutic that would disclose codes, models, and the place of the analyst herself, that would bracket the object of analysis, and understand the "analytic practice as 'nothing but' an operation in time …. reopen[ing] text and analytic process alike to all the winds of history" (216). Though Jameson's infamous dictum, "Always historicize!" (*The Political Unconscious* 9), renders him very visibly and self-consciously Marxist, he also has a penchant for close reading that demonstrates an attempt to overcome aphasic critical tendencies. Similarly, to think translation associatively, via contiguous relations, does not mean abandoning metaphor or the axis of selection altogether.

This book is not driven by a move to devalue the ripples produced by the arrival of foreign knowledges, proclaiming arrivals, *point final*, to be the destination of knowledges that are, via geographical remove, always distanced from their truth. I do think that it is important to recognize that when ideas move from one point to another, from origin to destination, they are transformed. Conditions of emergence become conditions for accommodation, and new uses do not necessarily speak to the versatility of ideas but rather to the forcible adaptation of ideas to make them applicable to new problems. There is a difference between here and there. Concepts are spatially and temporally contingent.

---

4  We might say that the Baltimore and New York conferences represent contiguity and similarity disorders, respectively. Whereas the Baltimore conference appears to be more concerned with importing a paradigm (or, at the very least, a controversy), the Schizo-Culture conference, describing itself as an event concerned with madness, imported cacophony, and is best described via the suggestive multiplicity of its roster. But, of course, this is not a question of the conferences themselves; instead, this distinction is a product of their translation into icon and cacaphony, respectively.

On the one hand, when 1966 is republished in 1972 as *The Structuralist Controversy*, the '68 years are elided and the trajectory of French theory is restricted to the interests of target language fields (like literary studies, for whom structuralism and post-structuralism represented paradigms that could replicate and complicate the formalist tendencies inherent in the New Criticism).[5] On the other, this trajectory is itself a delimited tracing. To emphasize the emergence of post-structuralism as a response to structuralism proper (Derrida's "controversial" Johns Hopkins paper, the rise of the Yale School, and a continuation of the project of close reading) is certainly to focus on a history whose effects are discernible in the field of literary studies, but this narrative is also a conventionalized one, on offer with variations in Terry Eagleton's *Literary Theory* and *The Function of Criticism*, Frank Lentricchia's *After the New Criticism*, and in introductory guides like Peter Barry's *Beginning Theory*, emblemizing the underlying narrative taught in university classrooms and graduate seminars. Ian Hunter's point that the moment of theory looks different depending on its moment of arrival in any of several disciplines – literature, sociology, critical-legal studies, political science, history – stands as a corrective to the notion that there is a single, traceable narrative for the translation of theory; there are indeed many, and the constitution of theory upon arrival is dependent upon the structuring relations within a given field at that given moment. Cusset's *French Theory* is even messier in this respect. Cusset moves beyond translation for and by academic fields to demonstrate how, in America, theory spawned identity politics, made inroads into the art world, and was transformed when it was used by students, or when it was applied to explore technological developments in cyborg theory and sci-fi. While it is tempting to scold translators and foreign users for their elisions, the mutations that result, as Cusset's book demonstrates, can be fascinating and productive in their own right. Insert platitude here: just because it (theory) is different (upon translation) doesn't mean that it is wrong.

---

5 The principle that texts take on new meanings when grafted onto a target language culture is not only central to translation studies, it is also fundamental to recent work in the growing field of the history of theory. While people talk about a "moment of theory," in "The History of Theory" Ian Hunter argues that one struggles to find consensus regarding even the objects that are proper to theory not only due to theory's own diversity of thinkers, but also due to the diversity of disciplines that have transformed theory according to their own constitution at the moment of theory's arrival. François Cusset invokes Pierre Bourdieu on this point, employing the language of symbolic capital as opposed to that of misappropriation, noting that there has been "a highly productive transfer of words and concepts from one specific market of symbolic goods to another" (xiv–xv).

In thinking about the translation of French theory herein, the task that I set out to accomplish is not to map its distant afterlives; instead, my aim is to work through what it means to think about French theory as a product of the global '68 years. My contention is that we do not need to wait for the linguistic translation of theory's texts to see how it ramifies in America; in the context of globalization and global revolt, French theory is already crossing national borders at its moment of conception. While the nation-state remains important to understanding "French" theory, that the moment of theory is one of global revolt means that its constitution is *irreducible* to the state.[6] This context of perpetual border crossings – the global '68 years – is itself a space of translation.

The act of situating one's scholarship in context with others is a convention that speaks to the centrality of contiguity in everyday scholarly practice: as we refine our paradigms, we of course do so in relation to others. Translation studies, like other domains, experienced a cultural turn, and historical, institutional, and economic questions are now given serious consideration when thinking about the movement of texts and cultures across borders.[7] Emily Apter's work on "drift" and "zones" considers translation, in the context of globalization, in its temporal and spatial dimensions, and her call for a politics of untranslatability[8] recognizes the danger imposed upon the nuances of marginalized cultures by cosmopolitan calls for a world literature driven by the principle of

---

6  In "Times of Theory," Warren Breckman points to a variety of reasons why we must think about the nation of origin, and not just destination point, when we consider the history of theory. With reference to the work of Alan Schrift ("'Is There Such a Thing as 'French Philosophy'?"), Marcel Lepper ("'Ce qui restera ... , c'est un style'"), and François Dosse (*History of Structuralism*, vol. 2), Breckman points out that, to understand why French theorists were writing as they were in the first place, one has to consider the restructuring of the French educational system, the rise of the human sciences, and the circulation of ideas in avant-garde movements and presses (343–4).

7  See Lefevere and Bassnett's "Introduction: Proust's Grandmother and the Thousand and One Nights," which heralded the turn. Subsequent collections from the 1990s and beyond brought discourse analysis; technological developments; memory studies; as well as feminist, queer, postcolonial, trauma, and legal theory – among others – to bear on the field. See, for example, Niranajana, *Siting Translation* (1992); Venuti, *Rethinking Translation* (1992); Álvirez and Vidal, *Translation, Power, Subversion* (1996); Simon, *Gender in Translation* (1996); Bassnett and Lefevere, *Constructing Cultures* (1998); Bassnett and Trivedi, *Postcolonial Translation* (1999); essays collected in the section devoted to the "1990s and beyond" (323–504) in Venuti, *The Translation Studies Reader* (2004); Bermann and Wood, *Nation, Language, and the Ethics of Translation* (2005); and Brodzki, *Can These Bones Live?* (2007).

8  The concept of untranslatability – as deployed by Derrida-inflected translation theorists such as Emily Apter, Barbara Cassin, and Jacques Lezra, in particular – has itself become a crucial term for thinking about philosophical concepts that are both unsettled and unsettling,

universality.[9] This work reminds us that borders everywhere abound, and we need to think about the politics of border-crossing in relation to translation that, in many ways, appears to render thought and writing borderless. While this cultural and geopolitical turn in translation studies is obviously pertinent to my thinking about the translation of theory, so too is recent work by Jane Bennett, Manuel Delanda, and Bruno Latour on assemblage theory,[10] and the field of postcolonial studies and work on the diaspora have of course long been at the forefront in considering the effects of border crossings on culture and modes of thinking, with concepts like Françoise Lionnet's "métissage" and Edouard Glissant's work on "creolization," for example, developed to account for the complexities of contact.[11] And when one considers the list drawn up by Ulf Hannerz to describe the terms that have emerged since creolization – "hybridity, collage, mélange, hotchpotch, montage, synergy, bricolage, creolization, mestizaje, mongrelization, syncretism, transculturation, third cultures" (13) – one can see that there has been a major proliferation of contemporary critical languages around, and theoretical obsessions with, the idea of cultural mixing.

Context matters. When Jakobson discusses Uspenskij's writing, he points out not only that his penchant for metonymy is related to his similarity disorder but also that his "metonymical style" was "obviously prompted by the prevailing literary canon of his time, late nineteenth-century 'realism'" (258). If I were, as per Jameson's suggestion, to make a self-conscious statement about my own context, it is that these contemporary concerns with questions of mixing and hybridity compel me to think theory contiguously. And I am not alone. Consider Françoise Lionnet and Shu-Mei Shih's call for a "creolization of theory" "to raise questions about the forms of intellectual and political entanglements that have marked disciplinary formations in the academy," a practice that might help to overcome the "melancholic tone" abound in decades of conversation about the death of theory ("The Creolization of Theory" 1–2).[12]

---

concepts that refuse to be translated, once and for all, into a definitive meaning. See, in particular, Cassin, *Dictionary of Untranslatables*; Lezra, *Untranslating Machines*; and Apter, *Against World Literature*.

9  See Apter *Continental Drift*, *Translation Zone*, and *Against World Literature*.

10  See Bennett, *Vibrant Matter*; Delanda, *Assemblage Theory* and *A New Philosophy of Society*; and Latour, *Reassembling the Social*.

11  See Lionnet, *Autobiographical Voices*, and Glissant, *Carribean Discourse*.

12  For reasons related to Apter's politics of untranslatability, I am somewhat more reluctant to appropriate the term "creolization" for Euro-American application.

Ultimately, while terms like contiguity, association, metonymy, and syntag-matic provide *something* of an original apparatus for the study of translation, I would by no means make any sort of grandiose claims about their originality, and, besides, I use these terms somewhat sparingly throughout the book, as my purpose is less to develop a new paradigm than it is to demonstrate the con-tiguity inherent in theory.

While it is easy to see the draw of thinking through the drafting of a book like *A Thousand Plateaus* associatively, this mode of rethinking the complexi-ties of translation does not restrict itself to thinking about the theorists and practitioners of the rhizome. In my first chapter, I consider, with Derrida, the contiguous relationship between campus and community using "margins" and "tympan" as concepts that help us to think about the politics of borders and the ethics of translation.[13] In "The Ends of Man," a paper delivered in New York in 1968, Derrida invokes, in the margins of a paper that otherwise considers re-cent developments in French thought, student unrest, the Vietnam War, and the death of Martin Luther King Jr. Derrida answers the question he was posed when he was invited to present a paper at the New York conference – "Where is France, as concerns man" (*Margins of Philosophy* 114) – by rehearsing certain common anthropological readings and misreadings of Hegel, Husserl, and Heidegger, but these philosophical considerations, which translate and work through "man" using philosophical concepts – concepts working towards uni-versal truth, the end of man – ring hollow when this conceptual work is al-lowed to run bracketed off from seismic developments with respect to the actual status of "man" (i.e., who gets to be one) in 1968. How are the icons and political movements of America's '68, very much on the margins of Derrida's earlier writing, associated with the development of his thought? The chapter considers, on the one hand, Derrida's provocations about the relationship be-tween philosophy and its margins and, on the other, student consideration of the relationships between the university, weapons development, and the real estate market. Under the rubric of eschatology, Derrida brings us to the nexus of the university and its outside where a surfeit of associations is brought to bear on the Western philosophical canon's approach to man. Theorizing mar-gins, Derrida helps us to identify relationships of reciprocal implication at the same time as he reminds us that there is a fine line between recognizing exclu-sions and assimilating them. The chapter is therefore self-conscious in its

---

13 The ethical thinking embodied in Derrida's "Ends of Man" fits well within the trajectory analysed in Julian Bourg's *From Revolution to Ethics*.

modelling of Derrida's politics of marginalization, with Derridean philosophy and '68 politics resonating with each other in separate sections, or on either side of a border.

In the second chapter, I not only document and analyse the encounters and relations that are effectively translated into Deleuze and Guattari's theory of the rhizome, as per my discussion above, but I also follow the combinatory lines that emerge when following Deleuze and Guattari's associations. In effect, the rhizome is a model for doing translation. On the one hand, following Deleuze and Guattari's associations involves scrutinizing the paths being forged by Lebel, whose relations with American and French political movements, thinkers, and writers make him an interesting case study in the messiness and intensity of associations, but it is also by reading the underground newspapers that collected and projected liberationist movements, from the Columbia University revolt to the '68 Democratic National Convention in Chicago and beyond, that we can see how the politics of association is related to movement building. Thinking translation by association does not involve considering only the importance of neglected lateral connections to other figures and cultures in the development of thought, but also the diachronic development of movement by associations. As it moves through Deleuze and Guattari's associations with the movement, the chapter, under the rubric of the rhizome, develops three additional models for thinking translation associatively: fold, event, and transcreation.

In chapter 3, I consider how Foucault's activist work with incarcerated people provides insight into the development of his thinking about the relationship between theory and practice. Key to this chapter is the concept of "relay," a term used to describe Foucault's activity at protests – where he relayed texts written by incarcerated people rather than speaking in their place – and also used by Deleuze and Foucault to describe the relationship between theory and practice. In both cases, we see a refusal to "represent" that corresponds to Foucault's rethinking of the role of the politically engaged, public intellectual. Thinking translation by association in this instance means thinking about the importance of Foucault and other prominent intellectuals to liberating the speech of prisoners, the importance of Jean Genet to introducing the work of George Jackson to a French and American public, and the importance of George Jackson and the massacre at Attica to understanding conditions, and legitimizing revolt, within France's own embattled prisons.

In my final chapter, I provide a history and analysis of the early years of the Semiotext(e) project. While Lotringer considered the Schizo-Culture conference a miss – it arrived too late, demonstrating a nostalgia for '68 and a

fantasy of instant connection between French and American contingents –
the French-American associations made at the conference, and in an early
run of Semiotext(e) journals, horizontalizes the relation between theory and
culture. Rather than seeing, in French theories, the interpretive value that
made structuralism and post-structuralism so suited to the analysis of cultural texts, the project operated conversationally – by juxtaposing French and
American thinkers, writers, and texts, thereby putting works into conversations that remain as suggestive today as they did at the "failed" 1975 event.
To do theory "conversationally" is yet another associative approach to the
question of translation.

Rather than examining and deeming the Anglo-American life of French theory to be a translation failure, or a sort of afterlife of the impossible-to-translate
thought that is left behind when a thinker's corpus crosses linguistic and cultural
borders, this book considers translation as a perpetual process of border crossings that, in many cases, precedes the inculcation of thinkers, texts, and concepts within discrete fields of study. Ultimately, this book is an exploration of
how French thinkers and American countercultural and political movements
mixed during the late 1960s and through the 1970s. Working from archives and
neglected publications like political pamphlets and underground and alternative
presses provides new narratives for the arrival of French theory in America.
Prominent political questions were elided in favour of conceptual ones when
French intellectuals and their theories crossed the Atlantic. That certain texts,
contexts, inflections, and interventions are lost in translation does not mean that
French thinkers left these elements behind when they travelled; it simply means
that they are not a part of the narrative drawn to situate French theory in the
Anglo-American academy. My purpose in this book is to recuperate these elid-
ed elements and to weave French theory's arrival through the transatlantic political and cultural movements that animated the late 1960s and early 1970s.
"French theory" is an effect of its associations.

# 1 Translating *Margins*: Paris–Derrida–New York, 1968

While participating in a roundtable on translation in 1980, Derrida argued that the essence of philosophy is translation.[1] The work of the philosopher is to find the truth or meaning that lies "before or beyond language," and "[t]herefore the thesis of philosophy is translatability" (*The Ear of the Other* 120). From being to meaning, "the passage into philosophy [is] the program of translation," and any failure in translation marks the defeat of philosophy (120). Part of the work of deconstruction is to mine philosophy for the paradoxes and aporias that litter philosophy's canon. Derrida, of course, was not out to destroy or discredit philosophy; instead he wished to save and activate philosophy as – or, using its concepts all the while, to translate philosophy into – something other than a metaphysics of Truth.

To understand that doing philosophy is doing translation is also to foreground the fact of philosophy's relations with others, a fact that forces us to think about the nature of those relations. To foreground translation as passage into philosophy denotes the limits or margins of philosophy as such. In the process of

---

1 The 1979 roundtable on translation collected in *The Ear of the Other* is situated between two of Derrida's most infamous texts on translation, "Living On: Borderlines," which was assigned to the participants in the Montreal colloquium, and "Des tours de Babel," which appears in a somewhat preliminary form in some of Derrida's replies to his interlocutors during the Montreal roundtable on translation. In a chapter that discusses Derrida's "Theologies of Translation" (a paper that Derrida presented at Columbia University in 1980), Emily Apter notes that Derrida was also lining himself up to deliver a seminar entitled "The Concept of Comparative Literature and the Theoretical Problems of Translation" in 1979–80 at Yale (*Against World Literature* 228). While explicit and overt theoretical concerns about translation are concentrated in this nexus, questions about translation are peppered throughout Derrida's corpus. Translation is fully central to Derrida's approach to philosophy.

relating its others, philosophy can never properly understand these others, or, put differently, in order for philosophy to understand and communicate its others, they must necessarily be translated. That which exists outside of philosophical language and conception is translated into philosophical language via philosophy's concepts. If philosophy is something of a translation machine on a bent towards universality, how do we ensure that it comes into ethical contact with others rather than merely subsuming and mutilating them for the purposes of this large-scale, Western philosophical project?

Derrida plays at these margins of philosophical integrity and contact throughout his oeuvre, often using typographic techniques to force his readers to think about the relations between different types of discourse. I will focus on two texts herein, both from his 1972 collection *Margins of Philosophy*. While "Tympan," something of a preface to *Margins*, discusses and performs the margin's relations with philosophy in several very illustrative ways, helping us to grasp at the thrust of Derrida's work in *Margins*, "The Ends of Man" ushers us to the limits of philosophical discourse, where we find, in 1968, concrete political subjects vying for recognition not in philosophical discourse, but in spite of it. Prefacing the latter paper with an acknowledgment of those who remain on the margins of philosophy, the structure of Derrida's talk mirrors the constitution of the field. If we consider Derrida's deconstruction of the relationship between margin and centre, however, the philosophical centre of his paper does not hold, or, at least, it is not made to hold the margins at bay.

## On the Margins of *Margins*

As a preface to *Margins*, Derrida's "Tympan" discusses and performs the margin in several ways. "To typanize – philosophy" (x). Infinitive, dash, noun: Derrida's essay begins by proposing a relation between criticism and philosophy. To tympanize: an archaic verb, translated transliterally by Alan Bass, means to ridicule or criticize (xi n.1). *Margins* is an exploration and performance of criticism's relation to philosophy: how does philosophy listen and react to criticism? Must those on the outside of philosophical discourse yell in order to be heard, and, when they are heard, how is this yelling translated? To tympanize philosophy one must address the ear of the philosopher – and Derrida is playing with "tympan" here – from the tympanization of philosophy to the tympanic membrane that receives and transmits the vibrations of the outside environment to the inner ear: "Can one violently penetrate philosophy's field of listening without its immediately …. making the penetration resonate within itself, appropriating the emission for itself" (xii). The dash between tympanize and philosophy thus denotes a passageway into philosophy (the ear canal), but passage (via tympanization) requires penetration of a protective border (the tympanic membrane).

Derrida does not waste time considering the tympanization of the mild-mannered; instead, he invokes Nietzsche, the philosopher who proposed that he would "philosophize with a hammer" (xii). Aggressive as it sounds, Nietzsche's proposition is not to batter philosophy into submission. Instead, in *Twilight of the Idols* he proposes to take a hammer to the idols of philosophy to see whether they are sound or whether, once hammered, he will "hear in response" from these hammered philosophers "that famous hollow sound which speaks of swollen innards" (3). While the hammer is an instrument used to determine whether philosophy will ring hollow when met with rigorous examination and critique, Nietzsche announces his intent as a "declaration of war" (3) on the "idols" (philosophers, philosophemes) that populate the tradition.

Whereas Nietzsche, the mad Dionysian philosopher, hammers away at the tradition, Derrida prefers to approach the tradition with surgical precision. In order to better understand how philosophy responds to the pounding of a hammer, Derrida examines the anatomy of the inner ear: "on the *internal* surface of the tympanic membrane," he notes, we find a series of small bones – hammer, anvil, and stirrup (xiii n.5, emphasis in original). The membrane takes on "the role of mediation and communication": it transmits sounds to these small bones, which transmit sound to the inner ear in turn. The hammer in particular "protects the tympanum while acting on it" (xiii n.5). When the tympanum is struck by powerful sounds coming from outside, the relaying and protective inner hammer "can weaken the blows, muffle them on the threshold of the inner ear" (xiii n.5). What do we take away from this anatomy lesson? On the one hand, this is a comment on the mediations of philosophy: the passage into philosophy is a program of translation. Mad Dionysian screams, tempered by the inner hammer, are calmed so as to protect the inner sanctum of philosophy. On the other hand, Derrida is here troubling the distinction between inside and outside. The hammer itself is already part of the inner structure of philosophy: it is part of its Apollonian form. Philosophy's outside – including the passionate Dionysian philosopher yelling into its ear – is mediated and internalized according to the workings of philosophy's internal structures. We might say that, in preparation for philosophers of Niezsche's Dionysian ilk, philosophy was always already doing philosophy with a hammer (or, in terms of the anatomy of philosophical criticism, awaiting Derrida's tympanizing, philosophy always already will have had an inner hammer). Those who tympanize philosophy are destined to be translated into its corpus.

It is important to pay some attention to the structural/performative aspects of "Tympan," which are conveyed – as is the case with many of Derrida's texts

– via its typography. Derrida's anatomical lesson on the inner hammer comes in a footnote, and therefore on the margins of his text. Similarly, many of the terms discussed in the essay also appear in a text that is written on its margins. While Derrida's text takes up about two-thirds of the page, a selection from surrealist/ethnographer Michel Leiris's memoir *Biffures* takes up the final third. In the selection, which remains outside of Derrida's essay – he never alludes to it or explains its presence – we find the terms "margin," "tympan," "perce-oreille," "writing machine," and so on. In order to properly understand what Derrida is saying with this typographical performance, we must turn to yet another definition of the word "tympan."

Although Derrida predominantly discusses the tympan as a feature of aural anatomy in his essay, it is also, in music, the membrane stretched over the head of a drum; in architecture, a decorative wall over an entrance; or, in hand press printing, the parchment-covered frame upon which the sheet to be printed is placed. Derrida discusses the tympan of the printing press towards the end of his essay, pointing out that one of its functions is to set the margins of the text (xxvi–xxvii). Derrida discusses how a large and small tympan work together with the lowered frisket to protect and set the virginal white space of the margins, and he uses this as a metaphor for a philosophy that watches over its outside as "homogenous," "undetermined," "negative" space waiting "to receive and repercuss type" (xxvii). Derrida's "Tympan" undermines this convention. His footnotes – a space for annotation and commentary on technical terms – supplement the text in the properly Derridian sense: while they may not be a part of the text proper, they are necessary in order for the text to properly function (the meaning of the text is not fully communicated without this marginal supplement). The marginal nature of the margins is further undermined by the inclusion of Leiris's text. That Derrida's and Leiris's texts run as two columns, with Derrida's text occupying slightly more space on the page, complicates the temptation to render literature to the margins of philosophy, a point further made by the fact that Leiris and Derrida complicate the figures of poet and philosopher, respectively.

As Derrida states towards the beginning of his preface, "almost constantly, in this book, I shall be examining the *relevance* of the limit" ("Tympan" xi, emphasis in original) – and we should think, here, of the limit or border that separates philosophy from its others. Derrida's interest in the "margins of philosophy" is based in a translation of the Hegelian term "*Aufhebung*." Derrida's uses the word "*relève*" in an attempt to capture the proper meaning of *Aufhebung*. *Relever* means to lift up, relay, or relieve (as in a changing of the guard). As Alan Bass clarifies in a translator's footnote later in *Margins*, Derrida's translation preserves and highlights the contradiction inherent in the term: it signifies both negation and conservation; it is a "conserving-and-negating" lifting up (20 n.23). In "examining the *relevance* of the limit" – note the play on *relève* – Derrida, in *Margins of Philosophy*, is "relaunching in every sense the reading of the Hegelian *Aufhebung*, eventually beyond what Hegel, inscribing it, understood himself to say or intended to mean" ("Tympan" xi). Indeed, what is the relevance of a limit if the end of philosophy is to be lifted up (*relever*) to the limitlessness of spirit?[2]

Derrida's translation of Hegel is not limited to the selection of a word. To "[relaunch] in every sense the reading of the Hegelian *Aufhebung*, eventually beyond what Hegel, inscribing it, understood himself to say or intended to mean" is to engage in fidelitious abuse of Hegel. Such is the politics of Derridean translation, and this is an illustrative example of why, as Derrida

---

2 Derrida would later give the term essay-length treatment in "What Is a 'Relevant' Translation," an oblique response to Ernst-August Gutt's application of Dan Sperber and Deirdre Wilson's relevance theory to translation. Rather than addressing Gutt directly, Derrida turns to Shakespeare's *Merchant of Venice* in order to do some translation work of his own, demonstrating the thought process that goes on behind moving a word from one language to another. In a move that ultimately demonstrates the racism at play when Shylock's Judaic conceptions of justice are translated into Christian mercy, Derrida proposes that "*relève*" be used to translate "seasons" in Portia's line "When mercy seasons justice" (195). Use of the term *relever* highlights Portia's prejudice: when she says that "mercy seasons justice," she believes that justice is being conserved and "lifted up," above base Judaism, to a higher, Christian plane. We see, here, that translation involves interpretation ("*relève*" is not a literal translation of "seasons"; instead, it is appropriate because it captures the essence of the exchange, as per Derrida's unconventional reading of Portia's line). We also see, in Portia's translation of justice, that translation is a process that involves diverse contexts – in this case, the Christian and the Jew – and questions of power. Never one to be literal, Derrida raises issues of untranslatability, undecidability, and multiplicity throughout his essay, inserting homonyms and generating cognitive dissonance by playing with his audience's expectations of "relevance." When "*relève*" ultimately appears as nothing more than an anachronism inappropriate to the task of translating Portia's speech, as Emmanuelle Ertel points out, one cannot help but notice the "suppression, negation, destruction," and indeed, the "violence against the foreign language" "that the relève, Hegel's *Aufhebung* entails" (15–16). For Derrida, translation and "relevance" are interwined, not in Gutt's sense of finding the perfect, cognitive-friendly fit for a term, but in the sense that multiplicity, context, and power are often muted parts of the translation process.

Credit must be given to Lawrence Venuti here, who implemented Philip Lewis's "abusive fidelity" theory of translation (see note 3 below) to translate Derrida's "What Is a 'Relevant' Translation." To take such an approach to translation means resisting the directive to use transparent and domesticating language to convey the sense of a foreign text and to instead reproduce, in Venuti's case, Derrida's "syntax and lexicon by inventing comparable textual effects – even when they threatened to twist English into strange forms" (Venuti "Translating Derrida" 253).

states elsewhere, "the question of deconstruction is also through and through *the* question of translation ("Letter to a Japanese Friend" 1, emphasis in original). Derrida is not out to destroy Hegel: in tympanizing Hegel in his *Margins*, he is very careful to be true to Hegel's *Spirit*. In an act of "abusive fidelity,"[3] he simply skews and renders visible margins and limits to the extent that we recognize the relations as differential rather than dialectical (the negative isn't lifted up, and we don't see a resolution in the negation of the negation: Derrida dwells in a world of difference without positive terms). In "Tympan," what is the difference between Leiris and Derrida, or Derrida and Hegel? Answers to those questions tell us something about poetic and philosophical discourse (on the basis of marked differences rather than the full presence of one or the other discourse). Fundamentally, in Derrida's subtle hands, we see that literature and philosophy (as well as biology, the technology of the printing press, and so on) exist in each other's margins, and, as each is peppered with the other's language, we see that the language and concepts used in each domain are not proper to them. Rather than full presence in any given discourse (or the desire of any one discourse to achieve full presence by appropriating and effacing others), we witness relations of difference and supplementarity.

The "marginal" work being done by the tympan of the manual printing press is interesting for another reason that helps us to understand what Derrida is trying to achieve in the essay that ultimately acts as the preface to *Margins*. As a part of the printing press, the tympan provides a type of padding, regulating the pressure between the type and the sheet being impressed upon. The tympan is thus a type of margin between writer (press) and reader (sheet). The tympan mediates, tempering the impression of the type on its target. "Tympan," much like the preface of *Dissemination*, also published in 1972, is not a gesture of mastery. Instead, it undermines the very idea that any discourse – whether

---

3 Philip Lewis makes note of Derrida's translation of "*Aufhebung*" in an essay that develops an "abusive fidelity" theory of translation. As Lewis argues, in Derrida's translation of the term "*Aufhebung*," one can glimpse an "inchoate axiology of translation," where, instead of opting for "common linguistic usage," that which "domesticates or familiarizes a message at the expense of whatever might upset or force or abuse language and thought," Derrida's translation practice in this instance, as elsewhere, "points to a risk to be assumed: that of the strong, forceful translation that values experimentation, tampers with usage, seeks to match the polyvalencies or plurivocities or expressive stresses of the original by introducing its own" (40–1). As noted above, "*relève*" is a word that captures the contradictions and inconsistencies inherent in the Hegelian concept, and it is therefore a term that resists the demand for transparency in the receiving language.

preface, philosophy, or Derrida's own critique of philosophy – can properly translate its proper other (its own other – in the case of the preface, the book proper). As a preface, "Tympan" is oblique, much like the placement of the tympan in the inner ear: it serves the inside/outside/marginal/supplemental function of priming readers to begin thinking margins as the texts of *Margins* should be thought: obliquely.[4] Where does this preface leave us? On the margins, to be sure, but it is with an interest in the margins that we therefore enter into *Margins* proper to think "The Ends of Man."

## On the Margins of "The Ends"

Why the "ends" of man? In the latter half of the 1960s in France, the "end of man" was being heralded by structuralists whose scientific study of everything human – anthropology, linguistics, psychoanalysis, literature – spelled the end of humanism. As Derrida put it, "[T]he current questioning of humanism is contemporary with the dominating and spellbinding extension of the 'human sciences' within the philosophical field" (*Margins* 117). The twilight of old philosophical idols (Jean-Paul Sartre and his existentialist humanism) was giving way to a new dawn marked by the arrival and consecration of new master thinkers: Althusser, Barthes, Foucault, Lacan, Lévi-Strauss, the leaders of the structuralist charge for whom human consciousness is the product of an ideology for which there is no accessible outside (Althusser); for whom the text must be freed from the interpretive tyranny of its creator (meaning lies in language itself and its influence on each new reader) (Barthes); for whom an "archeology of the human sciences" demonstrates that "man is an invention of recent date. And one perhaps nearing its end" (Foucault *The Order of Things* 387); for whom psychoanalysis is structuralized in a return to Freud with Saussure ("it is the whole structure of language that psychoanalytic experience discovers in the unconscious" [Lacan 139]); and for whom the "elementary

---

4 Pointing out that the texts of *Margins* straddle '68 and it is therefore a book where we can situate a pre- and (especially, as per its 1972-penned preface) post-'68 Derrida, Steven Helmling gives this oblique approach special significance: Derrida, here, is developing deconstruction as an ambush performance rather than as an exposition or antism: "Derrida's prose does not occupy 'positions' so much as it surges between them, toward and away from them, in a ceaseless agitation of assertion and qualification, saying and unsaying" (n.p.). Derrida discusses his position taking with respect to various thinkers in three interviews from 1972. See Derrida, *Positions*. For a discussion of Derrida's position among Althusserians and the Groupe Spinoza at the École Normale Supérieure, see Baring 259–94, and Peeters 207–29.

structure of kinship" informs all attitudes and behaviours (Lévi-Strauss). Rather than looking to man for meaning, man was everywhere the parcel and product of structure in a move from the "human" to the "subject" (of the sentence, language, ideology, culture, epistemes, various institutions and discourses, and so on).

While we are meant to reflect on this structuralism-announced end of man in light of Derrida's paper, structuralism is not his direct focus or target. If structuralism marks itself as the end of man, it is merely repetition, albeit with difference: phenomenology similarly heralded the end of studying the nature of being, of metaphysics, by turning towards the study of consciousness and the direct experience of phenomena. In a move that is meant to make us reflect on the most recently proclaimed ends (the structuralist approaches that mark many, simultaneous ends of man), Derrida demonstrates that man didn't need revival by way of the existentialist humanism of Sartre; instead, "man" is sublated – conserved at the same time as he is (nominally) negated in Hegel, Husserl, and Heidegger: in their attempts to break with the tradition of Western metaphysics, man becomes consciousness (Hegel), rational humanity becomes transcendental humanity (Husserl), and metaphysical we-men becomes proximity to being (Heidegger). In other words, if we hold up man's various ends for closer examination, we might find man intact.

Collected in *Margins*, "The Ends of Man" is, of course, concerned with reading "the *relevance* of the limit" ("Tympan" xi). In fact, "The Ends of Man" is the beginning of the *relève*: it is the paper that marks Derrida's translation of Hegel's "*Aufhebung*" as "*relève*," and Derrida's rigorous reading of phenomenology as the *relève* of anthropology demonstrates how this conserving and negating movement works. If phenomenology is the *relève* of anthropology, in "the structures of that which has *relever* man ... man remains in relief. His essence rests in phenomenology" (121). Here, the death of man is in unity with his accomplishment: the essence of man is realized, lifted up to a higher plane (*relever*), at the same time as man is laid to rest or put into relief (*relever*). Thus, we have the marriage of eschatology and teleology, end and truth, and natural and philosophical consciousness. This last union, which Hegel articulates with a *we* in his phenomonology, marks "the unity of absolute knowledge and anthropology, of God and man, of onto-theo-teleology and humanism" (121). Such is the all-consuming, conserving, and negating movement of the *relève*: it is a mass of contradictions.

Derrida's emphasis on the "we" is a theme that runs through his paper, and it is a theme that was meant to give the philosophers present at the colloquium pause. As Derrida puts it in a paragraph that links the thought of Husserl, Hegel, Heiddeger, and Sartre, "The unity of man is never examined in and of itself" (115); moreover, in a stab at Sartre in particular, who argued that struc-turalism was ahistorical,[5] "the history of the concept of man," Derrida points out, "is never examined. Everything occurs as if the sign 'man' had no origin, no historical, cultural, or linguistic limit" (116). More than staging fundamen-tal contradictions in the work of German phenomenologists, Derrida's paper stages, as per the final remark in his presentation, a question to the philoso-phers present at his talk: "But who, we?" (136).[6]

The movement of philosophy towards the absolute is premised on the idea that philosophy's other exists in order to be sublated, and this rather imperialist and fascistic movement is encapsulated in the "we." As Derrida puts it in "Tympan," philosophy "*insist*[s] upon thinking *its other*: its proper other, the proper of its other, an other proper? In thinking it *as such*, in recognizing it, one misses it. One reappropriates it for oneself, one disposes of it, one misses it, or rather one misses (the) missing (of) it" (xi–xii, emphasis in original). The other of a philosophy that aspires to the absolute is always *its* other. Teleologically speaking, all of philosophy's others are *its* others: the property of a philosophy to come. Derrida undermines this philosophical impulse in "Tympan" by out-lining philosophy's relation to its other while staging his margins – Leiris, ex-planatory footnotes, definitions – as being as distinct and unassimilable as "Tympan" proper (though the point should be made that "'Tympan' proper" is the sum of all of these different parts and not just Derrida's text). The question of "the ends of man" therefore becomes: what are "man's" unassimilable mar-gins? While eschatological and teleological ends are certainly part of Derrida's play, it is in his own margins, once again, that we find a significant discussion – and performance – of marginality. By exploring philosophical inquiry itself, we end up looking at "man" in the margins of philosophy, in close proximity, but never as the property of philosophy itself. To think "the *ends* of man" is not only to think about "the end" as a troubled theme with variations, it is to rein-state the limits of "man" as a philosophical concept, and the limits of philo-sophical discourse as it pertains to man.

Derrida prefaces his paper with a commentary on the political context of philosophical colloquiums, with a particular focus on the colloquium at hand.

---

5 See Sartre 110.

6 "But who, we?" should also be read as a question that Derrida himself continued to ask of philosophy throughout his career as he broadened its limits via deconstruction. For a discussion of Derrida's work on the university, and the place of philosophy in the curriculum within the broader context of Derrida's work on citizenship, rights, the nation state, and so on (all under the rubric of "belonging" or "not belonging"), see Wortham.

Much like "Tympan" as preface to *Margins*, Derrida's prefatory remarks do not offer up a kind of thesis or overarching explanation, but they are meant to, in an oblique way, temper his audience's reception of his paper. While Derrida's paper is about philosophy, his preface is about politics, or, more specifically, the relationship between politics and philosophy. Beyond the essential connection between these two domains, Derrida remarks that "[e]very philosophical colloquium necessarily has a political significance," a "political import," which is to say, a localized and immediate political significance that, as one is in the process of thinking and writing, is imported from the political domain into the philosophical one. This "aggravates," "burdens," and "determines" "the a priori link between philosophy and politics" (*Margins* 111). For the conference at hand, its political significance is the fact of its being "announced as an international colloquium" (111). Derrida thus begins by considering what "international" means in the particular context of the philosophical colloquium that he is attending.

In the age of networking and knowledge mobilization, we take the occurrence of international colloquia for granted now more than ever (even though it has become increasingly difficult for the academic precariat to attend such colloquia, demonstrating that invisibility is not relative to proximity). But Derrida takes a step back to consider what it means to link "international" with "philosophy." The implications of this linkage – the way that it makes us rethink the essence of philosophy, in particular – Derrida notes, are significant: "[C]ontrary to the essence of philosophy – such as it has always represented itself at least – philosophical nationalities have been formed" (*Margins* 111).[7]

---

7  The division of philosophy into national camps without singular vision is illustrated in the discussants' responses to Derrida's paper. Richard Popkin notes that he may have been selected to respond because he has spent a good deal of time in France and doesn't share "the positivistic or analytic attitudes towards Continental thought" that are characteristic of the American tradition (207); Wesley Piersol makes note of some of the structuralist currents that underpin Derrida's intervention, and that explain "the need for a changing of terrain or style" (222); and Marvin Farber takes a logical positivist approach to the question of man that exhibits a kind of deafness to Derrida's paper that is explained in Peter Caws's response: "Professor Derrida is not always intelligible even to his compatriots; given these differences of tradition and attitude he may well seem totally opaque to American philosophers, who as a class react to opacity with impatience and even intolerance" (Caws 220). Taken together, the discussants' compulsion to contextualize Derrida's talk and their own work as belonging to a particular nation, movement, or trend demonstrates Derrida's point about the lack of a "we" in the philosophical field. For a discussion of how Derrida's work on the place of philosophy in the university is simultaneously rooted in the French state and uprooted by Derrida's transatlanticism, see Orchard, *Jacques Derrida and the Institution of French Philosophy.*

As Derrida explains, these colloquia operate according to the assumption that the philosophers present represent national philosophical identities – and his role at the New York colloquium was to represent France. This, of course, undermines the whole idea of universality that forms the basis of the philosophical enterprise. Furthermore – and this is where the political import weighs most heavily on philosophy – while the idea of an international colloquium would have been becoming increasingly commonplace for the attendees of Derrida's talk, "it is of a no less remarkable rarity in the greater part of the world ... where the organization of a philosophical colloquium simply would have no meaning" (112). This observation is especially striking, Derrida notes, because the topic of the colloquium is the *anthropos*, or philosophical anthropology. It would seem that, from an international philosophical perspective, man, or, slightly less broadly, "encultured" and "civilized" men, exist only behind a limited and select set of borders (and, even within so-called great world cities, like New York and Paris, large swathes of the population are ghettoized, placed on the outer limits of the "great world city" proper – and the relation of the university with these marginalized, local populations was, of course, at the centre of the protests of '68). Derrida articulates the political significance of his observation in succinct terms that not only give concrete meaning to his immediate critique of the colloquium at hand but that further clarify the prefatory remarks that he makes about philosophy's relationship to its other in "Tympan":

> [T]he anxious and busy multiplication of colloquia in the West is doubtless an effect of that difference which I just said bears down, with a mute, growing and menacing pressure, on the enclosure of Western collocution. The latter doubtless makes an effort to interiorize this difference, to master it, if we may put it thus, by affecting itself with it. The interest in the universality of the anthropos is doubtless a sign of this effort. (112)

In the span of three prefatory paragraphs discussing the significance of an international colloquium, Derrida does the type of deconstructive work that generally takes him an entire essay to achieve: philosophy marginalizes/philosophy is on the margins. While Derrida's close readings often leave readers aghast, and were appropriated by Yale School critics such as Paul de Man to make readers marvel at uncovered and exploited aporia, the "political import" of this observed fact is immediately tangible. The ends of "man" are the limits of what is included in international fora, defined by those who are invited or are allowed to speak, or who are simply aware of the discussions taking place inside, in an imperialism of thought and culture (that mirrors the reckless abandon with which the West firebombs the other in an attempt not simply to stop the spread of communism but to smash the barriers that limit the spread and global dominance of free-market capitalism). Derrida's relevance to the field of postcolonial studies is on full display here.[8]

Derrida also prefaces his paper with a performative utterance that establishes conditions for his presence in America. Noting his initial hesitation to accept the invitation to speak at the New York conference, he remarks that he agreed to present a paper at the conference only on the condition that he could express his "agreement" and "to a certain point ... solidarity" with those in America who were "fighting against" their government's policy, particularly with respect to Vietnam (113). Derrida is not simply describing his conversation with the organizers here. He very purposively punctuates his comments, asking his audience to "let me be permitted to speak in my own name *here*," and he notes that he "was assured that I could *bear witness here, now*" to his political position with respect to America and its publics (114, emphasis added). Though his position is boldly stated and purposively performed, he does this to demonstrate that his declared solidarity with those in opposition to domestic policy is "not bothersome" (114): such freedom, granted by the authorities, simply demonstrates that "oppositions may freely and discursively relate to one another," and this particular declaration "does not upset the given order" (114). In other words, the current system allows for a certain amount of discursive freeplay, and this type of opposition – expressions of agreement and solidarity – is entirely unthreatening to America's imperialist political projects.

Solidarity, however, which involves a decentring of self, also makes us think in a differential – or, rather, deferential – direction. While Derrida explicitly discusses the metaphorics at play in Heidegger – and we're certainly invited to consider ends, dawns, eves, man, and so on, as metaphors that represent concrete beings and processes – these questions of context, agreement, and solidarity pull us away from Jakobson's vertical axis of metaphor and towards the horizontal axis of metonymy, or from selection to combination. To understand where Derrida stands, we look alongside him much in the same way as we look to the marginal preface for direction; this is where we find, in the margins of "Tympan," Michel Leiris as an unassimilated other. Derrida's philosophy does not stand in for – we cannot read "Ends of Man" proper as a metaphor for

---

8 Derrida's influence on the field of postcolonial studies – including a major impact on the work of Gayatri Spivak, Homi Bhabha, and Robert Young, in particular – cannot be overstated. For accounts of Derrida's influence on the field see Syrotinski; Attridge, *Reading and Responsibility* 39–42; Hiddleston; and Hall.

– resistance to America's foreign policy. Derrida, and his paper so situated, is part of a philosophical contexture that includes opposition to imperialist war.

While Derrida's preamble does not seem to be sutured to the philosophical discourse that characterizes the brunt of his paper, the whole contexture of his paper is focused on the status of "man." One must remember that Derrida is not only using his preamble to state his conscientious objection to a war; this political position is situated within a preamble that begins with the statement that "[e]very philosophical colloquium necessarily has a political significance" (111) and that considers the politics involved in holding an international colloquium on the *anthropos*. Derrida explicitly discusses the political context for writing and delivering a paper in New York in 1968: he notes that his paper was written in April '68, against the backdrop of the beginning of the Paris peace talks and the assassination of Martin Luther King Jr and, at the beginning of May, as students occupied university campuses – Nanterre and the Sorbonne – in Paris. In this context, the question posed to Derrida – "Where is France, as concerns man?" – appears rather deaf to the very questions it is asking. In a gesture that reflects and enacts the movement of philosophical discourse, Derrida demonstrates how "man" himself is marginalized when we discuss the philosophy of man (which is a discussion of proper names – in France: Sartre, the unnamed structuralists proclaiming the death of man, the uptake of German phenomenologists, Hegel, Husserl, and Heidegger). If we look at his intervention in another way, however, by prefacing his talk as he does, Derrida presents, in the margins of philosophical discourse, unassimilable others (who were fighting, at that very moment, for the various institutions of the West – the university, the law, the military, and so on – to recognize them in their difference).[9]

Thinking through the interaction between preamble and presentation proper is key to understanding how Derrida is answering the question posed to him. In his presentation proper, Derrida provides a straightforward answer to the question "Where is France, as concerns man?" France is working through humanism by reading, misreading, and re-reading German phenomenologists. A less straightforward, but ultimately more meaningful, answer lies in reading Derrida's prefatory remarks as part of his response. First of all, the two nouns included in the question are metonyms (not in Jakobson's sense, but in the

---

9 Only one of four discussants – Richard Popkin – tackled the disconnect between philosophy's staking claims on universality while students, racial minorities, and former colonies vied for voice, personhood, and independence.

literal sense, simply meaning that a word is substituted for an associated one): "France" is made to stand in for French philosophical discourse, and "man" is made to stand in for humanism. While these two metonyms are understood and unchallenged in Derrida's presentation proper (even as he challenges the philosophers' anti- or post-humanist claims), Derrida's preface challenges the idea of nationally unified philosophies, and it speaks of civil unrest that not only opposes the foreign and domestic policies of the (always already divided) nation state, but also the very idea of a unified entity called "man." When philosophical discourse is placed in contiguous relation with its consituent context, what emerges is a struggle for the inclusion of difference as such that runs counter to the very idea of a unified national or international philosophical discourse (that could ever stand in for its constituent parts).

And here, again, we should pay attention to the expressivity of Derrida's structure. In a move that mirrors the structure of "Tympan," a prefatory essay that considers philosophy's relations with its others, the marginal, prefatory remarks made at the beginning of "The Ends of Man" are a part of Derrida's presentation, but they are not subsumed by the presentation proper. Situated as such on the margins of Western collocution about man (the topic of Derrida's presentation proper), the figures that exist on Derrida's margins (students, Martin Luther King Jr, the Vietnamese) tympanize philosophical discourse proper, "burdening" and "determining" the link between philosophy and politics. Here we also find the characteristic Derridean reversal or, at the very least, a horizontal flattening of the verticalized valuation of margin and centre (structurally presented as prefatory remarks and conference paper proper): it is "France," or philosophical discourse as such, that is marginal in relation to these seismic movements pertaining to the status and constitution of "man": a Vietnamese people's army fighting for national liberation under the rain of American napalm, black Americans vying for civil rights in a country whose founding document states that "all men are created equal," and students expressing solidarity with racialized and working-class people who didn't have equal access to education or with Vietnamese people who were being decimated as a result of weapons research being conducted on American campuses. "Where is France [French philosophy], as concerns man?" Very much on the margins of these important conversations.

Again, this is not to say that, having identified philosophical discourse with the imperialist impulses and ambitions of the West, Derrida wishes to do away with philosophy once and for all. While the gravity and immediacy of concrete ends – dead and dying civil rights leaders and civilians – might make philosophy seem trite, such is the evaluative and exclusionary logic (of what use are the humanities today?) that leads to the university as a site where market-driven performance indicators favour endeavours like weapons research and petroleum engineering without regard for the associated costs of such research.[10] To place philosophical discourse alongside these concrete struggles is to force philosophy to think about the "political significance" of its inquiries; it is to force philosophy to think its material others without assimilating the differences they are struggling to express.

## Paris X New York: Reflecting, Admiring, Mourning, and Moving

What does it mean to reflect on the '68 years? What are we looking for when we look back, and how does what we find there reflect back on us? The '68 years were indeed a time of reflection, but they were also a time of admiration, which is to say that students looked to each other across borders and oceans and to the burgeoning civil rights movement not simply to find themselves reflected there but in order to locate where these movements exceeded their own, and to try to understand, with and through them, the limits of a form of democracy that was struggling to capture and suppress the excesses of the era (by force, misinformation, concession, assassination, infiltrations, and so on).

Université de Nanterre, sitting ten miles west of Paris in the suburbs, was built with the purpose of giving students a ground for expression, encouraging them to become involved in university governance for the purpose of reform. When bureaucracy reigned towards the end of 1967, and the Fouchet reforms – championing efficiency rather than a broader culture of learning in order to deal with the mass influx of students in the postwar period[11] – were imposed from above, a handful of students boycotted classes and a group of a few dozen students, naming themselves the *enragés*,[12] emerged. When the police invaded campus to break up a confrontation between the *enragés* and another student group, the *enragés* (whose practice of disrupting lectures in the name of Mao and Guevara was more often than not the object of ridicule) experienced a rapid swelling in their ranks as a result of widespread opposition to the police presence.

---

10 For a discussion of the roles and rhythms of philosophy and the humanities in relation to technological advances and the profit motive, see Derrida, *Eyes of the University* 83–182, and "The Future of the Profession."

11 The Fouchet reforms instituted yearly examinations to replace the certificate system. They also took control of the constitution of the baccalauréat away from professors and, by extension, removed their influence over the curriculum in the lycées.

12 "The angry ones" – a reference to a radical group during the French Revolution.

On 22 March, a group of more than 500 students occupied a faculty conference room to protest the dean's refusal to fight on behalf of four students who had been arrested for their participation in a protest against the Vietnam War and for his refusal to provide a bigger lecture hall for meetings of the burgeoning student radical Left. The result was access to the university's largest lecture hall, where perpetual meetings saw the ranks of revolt double, a mass boycott of midterms, and finally the shutting down of the university on 2 May. The next day, students from Nanterre went to the Sorbonne to join protesters who were beginning to organize around the closing down of the suburban university. This protest in turn led to the closing of the Sorbonne only a day after the doors at Nanterre were shut. Hundreds of protestors were arrested. On 6 May, more than 20,000 teachers and students marched in protest of the arrests, and on 13 May, with the support of major workers' unions, the number of people on the streets increased to over a million and continued to grow over the course of the month.[13]

It is important to take the geography of the university into consideration when looking at how student-worker alliances were established. At Nanterre, the industrial working class was permitted to emerge from the fictions within which they had otherwise been enrobed simply because the experimental university had been dropped into their midst, into the working-class suburbs of Paris. Access to the French academy was classed, and Nanterre's geography played a significant part in confronting French students with an image of the university as a beacon of privilege. As a result of this new geographical proximity, some of Nanterre's students started to form alliances with the workers, helping workers to organize and supporting their causes.[14]

---

13  The sources on the May uprising are numerous. Notable for their precise examination of the student revolts that led up to, and proceeded through, May '68 in Paris are Bourges, *The Student Revolt*; Feenberg and Freeman, *When Poetry Ruled the Streets*; Gregoire and Perlman, *Worker-Student Action Committees*; Schnapp and Vidal-Naquet, *The French Student Uprising, November 1967–June 1968*; and Seale and McConville *Red Flag / Black Flag*. The Bourges volume is useful for its inclusion of prominent student perspectives in the direct aftermath of May, and the Feenberg and Freeman, Schnapp and Vidal-Naquet, and Gregoire and Perlman volumes are significant in that they reprint a vast array of documents and communiqués from the revolt. Nanterre's *enragés* were inspired by the Situationist International, and their 1966 pamphlet *On the Poverty of Student Life Considered in Its Economic, Political, Psychological, and Particularly Intellectual Aspects with a Modest Proposal for Its Remedy* – which also references Berkeley – is a key document in this respect.

14  For a discussion of how the suburban, low-income landscape surrounding Nanterre was essential to dismantling traditional separations between students and workers, see Lefebvre 104–10. Kristin Ross briefly discusses the importance of Nanterre in her chapter "Forms and Practices," which provides an excellent, multifaceted analysis of how and why students and workers broke down these separations surrounding the events of May. See Ross 95–6.

Numbers swelled from twenty-five students protesting at Nanterre to ten million student and worker-led revolters in a matter of months. To overlook the way that protests reconfigured the space of university campuses and the streets of France in the vicinity of May, or the way that intellectual production was to a large extent determined by this material context, is to overlook the way that concepts – like complex compounds composed of bonded molecules boasting atoms of various charges – are infused with the volatile stuff of history. The relationship that various political camps had with the academy and the way that intellectuals at specific teaching and research institutions reacted to (became a part of, acknowledged, incorporated, denied) these political currents are significant factors to consider. Not only is a turn towards political engagement an important context for French thought, a context that, more often than not, falls into an imperceptible background in North American appropriations of theoretical terminology, but it also tells us something about the utility of French thought in that it *was* being used, thrown around by students that were at times inspired, and at others exasperated, by its form and content.

Although, in New York, the Columbia protesters did not explicitly invoke curricular issues among their official demands, as was the case with Nanterre and the Fouchet reforms, dissatisfaction with the distance that separated the curriculum and the world outside its walls was widespread. Speaking to this dissatisfaction among students, Robert Friedman hones his attention on an illustrative example. When faculty met in order to re-evaluate their approach to a course called "Contemporary Civilization" the weekend before the revolt – a course that had been a requirement for all of Columbia's students since 1919 – the result of the discussions was that they would lop off Plato, Aristotle, and Aquinas and begin with the Reformation. The irony is too much for Friedman to handle:

> Educational reform was once again a step behind reality. Studying old revolutions in the classroom while new ones were taking place on the Harlem streets just ten blocks away is typical of the University's relation to society. In recent years students had come to discover that ... the University was a social as well as an academic institution and would have to play an active role in the society it once attempted to avoid. (3)

Friedman goes halfway here, recognizing that the university *could* play a relevant role in society. What Foucault – and, of course, Althusser – so effectively and resolutely points out is that it already has its role to manufacture docile bodies, not agitated ones. As was the case with Nanterre, curricular design only helped to accent the disparity between the university classroom and

its immediate environs.[15] Student tympanizing was not met with adequate response on either side of the Atlantic, a fact rendered particularly clear as those
excluded from the discourses of "civilization" were also tympanizing, and had
found a sympathetic ear in students.

The crossing between the New York and Paris campus uprisings (and their
subsequent snowballing into much larger and generalized revolts) is not at all
surprising. As Joanne Grant points out in the preface to her book on the
Columbia uprisings, parallel uprisings were not the result of students mimicking one another but a response to "conditions which are general in this society"
(ix). Daniel and Gabriel Cohn-Bendit reference Columbia among the American
influences for the French student revolts of 1968. Wearing Columbia's (and
Berkeley's) influence on their sleeve in the pages of *Obsolete Communism* –
their rapidly translated late-1968 book – they provide the following comment:

> *Berkeley–Columbia–New York*: Students sickened by the imperialist policies of
> their country, especially in Vietnam, showed their solidarity with the Vietnamese
> peasants and workers and with the oppressed racial and ethnic minorities of their
> own country. They made known their refusal to become privileged members of the
> American bourgeoisie. (33)

Students in the Sociology Department at Nanterre were particularly upset
about the Americanization of their curriculum, with tests and competitive entry
exams that guaranteed fluency in the specialized language of the discipline;
from industrial sociology to political and advertising sociology, the Cohn-
Bendits declared that the discipline "has increasingly been used by the bour-
geoisie to help rationalize society without jeopardizing either profits or stability"
(Cohn-Bendit and Cohn-Bendit 36). The importation of the American model of
modernization was read by sociology students as an earmarking of the discipline for the rationalization of organized capital, clearing the discipline of the

---

15 Although dissatisfaction with the curriculum did not make it into the explicit demands
of Columbia students, the Cox Commission report on the Columbia uprisings includes a
subsection entitled "Uncertainty Concerning the Role of the University" in a section devoted
to "conditions giving rise to the disturbances" (19–24). In his introduction to Roger Kahn's
*The Battle for Morningside Heights*, Senator Eugene McCarthy agues that the university's
inability to recognize – or admit – that it "is involved in contemporary problems and in
contemporary history" was largely to blame for the Columbia events (11). At the centre
of his argument is the government and private funding sources that determined not only the
university's research projects but also the way that results were reported (11–12), a criticism
amplified in the context of the neoliberal university.

potential to reflect critically upon the manner in which society is run, and for whom. Beyond sharing a focal point in opposition to the Vietnam War, then, this more general "refusal" – to become a part of the middle class (and all of the complicities that the conversion entailed) – was a common ground. If this is what French students recognized in American uprisings, what did the "poetry" of the Parisian uprisings – their marches, building occupations, barricades, graffitied and hollered slogans, and so on[16] – signify if not the refusal of a whole way of life?

To say that the parallel uprisings were conducted in concert against global capitalism, however, is not to forget that the uprisings were acted out upon local stages, against global capitalism's local effects. It is important and illustrative to note that when we attune ourselves to the local details underlying the parallel uprisings, rather than pushing the revolts further apart in the process of outlining their specificity, we find another crossing. If the events at Nanterre were, to a large extent, sparked by its geography – the suburban space in which the new, experimental Université de Nanterre was built – Columbia's uprising had a lot to do with its location in New York. Around the same time that Nanterre was being built in the industrial suburbs of Paris, Columbia was expanding into Harlem, driving out the local black and Puerto Rican population by buying real estate out from under them, raising rents, and establishing policies that enforced segregation. At the centre of the Columbia uprising was the proposed site of a new gymnasium on parkland heavily used by local residents. The mostly black local population would be permitted to access basement facilities via a back door, prompting protestors to label the project "Gym Crow."[17]

Columbia's development plans for the neighbourhood had been a source of clashes since he mid-1960s. As Grant notes, although the expansion of the

---

16  My use of the term "poetry" is in reference to Feenberg and Freeman's collection of posters, manifestoes, and graffiti from the May '68 events in France, in *When Poetry Ruled the Streets*.

17  The most substantial accounts of the Columbia events of 1968 were published in its immediate aftermath by journalists who witnessed the events and conducted interviews from their midst. See Grant, *Confrontation on Campus*; and Avorn et al., *Up Against the Ivy Wall*. Until recently, the history of the struggle against the gym has been whitewashed. For an account that focuses on the Students' Afro-American Society (SAS) and the development of the Black Power ideology at Columbia over the course of the 1960s, see Bradley, *Harlem vs. Columbia University*. Considering the legacy of Columbia '68, that the SAS protest at Hamilton Hall fulfilled its task of blocking the gym without erupting in or provoking violent clashes makes the omission of SAS participation from most of the narratives that relate the history of the events of April 1968 particularly curious and troubling.

campus was not driven by an explicit policy of displacing racialized people from their neighbourhoods, by 1968, community leaders estimated that 7,500 tenants had been pushed out of their community as Columbia took over buildings, and 85 per cent of these tenants were black or Puerto Rican (29). Statements made by a coordinator of campus planning that Columbia was "looking for a community where the faculty can talk to people like themselves," or by Provost Jacques Barzun that the community was "uninviting, abnormal, sinister, dangerous," reinforced the fact that Columbia, a university that did not yet have any tenured black faculty, did not want to share its space with the racialized community that it was in the process of pushing out (Grant 29). In 1965, Columbia submitted a map of "current and anticipated holdings in the Morningside Heights area" to the board of estimate (Grant 30); though somewhat of a public relations disaster, the map demonstrated Columbia's bold and reckless pursuit of community properties. The plan to build a segregated gym over public, locally frequented parkland was not an isolated incident somehow deviating from the university's otherwise considerate and friendly relations with its neighbours; it was the work of its board of trustees, stacked with developers and realtors, who had become emboldened by their otherwise effortless decimation of a community.[18] While the gym symbolized the brutality of expansion, that students and community members were eventually able to stop it from being built was also, as Columbia's current expansion into the West Harlem community of Manhattanville attests, somewhat of a symbolic victory. Such is the university's relations with its others.

That the Columbia protest split along racial lines provides further instruction on issues regarding the margins. When members of Columbia's chapter of Students for a Democratic Society (SDS) met with several students at the sundial on April 23rd, they were joined by members of Columbia's Students' Afro-American Society (SAS). Members of SDS and SAS worked together for the duration of the day in an initially unsuccessful attempt to occupy Low Library, followed by a march to the gym site and scuffles with police at 113th Street and Morningside Avenue, and ending with the occupation of Hamilton Hall. Once there, members of SAS and SDS formed an impromptu joint steering committee and co-produced a list of demands. At 3 a.m., when police were reported to be on their way, a black student caucus decided that white students

---

18 For analysis and charts of the real estate, military, intelligence, and corporate interests that drove Columbia's various agendas in the 1960s, see *Who Rules Columbia*.

should leave because the black students wanted to run their own protest against the gym and they felt that the white students were not disciplined enough. The suggestion by black students that white students were just playing at being revolutionaries echoes comments made by Stokely Carmichael and Charles V. Hamilton in *Black Power: The Politics of Liberation in America*:

> It is our position that black organizations should be black-led and essentially black-staffed, with policy being made by black people. White people can and do play supportive roles in those organizations. Where they come with specific skills and techniques, they will be evaluated in those terms. All too frequently, however, many young, middle-class, white Americans, like some sort of Pepsi generation, have wanted to "come alive" through the black community and black groups. They have wanted to be where the action is – and the action has been in those places. They have sought refuge among blacks from a sterile, meaningless, irrelevant life in middle-class America … Many have come seeing "no difference in color," they have come "color blind." But at this time and in this land, color *is* a factor and we should not overlook or deny this. (83)

Carmichael and Hamilton's assessment illustrates a tension writ large, not only as regards the revolt at Columbia but in general over the course of this period of protest. Beyond immediate tensions regarding the constitution of protest, the often well-intentioned actions of a generation seeking refuge from white middle-class America has had the effect of obscuring many of the important battles waged by black and brown groups during this same period. The whitewashed history of the Columbia revolts is one such instance. Considering the legacy of Columbia '68, that the SAS protest at Hamilton Hall fulfilled its task of blocking the gym without erupting in or provoking violent clashes, makes its omission particularly curious and troubling.

The lesson from this is that margins are not singular; they emerge as unequal power relations within movements and must be accounted for in every interaction with others. As Stefan Bradley notes, in the midst of black student activist protests at Rutgers, Harvard, the University of Pennsylvania, and Cornell, where a focus on the institution of black studies programs was the primary goal, "Columbia's proximity to Harlem allowed SAS to focus on an issue that directly affected the surrounding black community" ("Gym Crow Must Go!" 164). Black students therefore became a voice for the embattled communities on the campus's margins while aiming to ensure, via the lessons of Stokely Carmichael and Malcolm X, that their own voices would not be co-opted and marginalized, translated by white protestors who, comparatively speaking, had more political and economic clout and who might misrepresent or redirect the protest via their own inclinations.[19] As Bradley points out, while black students did not want to lose the support of white students – they needed their support, just as white students needed black student support – the black takeover of the Hamilton Hall protest against the gym was a victory in itself – like an "invasion of the ivory tower," as one local resident put it – by a group of students who were not only black but who were first-generation, working-class students who were "structurally closer to their community" (*Harlem vs. Columbia University* 79). The movement of Columbia outwards, over top of its black, brown, and working-class neighbours, was perceived by black students as a threat within the movement itself, an absolutely legitimate concern considering the marginalization of black students in accounts of this history. In other words, while black students were successful in stopping the gym because they retained their independence, history has, with a notable exception in the work of Bradley, proceeded to erase this activist history, just as Columbia has proceeded to displace its neighbours since 1968. History – like philosophy and the university as real estate developer – is also a translating machine.

Although white student activists relinquished control of the Hamilton Hall occupation, white protest efforts remained in contiguous relation with black activism. The Columbia uprising was set against the backdrop of the assassination of Martin Luther King Jr at the beginning of April, which only fuelled the fire against the politics that Columbia's expansion practices represented. In the days prior to the Columbia revolt, the SDS staged a walkout at Columbia's King memorial in recognition not only of the contradictions embodied by the university's expansion practices but also of the dissonance between King's recently declared opposition to the Vietnam War and Columbia's membership in the Institute for Defense Analyses (IDA), a weapons research and development group, and of the impossibility of reconciling his late focus on improving conditions for the working poor[20] with Columbia's paying cafeteria workers an unlivable wage of $1.65/hour (Feldman). In his final year of sermons and public addresses, King himself emphasized how his concern had widened over the years, from a focus on black Americans, to all Americans, to all people of the

---

19  For discussions of the necessity of racial separatism in social movements, see Bradley,
     *Harlem vs. Columbia University* 74–92; and Malcolm X, "Message to the Grassroots."
20  King was assassinated in Memphis while supporting sanitation workers as part of the "poor
     people's campaign" of 1968. The campaign was planned by the Southern Christian Leader-
     ship Conference (SCLC) under his leadership in late 1967 and was to run from February to
     May 1968, culminating in a poor people's march on Washington. For King's appeal for a
     multiracial movement for economic justice, see King, "The Other America."

world (a broadening most emblematically encapsulated in "Beyond Vietnam," a sermon delivered exactly one year before his assassination, where King argued that America's soul can "never be saved so long as it destroys the deepest hopes of men the world over" [144]).

The Columbia protest against the presence of the IDA on campus was the latest in a string of targeted protests against the militarization of campus. The intensification of student revolt began in 1965 with the formation of a human chain to block the Naval Reserve Officers Training Corps from holding their annual awards ceremony in Low Plaza. While the event had the immediate effect of drawing in police to end the protest, within two years the awards ceremony was ended due to the prospect of violence (Cox Commission 63–4). The Columbia SDS took similar stances regarding CIA recruitment, disrupting interviews by showing up en masse with questions of their own in November 1966, and by blocking interview room doors via sit-ins in February 1967. Both picketing and sit-ins were employed to block Marine recruitment in April 1967, which drew in counterdemonstrators and led to a blanket ban on picketing and demonstrations in campus buildings (Cox Commission 64–9). SDS challenged the rule with an October 1967 march to President Grayson Kirk's office to demand that all ties be cut to the military establishment and by picketing Dow Chemical recruitment in February 1968 – Dow Chemical was a manufacturer of Napalm, heavily used in Vietnam – before the administration finally invoked the rule, starting disciplinary proceedings against several students after the Columbia SDS held a demonstration in Low Library to mark its presentation of a letter to President Kirk, signed by 1,500 faculty and students, demanding an end to IDA affiliation (Cox Commission 69–73).

Student protest against the IDA was like a confrontation between networks. The IDA is a federally sponsored weapons research initiative that also conducts studies on counterinsurgency and riot control. In 1968, its membership consisted of twelve private universities,[21] and it conducted research for the Weapons Systems Evaluation Group of the Joint Chiefs of Staff, the Advanced Research Projects Agency of the Defense Department, the National Security Agency, the State Department, the Office of Civil Defense, and the Federal Aviation Agency (Grant 34). The April 23rd events at Columbia must be

---

21  Original members of the IDA included the Massachusetts Institute of Technology, the California Institute of Technology, Case Institute of Technology, Stanford, and Tulane. Columbia, the University of Michigan, and Penn State joined in 1960; the University of Chicago in 1961; Princeton and the University of Illinois joined in 1962; and the University of California Berkeley joined in 1964 (Grant 34).

understood in this context of protest against military ties and recruitment, and against the university's response of downplaying and obscuring ties while drawing up regulations to stifle participation in actions aimed at drawing attention to the university's dealings. The connections between King's legacy – sit-ins, marches, opposition to the war – and campus unrest cannot be overstated. As government organizations, weapons manufacturers, and university researchers combined their efforts to invent new ways to kill people and control crowds, purportedly to pave the way for democracy, students and citizens stood up for – and as – those who were actively being marginalized by the democratic vision of those in established positions of power.

We should also recall the first lines from Ho Chi Minh's "Declaration of Independence of the Democratic Republic of Viet Nam." The lines are recognizable, they admire and reflect: "All men are created equal. They are endowed by their Creator with certain inalienable rights, among them are Life, Liberty, and the pursuit of Happiness" (51). Ho quotes the American Declaration of Independence, noting that, in essence, it extends to all people of the earth, and that it was echoed by the 1791 Declaration of the French Revolution, that "All men are born free and with equal rights, and must always remain free and have equal rights" (51). Writing in 1945, while Vietnam remained a French colony, Ho observes that French imperial relations with Vietnam represent a violation of these universal and inalienable truths. As Ho compiles the deprivations of democratic liberties, the building of more prisons than schools, obscurantism and the fettering of public opinion, economic impoverishment, the use of drugs and alcohol to weaken the Vietnamese, and the devastation of Vietnamese lands with the extraction of its natural resources, one sees not only the parallel imperialist paths forged by French and American republics living in contradiction to their declared ideals but also the domestic parallels, which have only intensified since, that led to the defection of so many black American soldiers and that ultimately drew King into the antiwar camp. To tympanize – a form of democracy: "We the People" – "But who, *we*?"

## Mourning King

To make political sense of Derrida, we could do worse, at this juncture, than to look to his only named, marginalized tympanizer, Martin Luther King Jr. It is, after all, the end of this man's life that he uses to "date quite precisely" his writing about the ends of man (*Margins* 114): Derrida is no doubt memorializing King when he invokes King's end as a context for the beginning of his writing. Though "The Ends of Man" precedes Derrida's work on mourning, if we turn to the former, we can see how King's presence on the margins of this paper is a negotiated tribute that allows King to retain his political force. In *Memoires for Paul de Man*, Derrida discusses the paradox of mourning, where successful mourning, which would be to fully interiorize the other, denies others their alterity, whereas failure to mourn, or impossible mourning, fully respects the alterity of the other, "refus[ing] to take ... the other within oneself, as in the tomb or vault of some narcissism" (6). It is easy for an America still wrestling with Jim Crow to take King as one of its own, cutting him off from the promised lands where he dwelled and desired to take the country (and it is precisely for this reason that the Columbia SDS staged a walkout at the King memorial service). But, to fully other King, to refuse to mourn him in some way, amounts to the same thing; it is another way of aborting his project, because it is a refusal to engage the otherness that King represents. Mourning King – today, as much as in 1968 – is therefore a delicate, political matter: to respect and retain otherness while finding a way to continue to converse allows the absent other to remain a force for transformational change. "The only fitting eulogy for Dr. King," the Columbia SDS stated in a pamphlet circulated shortly after the King memorial walkout, "is to join his widow and Dr. Abernathy and continue the struggle for Black Liberation in *everyday practice* – and in the everyday functioning of this university" (qtd. in Grant 33). Turning towards Derrida's work on mourning helps us to understand both the Columbia walkout and the politics behind Derrida's positioning of King on the margins of his 1968 intervention. But how does it sit with King?

While Derrida's opposition to the Vietnam War was not bothersome to the American authorities, who let a French philosopher, as a condition of his appearance, make such a declaration,[22] King, jailed many times and assassinated just months before Derrida's presentation, was absolutely bothersome to the established order. In *The Work of Mourning*, Derrida writes that "[d]eath takes from us not only some particular life within the world, some moment that belongs to us, but, each time, without limit, someone through whom the world, and first of all our own world, will have opened up in a both finite and infinite – mortally infinite – way" (107). King dwells within Derrida's paper – lives on and is mourned, politically – as an absent alterity whose method, in life, was to be non-violently present. This presence, in the form of boycotts, marches, and sit-ins, was meant, as King notes in "Pilgrimage to Nonviolence," to "awaken a sense of moral shame" (50); it was not meant to "defeat or humiliate the opponent, but to win his friendship and understanding" (49) for the purpose of

---

22 Regarding the position takings of faculty, see Greenman.

creating a "beloved community" (50).[23] It is in this way that King is associated profoundly with the opening up of worlds, and it is for this reason as well that he is appropriately placed on the margins of a text that stylistically brackets the ends of man: "man" is a heretofore closed project that the presence of the other causes to tremble. Whereas Derrida is a welcome foreigner, King was not, and the presence of America's others looms large over Derrida's discussion of the ends, or limits, of man as represented in philosophical (and democratic) discourse. Whether or not this looming that perpetually repeats itself throughout Derrida's deconstructive project is really all that bothersome is another question.

We should also be mindful of the place of futurity in Derrida's margins. While the futurity that Derrida speaks – the eve of the end of man – flirts with a type of permanent exoticization or suspension of the other as pure, future potential, it also, in some ways, represents the contemporary work being done by student and civil rights activists. Over the course of the sixties, King and students alike pointed to the contradictions within systems and looked towards the futures that had long been promised by the languages of American democracy and the university, but the police, courts, segregated public spaces, curricula, weapons research, gentrification, and so on, foreclosed any possibility of realizing these futures.[24] Speaking still in the language of reflection, this is why we might recognize a piece like "The Ends of Man" as a kind of translation of the consciousness-raising work being done on the margins of the university: Derrida is translating the sentiments of those who are marginalized by the university and by American democracy into the margins of a philosophical address that deconstructs the logic of margins and centres.

If we can agree to read this marginalization as a kind of snapshot of the political field in 1968, it remains in contrast to the mourning being done by students in the wake of King's death. Not only did Columbia's students walk out

---

23  The overlap between Derrida's *Politics of Friendship*, oriented towards the other and aimed at a democracy to come, and King's work on friendship and love (*agapé*), which is oriented towards the enemy from whom one can expect nothing in return, and which is practised for the purpose of creating community, demands devoted study.

24  In responding to a letter penned by a group of clergymen condemning King's method of direct action as the unwelcome and impatient action of an outsider, King's "Letter from Birmingham Jail" not only demonstrates that he is more versed in scripture, the American Constitution, and American philosophy than those who penned the critique but also that he uses the traditions to undermine the very idea of an American outsider. Consider, for example, his argument that "anyone who lives in the United States can never be considered an outsider anywhere in this country" (290). For an excellent rhetorical analysis of his letter, see Haslam 109–34.

of the university's memorial service in a gesture that was meant to make people reflect upon the contradictions inherent in the institution's assimilation of a bothersome spirit, but the occupations SDS staged in the following months were non-violent direct actions against the continuing practices of segregation and displacement and the development of weapons technologies to be used against racialized others. Furthermore, to mourn King by refusing to deaden his spirit was not an aberration for students; it was a continuation of the student movement against racism that had been developing over the course of the sixties. If the Columbia revolt had an iconic predecessor in the University of California Berkeley campus's free speech movement (FSM) in 1964, the FSM grew out of the civil rights era of the black liberation movement. As Angela Davis points out in her introduction to Bettina Aptheker's *The Academic Rebellion in the United States*, Berkeley students had been participating in sit-ins organized by the civil rights movement against the hotel industry in San Francisco in the months leading into the sit-ins on campus, student sit-ins that themselves had precedents in the sit-in conducted by black students at the Woolworth lunch counter in Greensboro, North Carolina in 1960 (11). Two months after Greensboro, the Student Non-violent Coordinating Committee (SNCC) was established. One of the SNCC's first actions was to co-organize, with the Congress on Racial Equality (CORE), Freedom Rides, where black and white activists rode interstate buses from northern cities into the South, with the aim of desegregating transportation in the South. The lineage is important, because it saw white students participating in the black liberation movement in 1961 before establishing the SDS a year later. The impact that the civil rights and black liberation movements had on the American student movement cannot be overstated. While Derrida's philosophy aims at an ever-inclusive democracy-to-come, the complexity of the margins – the theories, discoveries, arguments, and alliances that were built in the '60s to disrupt hegemonic centres – have little place within his discourse.

The problem with Derridean deconstruction is not simply that it is a celebration of the margins that leaves those on the margin wed, in Derrida's writing, to an elaborated, albeit deconstructed centre, it is also that the ethical move of leaving the other in a state of indeterminacy – the infinite deferral of *différance* and the *à venir* – is disabling at the same time as it is liberating. On the one hand, the ethical commitment to not speaking for, or in place of, the other, is an ethic that should be at the heart of any political alliance, but, on the other, Derrida's dyadic thinking – even if it is used to dismantle pairings and hierarchies – reifies the centre it deconstructs, reaffirming its hold on the margins in a set of moves where, as Françoise Lionnet and Shu-Mei Shih point out, "the other never 'arrives,' he or she is always 'à venir,'" an ethics that is, perhaps, they "bluntly" point out, "analogous to the illusive and elusive promise of equality in Republican universalism" ("Introduction: Thinking through the Minor" 3).[25] Good intentions aside, where do we go when we read Derrida? As Lionnet and Shih point out in "The Creolization of Theory," we need to be careful about conflating the politics of difference being elaborated in Departments of Ethnic Studies with *différance*, as, in the heyday of high theory, the former was marginalized for its lack of theoretical sophistication, or, to put it another way, its unwillingness, in its concrete fights for the inclusion of minority voices and cultures in university curricula, to speak in the then dominant, high theoretical tongue (12–21). One must take note of the naming of names: when we read "The Ends of Man," we intuit Sartre and read all about Hegel, Husserl, and Heidegger, and then, following Derrida, we marginalize King, the movement against Vietnam, and the student voices who were, in the sixties, questioning the legitimacy of a university paving its way to audit culture and a discourse of excellence. Rather than translating his work into an impasse, to truly reflect upon and admire Derrida is to recognize his oeuvre not as a set of works with beginning and end, but as an opening up to the others that reside in its margins.

### Spontaneous Collectives

Derrida deconstructs the progress of philosophy, its drive towards universality, the end of man, by collecting, at the margins of the Western philosophical project, a world of exclusions that bear down on its universalist ambitions and claims. Although these exclusions undermine the project, the translative movement of philosophy is insidious: it internalizes those differences that complicate its claims. Such is the nature of that "form of democracy" whereby one is permitted to declare opposition to official policy. While some may feel absolved by having the "right opinion" and registering their dissent, such articulations are not at all bothersome to the unhindered, imperialist progress of the West. Those with unassimilable differences, on the other hand – those that we find on the margins of Derrida's paper: the Vietnamese National Liberation Front, civil rights and black nationalist leaders, students engaging in non-violent direct action to stop weapons development on campus and development plans harmful to the surrounding communities, movements aimed at stopping the violent, imperialist movement of "progress" – are deemed outsiders, are

---

25  On the exclusion and futurity of the other, see also Chow 61–9.

outlawed, are murdered or suppressed with batons and firehouses, and are, as per the mourning of King, retroactively internalized as representative heroes of Western democratic principles.

If we pay attention to the zone – the precise time and place – of Derrida's intervention, of this meeting of French and American philosophers, we find this meeting of Paris and New York expressed otherwise. In 1968, while American and French philosophers met to discuss "language and human nature" in an academic setting, students in Paris and New York – at Nanterre, the Sorbonne, and Columbia – were quoting each other in their respective revolts, marking, at the margins of French and American universities, another site of Western collocution. The extra-curricular events in Paris and New York did not only correspond to one another, they corresponded with one another in the underground press and through sentiments and actions readable in mainstream newspapers and television images. Like international colloquia, these concurrent events marked a pronounced line of communication between continents, a transatlantic channel for the movement of impulses and dispositions that were, of course, very different from those being exchanged and consecrated at international colloquia. As we have seen, Daniel Cohn-Bendit cites the influence of Berkeley and Columbia on Parisian students in *Obsolete Communism* (23–4, 33). Similarly, in his memoir, *Underground*, Mark Rudd notes that Columbia strikers were "intensely aware of the revolutionary events taking place in France" in spring 1968, and he recounts the exhilarating effect of seeing a newspaper image of a French student carrying a sign with two words, "Columbia, Paris," as well as the receipt of a telegram at Columbia Strike Central from the Sorbonne: "WE'VE OCCUPIED A BUILDING IN YOUR HONOR. WHAT DO WE DO NOW?" (113). In her book on the Columbia uprisings, Joanne Grant notes that, during a 21 May protest, with protestors singing "La Marseillaise," "people were pulling up bricks from the walks and hurling them at police" and windows, prompting someone to comment that "the mobile tactics of European students – diverting the police to all parts of the campus – were being used" (122). This is the context of "The Ends of Man"; it is a reflection of the relations that were making the very foundations of the university, and also "Man," tremble.[26] Structurally and significantly, "The Ends of Man" is a reflection on not only the troubled relationship between

---

26 While Derrida notes that his distrust of spontaneism led him to distance himself from the movements of May ("A Madness Must Watch" 347–8), the anti-imperialist and inclusive orientation that students expressed in the face of exclusionary curricula and policies is reflected in Derrida's oeuvre and in his work with GREPH.

philosophy and politics, or France's reckonings with humanism, but also the ethics of revolt; in the unassimilated contiguity of his margins, Derrida reflects the "solidarity" that was central to the student movements of 1968.

What is significant about the correspondent launching of inert matter? Why emphasize the crossing of campuses via cobblestones? Cobblestones made for a convenient and readily available projectile, to be sure, but their significance runs deeper. If we understand the term "modernity" to describe a relatively lengthy journey to the present – centring around the rise of capitalism, urbanization, and the increasing role of science and technology – the emergence of the cobblestone in the fifteenth century marked the transformation of the street into a route for commerce, suited for heavy traffic the whole year round. Following in the barricade-building footsteps of the June rebellion in 1832 (memorialized by Victor Hugo in *Les Misérables* with the death of Gavroche), the February revolution in 1848, and the communards of the Paris Commune in 1871, students disassembling the streets of Paris and New York were also undoing the roads that had paved the way for capitalism's flows. As a May '68 slogan went, "*Sous les pavés, la plage!*"[27] In the process of battling with police, students were uncovering collective spaces that had been covered over by modernity's steadfast march. As Daniel Cohn-Bendit put it, "People were building up the cobblestones because they wanted – many of them for the first time – to throw themselves into a collective, spontaneous activity" (qtd. in Fraser 9). The unearthing of cobblestones made for the emergence of collective spaces; the act of throwing a cobblestone became a collective-building act. To situate this within the discourse of translation, Columbia students were engaging in an act of translation by launching cobblestones as a part of their own revolt (quoting a French text in another context); in addition, the throwing of cobblestones is in itself an act of translation that transforms whole sets of relations (one's relation to space, people's relations with one another).

To translate Derrida isn't simply to substitute his signifiers for their equivalent in another language, it is also to take his sentiments elsewhere in a horizontal move across time and space. Paying careful attention to the time and place of his intervention, what would it look like to move laterally towards Derrida's margins rather than trying to "get to the heart of" his speech? Rather than being limited to instances where texts are made available in another

---

27 "Under the cobblestones, the beach," a reference to the fact that, if enough cobblestones were pulled up, the sand underneath transformed the street into an urban beach.

language, translation is any subsequent usage of a text, which is necessarily a transformative act. As Apter notes, while "translation failure demarcates inter-subjective limits" – a point that certainly applies to Derrida's 1968 critique of the Western philosophical project – "translation is a significant medium of subject re-formulation and political change" (*The Translation Zone* 6). To set Derrida at the crossing of Paris and New York in 1968 – before, above, and beyond his appearance at Johns Hopkins in 1966 – is an act of "subject re-formulation and political change." Not only does such an act unmoor Derrida from a trajectory whereby he undoes structuralism upon arrival and joins the Yale School in 1975, it also situates him at a site where the political subjects at the margins of philosophy are visible.

While the solidarity expressed by Derrida at the conference in New York was not particularly "bothersome" (authorized, as it was, by the authorities, it did not, he notes, "upset the established order"), in a way, "The Ends of Man" does "bother" the way that Derrida was established in America. Derrida presented "Structure, Sign, and Play" to an American audience in 1966, but it wasn't published in translation until 1970. Interestingly enough, "The Ends of Man" was published in the International Phenomenological Society's journal *Philosophy and Phenomenological Research* in 1969, making it Derrida's first paper to appear in English translation. While Derrida is certainly cautious about putting stake in origins, it is significant that, at the outermost margins of his entry into Anglo-American writing, we find him positioning himself politically in relation to the philosophical discourse that will follow. "The Ends of Man" allows us to translate the early Derrida differently – to put these crucial politics of difference first. These are, after all, the conditions that he places upon speaking in America in the first place.

Following Derrida's thinking about the impossibility of full presence – meaning is derived from difference, languages are a system of differences without positive terms – there can be no equivalency or fidelity in the crossing from one language to another because each language, though by no means impenetrable, is, in essence, its own system of differences. Accordingly, translation can never be done with absolute fidelity. Rather than trying to grasp at the ungraspable full presence of the proper name "Derrida," it is perhaps better to reconstitute him via the difference he introduced into philosophical discourse. This would be to translate by moving horizontally through and beyond the field of Derrida's discourse rather than trying to substitute, for his speech, other signifiers that grasp its "true" meaning. Conceived and enacted in this way, translation is a political act that reformulates discourse away from the authoritative, central-izing, phallogocentric subject of Derrida's critique.

In the end, this horizontal impulse, this movement away from the centre that is at centre of Derrida's philosophical project, is an impulse that was also at centre of "the margins" in 1968. To abandon Derrida for these margins is to take seriously both the context out of which Derrida's philosophy was born and his contention that philosophy misses its others when they are translated into philosophical discourse. It is the impulse towards, and an ethical relationship with, the margins (and not an arsenal of Derridean concepts) that comes from this zone, or passage, I notate as Paris–Derrida–New York, 1968.

Contiguity is not built of a moment, it is, as per Roman Jakobson's equation of contiguity with the narrative movement of prose, a movement where margins beget margins on a troubling and sometimes troubled route towards a more equitable future. In the midst of movement, each moment is a preface for the next, even if it is oftentimes presented as a recollection, written after the fact, for the purpose of moving ahead. In 1968, movement was in the margins, or, rather, it was that which was writing itself out of the margins as causes were being put in contiguous relation with one another, in campus newspapers, for example, where the tympan of the printing press presents itself as the blank spaces where connections are made.[28]

---

28  The issues of the *Columbia Spectator*, printed daily during the uprising, are available as pdf downloads as part of Columbia University Library's Digital Collections. While all issues dated 24 April through 8 May have been made available, the 22 April issue (with the masthead "*Up Against the Wall Motherfucker*" rather than "*Columbia Spectator*"), printed on the eve of the revolt, has not been made available. See http://www.columbia.edu/cu/lweb/digital/collections/cul/texts/ldpd_8603880_000/index.html.

# 2 Translating Movement: Going Underground with Deleuze and Guattari

Some leftist theorists might talk about building a bridge between Marx and Freud, but no one could possibly devise a structure to encompass this Movement. It would have to be a grand geodesic dome fitted together from pieces of Marx, Freud, Zen, Artaud, Kesey, Lenin, Leary, Ginsberg, Che, Gandhi, Marcuse, Laing, Fidel, and Lao Tzu, strung with the black banners of anarchy to which the sayings of Chairman Mao have been embroidered, and with a 40-watt rock amplifier strapped to the top – a gaudy, mind-blowing spectacle and an impossible intellectual synthesis.

Laurence Leamer, *The Paper Revolutionaries*

America is a special case ... everything important that has happened or is happening takes the route of the American rhizome: the beatniks, the underground, bands and gangs, successive lateral offshoots in immediate connection with an outside.

Gilles Deleuze and Félix Guattari, *A Thousand Plateaus*

Spontaneous collectives did not only manifest through the launching of cobblestones; they appeared in newspapers, too. The underground press displaced icons and networked alternatives; it made available a set of coordinate points that circulated marginally or not at all in university classrooms and the mainstream press. That Gilles Deleuze and Félix Guattari appear in a New York underground newspaper in 1968 displaces the origin of their work in America. What opens up in the process is a vast and intricately networked set of unsynthesizable struggles that scores of late sixties politicized youth called "the movement." Not only is the "grand geodesic dome" – the network of points and connections – that Laurence Leamer describes obscured when French theory is pursued via its translation for academic books, journals, and university departments, but connections are similarly obscured when we focus solely on the proper names that come to emblemize thought. Although a proper name designates an oeuvre and intellectual property, the fact that, as Deleuze and Guattari note, each of us is several reminds us that every oeuvre is the net work of innumerable influences. Moreover, translation demonstrates that foreign words can be assigned to proper names as well, expanding the oeuvre beyond anything actually said or written by an author. Such is the case with Deleuze and translation.[1]

While Deleuze and Guattari's concepts can be compiled, and their production together can be assembled into a system understood in relation to others articulated in the history of philosophy (it is, after all, a collaborative relationship that culminates in *What Is Philosophy?*), their writings are wrought of relations extending in a number of directions that are opposed to and/or have little to do with the trajectory of philosophy. This renders metaphoric readings, interpretations, and translations of Deleuze and Guattari – readings that singularize and substitute, that overlook and/or obscure associations – problematic. Concepts are not the exclusive property of the domains where we usually seek them out. As they note in *What Is Philosophy?*, "The greatness of a philosophy is measured by the nature of the events to which its concepts summon us or that it enables us to release in its concepts" (34). In a sense, this chapter is an exploration of the events to which "rhizome" summons us. As Deleuze and Guattari state at the beginning of *A Thousand Plateaus*, the rhizome is not a metaphor; it exists, for example, as crabgrass. The rhizome also existed as the countercultural and political movements of the sixties and seventies, and it ran through the underground press. The lesson of this chapter, however, isn't simply that "rhizome" is a translation of these networks and movements; I also offer the more encompassing proposition that "rhizome" is the movement of translation: it is the perpetual movement of collection and projection. When movement ceases, so does translation.

This chapter is divided into three interrelated sections. In the first section, I discuss Deleuze and Guattari's relationship with Jean-Jacques Lebel through

---

1  I am indebted to Barbara Godard here. In her two essays on Deleuze and translation, Godard not only provides an account of the disciplinary and geopolitical relations that have had a determining effect on the way that Deleuze is taken up in translation, but she also develops a Deleuzian theory of translation. Although Deleuze had little to say about translation specifically, Godard focalizes Deleuze's work on the fold, the event, and transcreation through the question of translation in order to develop a model that takes both Deleuze and the field of translation studies in novel and productive directions. See Godard, "Deleuze and Translation" and "Signs and Events"; and Demers, "Taking Deleuze in the Middle."

the concept of the fold. The fold is one of the ways that we can read the "and" that is central to Deleuze and Guattari. "And" does not mark a simple relationship of correspondence between two terms. It is a relation of reciprocal implication or mutual exchange: the inside folds out and the outside in. Lebel is an artist and activist, and he was a friend of Deleuze and Guattari who participated in the '68 revolts on either side of the Atlantic. We are pulled away from privileging Deleuze and Guattari themselves when we follow the foldings embodied by Lebel. In Lebel's travels, we see the building of assemblages – groupings of figures and ideas – many of which would appear in *Anti-Oedipus* and *A Thousand Plateaus*, and we witness the elaboration and transatlantic distribution of concepts like the "body without organs" and "lines of flight." The fold is not just a useful heuristic device, it is a naturally occurring translator whose work we can follow to better understand the complex dynamics of a social sphere inhabited not by insular singularities writing philosophy books but by networks of relations.[2]

In the second section, I pull Deleuze and Guattari down an intensive line through the American underground that they celebrate in the introduction to *A Thousand Plateaus*. The section bridges two *events*; it moves from the building occupations at Columbia University in April 1968 to Chicago's Democratic National Convention (DNC) in August. Similar to the fold, events are plateaus, intensive middle grounds built of collaboration, intersubjectivity, and reciprocal implication. For Deleuze and Guattari, events are not something to marvel at; instead, they represent the collection of a vast amount of potential that should be plugged into something else to keep that potential alive. This is the anti-teleological premise of becoming.[3] It is in this sense that events are inseparable from *transcreation*: events *collect* a complex of folds that are *projected* in a transcreative process of becoming. My purpose in the second section of this chapter is to map the diachronic development of movement by associations and to develop, in the process, the work of two more Deleuzian translators: event

---

2 Deleuze not only writes about the fold in *The Fold*, but, significantly, he also uses the concept to trace the relation of inside and out throughout Foucault's oeuvre in the final chapter of *Foucault*, 94–123. On the "disjunctive synthesis," see, in particular, Deleuze *The Logic of Sense* 42–7, and Deleuze and Guattari, *Anti-Oedipus* 9–16, 75–84.

3 The concept of "becoming" is given a chapter in Deleuze and Guattari *A Thousand Plateaus* 232–309, but it is ultimately developed out of Deleuze's reading of Nietzsche's eternal return as a process that abolishes the possibility of origins and ends. See, in particular, Deleuze *Nietzsche and Philosophy* 47–9, and *Difference and Repetition* 52–8.

and transcreation.[4] One of the effects of following and analysing the work of concepts that can be situated and understood only in process is that this section and the next have a narrative thrust that foregrounds the importance of metonymy to social movements.

In the third and final section of this chapter, I describe the takeover of *RAT Subterranean News* – an underground newspaper I employ to follow the development of the movement throughout this chapter – by a women's collective. While the second section ends with a discussion of the movement being mobilized in *RAT* as a nomadic war machine forging relations outside the purview of the state while trying to evade capture, the takeover of *RAT* is an important reminder that "statist" ways of thinking and organizing can creep into social movements. For Deleuze and Guattari, the state apparatus is not simply the state, it is any despotic regime of signification that organizes and ultimately verticalizes relationships between elements within an assemblage. While women's liberation is a final destination point on a narrative journey through the development of the movement in *RAT Subterranean News*, it is also a site that compels us to revisit the complicated relationship between metaphoric and metonymic modes of translation.

As philosophers of becoming, Deleuze and Guattari have little to say about origins and ends; instead, they are invested in the middle. The middle is the space of the disjunctive synthesis, the space of the "and" or "with" that breaks free from the dualism of either/or, allowing for combination and autonomy at once. And so in this chapter we collect *with* Deleuze *and* Guattari: May '68 and Lebel and UAW/MF and Columbia '68 and the movement and affinity groups and national mobilization and the festival of life and Woodstock and Weatherman and women's liberation ... and ... and ... and ... More than a collection of proper names, events, and concepts, however, what this chapter examines is the movement of a movement driven by association. And (this) is how translation works.

---

4 While it is useful to separate out these three concepts to consider how Deleuze's thinking about the fold, transcreation/becoming, and events can help us to think about translation in creative new ways, the concepts, of course, form part of a philosophical system – Deleuze called himself a "pure metaphysician" ("Responses" 42) – within which these terms are inextricably linked to one another. Deleuze's writing on the "event" demonstrates the extent of this overlap. See, for example, Deleuze *The Fold* 76–82, and *Logic of Sense* 169–76.

## I. Paris X New York with Jean-Jacques Lebel

Jean-Jacques Lebel, who will, in chapter 4, take Deleuze and Guattari on a road trip from New York to San Francisco in 1975 – during which they will meet Bob Dylan, Allen Ginsberg, and Lawrence Ferlinghetti (French philosophers "on the road" with a stop-off at Big Sur: Deleuze was enamored of Kerouac) – crosses Paris and New York in 1968, with a foot in either revolt, and in underground newspaper articles that are at once Burroughsian, Deleuzo-Guattarian, and relevant to the movement to whom they are being addressed. Accordingly, the assemblage that will manifest itself in 1975 – in the form of the Schizo-Culture conference and the roadtrip that followed – was already in the making in 1968 and, as I explain below, had been for many years prior.

### Burroughs–Artaud–Deleuze–May '68–Guattari

Lebel first came to know Burroughs, Ginsberg, Brion Gysin, Gregory Corso, and Ian Somerville during the infamous "Beat Hotel" years at 9 Rue Git-le-Coeur in Paris (when the so-called Beat scene saw Burroughs at the centre of a collaborative experimental turn stemming from Gysin's discovery of the cut-up method). Lebel translated the books and poems of several Beat writers during the sixties and seventies, making their writings available to an audience that resided across the Atlantic. Beat writers became something of a sensation in France; they were given extensive coverage in underground publications like *Actuel* and were read by French philosophers such as Deleuze, Guattari, and Foucault.[5]

When we turn towards Lebel, we see the body without organs (BwO) crossing continents in 1958 in the form of Antonin Artaud's radio play *To Be Done with the Judgment of God* – travelling from France to America and back – before appearing in Deleuze and Guattari's books (in fact, the play did not even air in France until after May 1968). The BwO in Deleuze and Guattari's collaborations differed from Deleuze's first forays with the BwO in *Logic of Sense*, where he contrasted Artaud's exploration of limitless depth with Lewis Carroll's mastery of surfaces (93). In *Anti-Oedipus*, the BwO is re-articulated as a recording surface – as opposed to limitless depth – over top of which "co-ordinates that serve as points of reference" are distributed (4). Artaud can be

---

5 François Cusset discusses Deleuze and Foucault's "keen interest ... in the American counter-culture" in *French Theory* (67).

his father, son, mother, and himself, Deleuze and Guattari explain in reference to *To Be Done with the Judgment of God*, because "he has at his disposal his very own recording code, which does not coincide with the social code, or only coincides with it in order to parody it" (15). Artaud, here, is scrambling the codes of the Freudian analyst who always wants to Oedipalize the patient (mommy-daddy-me). Deleuze and Guattari's BwO operates by way of the disjunctive synthesis, an "either ... or ... or" relation (not to be confused with either/or) that presents itself as a "system of possible permutations between differences that always amount to the same as they shift and slide about" (*Anti-Oedipus* 12). The BwO is an inclusive surface that records and retains all alternatives without being organized by a code. For Deleuze and Guattari, literature – and particularly Anglo-American literature – is an exploration of the body without organs that breaks down barriers, causes flows to circulate, and helps us to think otherwise (*Anti-Oedipus* 132–3).

Lebel played a part in liberating Artaud from French vaults, finding passage for Artaud into America. When Lebel's partner smuggled a copy of Artaud's French-banned radio play *To Be Done with the Judgment of God* from ORTF (French public radio), Lebel gathered Burroughs, Ginsberg, Corso, Gysin, and Somerville into his apartment to listen to the performance. The group dropped acid and listened to the recording backwards – without realizing it until somewhere near the end, because the piece was supposed to include sections in which Artaud spoke in tongues – revelling in its brilliance. After twenty minutes of backwards listening, they adjusted the reel and remained transfixed. Ginsberg borrowed the recording the next day and sent several copies back to the United States to recipients who included LeRoi Jones, Michael McLure, Julian Beck, and Judith Malina (Lebel "Burroughs" 85).

If Deleuze and Guattari, champions of Artaud's body without organs, are admirers of Burroughs, it is, in part, because they see something of Artaud folded into him. Deleuze and Guattari invoke Burroughs in their chapter "How Do You Make Yourself a Body without Organs?" in *A Thousand Plateaus*. As they explain, the chapter, dated 28 November 1947, marks Artaud's penning of *To Be Done with the Judgment of God*, his declaration of war on the organs (150). Towards the beginning of the chapter, directly following their explanation of the significance of the date, Deleuze and Guattari, without attribution, quote a passage from *Naked Lunch*:

> The human body is scandalously inefficient. Instead of a mouth and an anus to get out of order, why not have one all-purpose hole to eat and eliminate? We could seal up the nose and mouth, fill in the stomach, make an airhole direct into

the lungs where it should have been in the first place. (qtd. in *A Thousand Plateaus* 150)

For the authors, Burroughs's body without organs is rife with intensity, but it is closed off; it is an "experimental schizo" that is laudable because it has waged "active war against the organs," but this comes "at the price of catatonia" (150). Burroughs's "drugged body" is a failed experiment, to be sure, but it is nevertheless a part of their call to experimentation: "Find yourself a body without organs," they go on to state. "Find out how to make it. It's a question of life and death, youth and age, sadness and joy. It is where everything is played out" (151). When Beat writers were introduced to Artaud's body without organs, the BwO became part of their project. Their writings traversed Artaud's text – and were traversed by it – extending his experiments with new ones. In the Artaud example, we see Lebel sending Artaud to the United States and bringing him back again in the form of French translations of Beat writing. As per the work of reciprocal implication, the work of both the Beats and Artaud were forever changed by the theft from the vault.

To what extent was Lebel a translator for Deleuze and Guattari, and to what extent did materials pass through him unaltered, provoking them to pick up a book, for example, without influencing the way they would read it? In other words, what kind of groupwork did Lebel do for Deleuze and Guattari? Was he a mediator or an intermediary? I would argue that such a line of inquiry is extremely limited. Whether or not Lebel is a key piece in this sort of Deleuze and Guattari puzzle – the determination of influence – is interesting, but it simplifies matters not only because Deleuze and Guattari's output was constituted of many influences from many registers but also because it is reductive to read lines of influence uni-directionally. Deleuze and Guattari are themselves a part of the transcreative Artaud rhizome that was criss-crossing the Atlantic through the sixties.

How might Deleuze and Guattari's theorization of the BwO as an abstract, non-totalizing whole be rendered useful for the context of a re-reading, or re-assemblage, of French theory? Short of indicating that the possibilities and permutations for French theory are endless, it is certainly a reminder that, as articulated, "French theory" slices thinkers from traceable associations. Why not take the idea of the BwO as recording surface literally and look to things like tape reels, books, journals, and newspapers as surfaces that render traces recuperable. The body without organs is itself distributed over the surface of several recording surfaces. It is recited into a magnetic tape banned from national radio, but smuggled and played for American writers in Paris, who translated the BwO into their own textual accounts, that were then translated into French for philosophers who read these translations of Artaud in relation to their own version of the BwO (as full body and recording surface). This circuit of translations is an assemblage rendered visible on a circulating set of recording surfaces. That the turn of the seventies was itself an attempt to build a body without organs is what Deleuze and Guattari's Capitalism and Schizophrenia books were about in the first place.

It is far from a revelation that Deleuze was interested in Artaud and Burroughs, or that Burroughs was interested in Artaud and Surrealism in turn,[6] but the presence of Lebel in this assemblage is enticing, because he brings a whole other set of associations to bear upon it, particularly if we continue to understand and use him as a figure through whom Deleuze and Guattari might be reassembled. Beyond revealing the points at which different groups come together (Burroughs listens to Artaud and is read by Deleuze in translation), it is crucial to understand that mediators, having encountered both sides of the equation that they bring together, are themselves marked by these crossings (Lebel as translator and friend of the Beats *and* a participant in Deleuze's seminars at Vincennes and St. Denis *and* a friend of, and co-conspirator during May '68 with, Félix Guattari: an assemblage). The point is not to locate originary moments or to definitively state the end results of such crossings, but to recognize the way that individuals and groups are multiply, persistently, and subtly *enfolded* in a process that cannot be reduced to the singularity of contact.

The fold is important because it introduces a theory of complex intersubjectivity. Consider *Dialogues II*, Deleuze's collaboration with Claire Parnet. *Dialogues II*, Deleuze points out, came out between *Anti-Oedipe* and *Mille plateaux*, and it was written therefore "between Félix Guattari and me" (ix). The collaboration with Parnet was "a new point which made possible a new line-between" (ix), one that moved with its own force and carried with it multiple elements from either side. As Deleuze and Guattari famously argue at the beginning of *A Thousand Plateaus*, names are temporary points of subjectification; each one of the writers involved in a collaboration is already multiple (3). In his preface to the English language edition of *Dialogues II*, Deleuze reflects on his collaboration with Parnet as follows: "As we became less sure what came from one, what came from the other, or even from someone else, we

---

6 On the complex relationship between surrealism and Beat literature, see Pawlik.

would become clearer about 'What is it to write?' … This really was a book without subject, without beginning or end, but not without middle" (x). The book is without subject because it is not rooted in one. The "middle" ground of collaboration is the fold. The inside folds out and the outside folds in. There is a becoming-Deleuze of Parnet and a becoming-Parnet of Deleuze. Not only is this a relation of reciprocal implication, but each of the subjects entering into intersubjectivity is already constituted by many folds, which in turn relate with one another.

A logical place to look for this complex intertwining of French and American individuals and groups is in Lebel's own writing, where crossing concepts leave a trace. If part of what I am arguing is that concepts are not the exclusive property of Philosophy and its constituent books and journals, before examining Lebel's writing, it is important to take stock of where it appeared: the underground press in which we find mapped the various routes of an American rhizome.

### In the Beginning, There Were Six: A Brief History of the Underground Press Syndicate

If American academic journals, in the process of importing post-structuralism, neglected the contextual bottom in order to cast nets at a conceptual top, young radicals did not only have their feet planted firmly on the ground: they were under it, forging connections between movements that were both cultural and political, both local and global. Just as there was a relay between various high schools and universities in Paris – when police and the administration sought to lock down a campus, an uprising, in solidarity, would pop up on another – campus movements across the United States and across continents were linked to each other. The most efficient and effective way that continental shifts were linked was by the Underground Press Syndicate (UPS),[7] a network that circumvented the mainstream media that (as was made clear by a letter to *Le Monde* co-signed by Lacan, Lefebvre, and Sartre on the eve of the barricades

---

7 The *Los Angeles Free Press*, the *Berkeley Barb*, the *East Village Other* (New York), the *San Francisco Oracle*, the *Fifth Estate* (Detroit), and the *Paper* (East Lansing) are the six papers that started their runs in quick succession (beginning with the LA "*Freep*" in 1964), becoming the first members of the Underground Press Syndicate, launched in 1966 in order to increase the six papers' chances of survival.

in Paris)[8] downplayed and misrepresented the international student movement. By means of the UPS, students across continents shared both cultural coordinates and political strategies.

In the underground press, one finds the position papers, manifestoes, and communiqués of the Black Panther Party (BPP), Students for a Democratic Society (SDS), the Weather Underground Organization (WUO), and the Youth International Party (YIPPIE!). It is here that we find primary documents of the movement, the papers that trace revolutions in both culture and politics among an extremely engaged youth, papers that were, in large part, responsible for producing the movement itself: bolstering the movement's numbers, disseminating its cultural and political codes, and coordinating various attacks on what were considered to be "enemy" institutions (not only national, state, and municipal governments, but also the larger institutions of racism, sexism, imperialism, and corporatism, enemies that the newspapers collectively worked to define, locate, and combat).[9]

---

8  The letter, dated 10 May, reads:

> The solidarity we affirm here with the movement of students throughout the world – this movement that has abruptly, in the course of a few shattering hours, shaken up that society of well-being that is perfectly incarnated in the French world – is first of all an answer to the lies by which all the institutions and political parties (with very few exceptions), and all the newspapers and tools of communication (practically without exception), have been seeking for months to alter this movement and pervert its meaning and even to portray it as laughable. (qtd in Dosse, *History of Structuralism*, vol. 2, 113)

> The full list of co-signatories included Maurice Blanchot, André Gorz, Pierre Klossowski, Jacques Lacan, Henri Lefebvre, Maurice Nadeau, and Jean-Paul Sartre.

9  In *Smoking Typewriters*, John McMillan argues that, while there is no shortage of books that tackle and exposit the phenomenon of youth ennui in the sixties, there is a shortage of scholarly work that examines "the internal dynamics that propelled the movement" (5). He cites James Miller's *Democracy in the Streets* and Todd Gitlin's *The Sixties* as texts that document the rise and fall of the New Left via the institutional history of the SDS, but, in situating his book, he argues for the necessity of understanding how these ideas were put into circulation, including the linking of local issues with the larger movement via the Underground Press Syndicate and the Liberation News Service (5–6). My chapter's tracing of "the movement" from the student occupation of Columbia University through to the 1968 Democratic National Convention in Chicago and the development of the women's liberation movement in *RAT Subterranean News* is part of the "revisionist effort" identified by McMillan (5). See also Leamer, *The Paper Revolutionaries*; Peck, *Uncovering the Sixties*; Fountain, *Underground*; Stewart, *On the Ground*; and Wachsberger, *Insider Histories of the Vietnam Era Underground Press*, Parts 1 and 2. A number of books collect original documents from underground newspapers. These include books that collected documents from underground

In July 1966, Allan Katzman, managing editor of the *East Village Other*, wrote an editorial entitled "Underground Press Syndicate" that laid out the purpose that a syndicate would serve and the principles by which it should operate. The six principles that Katzman proposed were:

1. Communication of the news that the middle class press won't print or can't find.
2. Some sort of teletype service between New York, Chicago, L.A., San Francisco, England, etc.
3. Dividing of all income between members.
4. A clearing house, where members can choose to syndicate other members' by-lines, columns and comic strips.
5. An advertising agency which will represent and procure advertising for all members from sources around the country.
6. An agent for all member newspapers to the whole communications industry to represent them and sell news for them to A.P., U.P.I., radio and television networks. (2)

At core, the reason for establishing a syndicate was to build an income- and information-sharing network. Beyond pragmatically keeping the papers afloat, a network could both sustain and move the culture and politics of the young counterculture.

When the UPS was officially founded, nine months after Katzman's editorial, the three qualifications for membership were: 1) the free exchange of material among members; 2) the occasional printing, by each affiliated paper, of a

---

newspapers in the early 1970s while they were still in vibrant existence, and that therefore could be considered works that attempted to take stock of the movement to orient the press's energies (a project encapsulated in the titles of Bruce Franklin's and Mitchell Goodman's collections). These earlier collections include Hopkins, *The Hippie Papers* (1968); Paul, Jon, and Charlotte, *Fire! Reports from the Underground Press* (1970); Goodman, *The Movement toward a New America* (1970); Franklin, *From the Movement toward Revolution* (1971); Fenton, *Shots* (1971); Stansill and Mairowitz, *BAMN (By Any Means Necessary)* (1971); Howard and Forçade, *The Underground Reader* (1972); Forçade, *Underground Press Anthology* (1972). More recent, retrospective collections include Bizot, *Free Press,* as well as single publication retrospectives like Hilliard, *The Black Panther Intercommunal News Service, 1967–1980*; Bizot, *Underground* (a collection of documents from the French underground magazine *Actuel*); and Dreyer, Embree, and Croxdale, *Celebrating* The Rag. Jeff Shero Nightbyrd is currently editing a collection of documents from *RAT Subterannean News*.

list of UPS members; and 3) the free exchange of subscriptions among member papers. As Robert Glessing points out, the first of these rules was perhaps the most significant, because it "served to break down the concept of copyright among underground papers from the start" (70). The purpose was not to make money, but to *make available* a people's culture and, eventually, to string together a people's movement.

The UPS expanded at an astonishing rate. In his 1972 introduction to *The Underground Reader*, Forçade takes note of the progress that the syndicate made in just a few years' time:

[T]here are over 450 papers scattered from Hong Kong to Copenhagen and from Winnipeg to Buenos Aires, reaching a conservatively estimated 20 million people. As a result, there is now a sizable part of the world that is functioning within an entirely different reality that has bare tangents at a few points of critical survival with the old, obsolete, decadent world. ("Introduction" *The Underground Reader* 2)[10]

The UPS was instrumental to the networking of millions of youth from around the world, carrying and bolstering, in the process, a thriving anti-capitalist – if not altogether anti-establishment – counterculture, and an energetic and active Left. If the problem with establishment media was the lie of the news – its empty core – the underground press, rather than simply offering the substance that would fill in empty forms, shifted the coordinate points altogether. In his

---

10  Official statistics regarding the production and circulation of UPS papers are impossible to gather. In 1972, Leamer wrote that:

Some two hundred papers, publishing at any given time, are a part of the loose confederation known as the Underground Press Syndicate (UPS). The narrowest possible definition of the underground press would be membership in the UPS, and that alone adds up to a circulation number of over 1,500,000. The formula employed by mass magazines (estimating six readers for each magazine) suggests a readership of over 9,000,000. And by including high school undergrounds, re-upholstered old left papers, rock-culture papers, and other publications that identify with youth culture, it's possible to come up with a circulation figure of at least 3,000,000 papers, or 18,000,000 readers, an even better indication of the enormous audience for a medium that is blatantly anti-Establishment. (14–15)

See, as well, Glessing's chapter "Audience Analysis" in which he provides a rough list of circulation numbers for a select number of papers and speculates about the demographics of the papers' readership (120–5).

introduction to the *Underground Press Anthology*, also published in 1972, Forçade notes that, with the underground press,

> a whole system of reality was created that was more accurate than the one before. Instead of cops, pigs; instead of drugs, mind expansion; instead of consumption, ecology; instead of the Democrats versus the Republicans, the imperialists versus the revolutionaries; instead of noise, hard rock. The list could go on indefinitely. The underground press not only set up an alternate culture, it set up an alternate reality, a new world qualitatively different, where the papers quoted the price of drugs, not stocks (think about that for a minute), printed news of what ideas had been born, instead of who died, where instead of reality being fed downward from the top, reality was everybody's. (7)

The UPS served as a clearing house for inquiries from members, scholars, and the general public, and it was also, more generally, a clearing house for the language and forms of the emergent revolutions in youth culture and politics. The underground press was a crucial site of mass displacement, a shift in coordinate points out of which an entire network of combinatory "ands" and "withs" was produced. To cite one of Deleuze and Guattari's concepts that I will develop below in the context of the 1968 Democratic National Convention in Chicago, the movement was a war machine: a set of personalities and practices – an "alternate reality" – distributed external to the state.

UPS papers were extremely self-conscious and sophisticated in their presentation of revolutionary form. William S. Burroughs, a frequent contributor to many underground newspapers from the UPS's founding in 1966 until its unravelling in the mid-seventies, wrote about the revolutionary potential of the underground press in a short article entitled "Storm the Reality Studios."[11] In his essay, Burroughs argues that, if the mainstream press alters reality by forming lines of association (juxtaposing news items, advertisements, and graphics), the underground press should follow suit, experimenting along the lines of the cut-up, "stir[ring] in news stories, TV plays, stock market quotations, adverts, and put[ting] the altered mutter line out on the street" (34). According to Burroughs – who plays out this endeavour in his turn of the sixties "Nova Trilogy" – the way to alter reality was to "storm the reality studios" that were responsible for manufacturing society as it was. To storm the reality studios was to shift coordinate points, to commit the

---

11  Originally printed in the London UPS paper *Friends* and reprinted in Howard and Forçade, *The Underground Reader*.

insurgent act of forging a new assemblage as a temporary escape plan from the current social order.[12]

The underground, united by its press, was not only a Burroughsian project articulated in his "Storm the Reality Studios," it was a Deleuzo-Guattarian one as well; the UPS was a vast entity of syndicated cultures and politics internationally networked and dispersed. What Burroughs suggests is akin to a delicately drawn but aggressively pursued line of flight, one that marks not a complete escape from society but an escape plan that is forged with tools inherent in society, turning society against itself by means of the coordinates that society itself provides; it is about rearranging what is given, undermining social integrity, and making space for the articulation of new ways of living. This is an important point of resonance between Burroughs and Deleuze and Guattari (who, in a discrete but significant way, cross paths in the pages of *RAT Subterranean News*).[13]

---

12  The potential for UPS experimentation was inherent in the technology that was used to produce the papers, and underground newspapers certainly took advantage of the possibilities that were inherent in the medium. If establishment news was set in sober columns, underground newspapers used offset printing not only to drastically reduce the cost of producing the papers but also to open up creative possibilities in terms of its layout. Photo-offset printing, which most UPS papers employed, was an inexpensive method whereby assembled columns and graphics would be transferred from film negatives onto printing plates and then onto rubber blankets for ink rolling. That pages were assembled and photographed rather than typeset left room for creativity: the columns could bleed into, and explode with, each other, going off in every direction. The papers were a collage of colours, comics, and columns, with photographs of urban guerillas, poverty, and war shuffled in. In this way, the graphic representation of the movement was also a snapshot of its chaotically dispersed core. For a more detailed analysis of the cost-and-effect relationship that led to such an explosion of experiments in form among UPS papers, see Glessing 39–49. (Glessing focuses his sights on a small number of papers in order to provide specific details regarding cost, technology, and resultant layouts.) For a discussion of the importance of the mimeograph machine to SDS, and the importance, in turn, of the SDS to the mimeograph revolution see McMillan 12–20. For an account of the centrality of the mimeograph revolution to the literary scenes in New York and San Francisco, providing further insight into how this particular, inexpensive, DIY technology was at centre of a number of grassroots movements in the mid-twentieth century, see Clay and Phillips.

13  It is also the space of resonance between Burroughs and Foucault. Although Foucault did not mention Burroughs in his writing, he was a great admirer of his work. Foucault met Burroughs on two occasions (the first of which will be explored in greater depth in chapter 4): in 1975 at the Schizo-Culture conference organized by Semiotex(e) in New York, and in the spring of 1984, at Foucault's home in Paris only months before Foucault's death (see Grauerholz). The latter should be taken as a significant invitation, as it was at this time that Foucault was also trying to get in touch with Deleuze after almost a decade of silence between them. See Eribon 259–61.

## Lines of Flight: Paris–Subterranean–New York

Lebel brings Paris to New York in a feature called "A French Diary," printed in the 1–14 June 1968 issue of *RAT*. Lebel was a participant in, and a continued proponent of, the March 22nd movement, which was the catalyst for the Paris uprisings that began at Nanterre. With a foot in either revolt (and always in mixed company), Lebel was in both Paris and New York in 1968, a crossing documented in the pages of *RAT*. The UPS was responsible for collecting the revolution bit by bit via the intensive lines that were being drawn across the globe, intensities that were "exclusive to the Free Press."[14] If the dispersion of Artaud is a clear example of how a radio recording can catalyse the development of an entire counterculture – a rhizome that saw the transcreative spread of Artaud through the Beat generation, Off-Broadway theatre, and beyond – May '68 was also produced of rhizomes decades before its explosion onto the social field. This is the rhizome that will concern me the most in this section, a rhizome that is apparent in Lebel's *RAT* writings.

The value of the underground press, as I have been arguing, lies in its propulsion of the movement; what makes Lebel's *RAT*-published "French Diary" so interesting is that movement is the very thing that he is participating in and celebrating in the article. Whereas the return of de Gaulle and the decades-long process of de-Marxification that followed in France are apparent from the standpoint of the present, Lebel's piece, which is in the moment, begins in an overwhelmed ecstasy: "This is turning into a revolution. The revolution we've been working toward and pushing for, in desperation, for more than 10 years. At last the spark has hit the wick. When I say 'we all have been working' I

---

In print, the most concrete space of correspondence between Foucault and Burroughs comes in Deleuze's late work on Foucault. Burroughs is literally inserted *into* Foucault, becoming a part of Foucault's body when he is mentioned in an appendix of Deleuze's *Foucault*, and in the essay "Postscript on Control Societies," one of the last pieces that Deleuze ever wrote, where Deleuze muses that the "disciplinary societies" that Foucault associated with the eighteenth and nineteenth centuries had become, in the twentieth century, the "control societies" that Burroughs described (177–8). The task at hand was to come up with "new forms of resistance" against control (182). Foucault's concern was always to uncover the apparati articulated and used by social formations to exercise power over others, and his inclination was to elaborate forms of resistance, elaborations that he demonstrated, bodily, in Tunisia, Vincennes, and under the auspices of the GIP in the global prison movement.

14 Lebel's "French Diary," as a note at the top of his piece indicates, is "exclusive to the Free Press from a Paris strike participant" (3). Lebel's piece is an example of how the underground press reproduced, in practice, the first of its founding principles: "communication of the news that the middle class press won't print or can't find" (Katzman 2).

mean ALL the non Stalinist nuances on the extreme left" (3). What is particularly useful about Lebel's characterization of the situation in France – even though his last line is obviously a specific swipe at the Parti communiste français (PCF) (considered Stalinists for their position regarding Algeria, their defence of the Soviet invasions of Budapest in 1956 and Czechoslovakia in 1968, and their conservative policies in the social and cultural fields)[15] – is that the trajectory that Lebel champions is analogous to what American students and radicals were beginning to articulate at this time: movement. This is what makes the "beginnings" of '68 at Nanterre so important: even its name, the "March 22nd *movement*" reminds us that looking for origins and ends is beside the point. In Lebel's presentation, the (March 22nd) movement is one that is antithetical to stasis, a driving force accumulating a diverse set of orientations, struggles, and strategies along its path. In the face of petty and static divides among Marxist factions in late-sixties France, the March 22nd movement emerged as a *collection* of contingents – "Gueverists, Anarchists and Trotskyites" – which, rather than competing, were reined in under a movement that had "many leaders and dynamos" (Lebel, "A French Diary" 3).[16]

The potential of the March 22nd movement lay in its being driven by a creative force. As Lebel described the situation, militants at Nanterre and the Sorbonne were "push[ing] for a *creative* insurrection," yelling, on a mass march, "étudiants, ouvrières, un seul combat, pas dans la salle, dans la rue" (3, emphasis added). Although this translates into a call for students and workers to unite in a single struggle in the streets and not in union or lecture halls, Lebel translates the slogan to mean "get up off your ass, you 'spectators' and participate, the only revolutionary theatre is in the streets" (3). Lebel's emphasis on theatre and creativity reveals a movement whose impetus is outwards, rife with constitutive energy, calling for collection in the streets, where ten million would soon march with such force that de Gaulle was forced to flee.[17] It is also

---

15  For an account of the PCF's demise in the decade leading up to 1968, see Christofferson 37–74.

16  See Cohn-Bendit and Cohn-Bendit. Their sections "The March 22nd Movement" (48–57), "The Battle of the Streets" (57–80), and "The Action Committees" (80–90), in particular, describe, with some specificity and detail, how the movement was constituted by moments of spontaneous unity without recourse to a vanguard, how splinter groups enjoyed autonomy while being plugged into the larger struggle, and how organization was "not an end in itself, but an evolving means of coping with specific situations" (79).

17  Lebel wrote articles on street theatre and "happenings" (which Lebel and Al Hansen, as Dick Higgins points out, introduced to European streets in the form of "wild, irrational free-for-alls" that "caught the journalistic eye," popularizing the term in the mid-sixties [269])

notable that Lebel participated in the May events alongside founders of the New York Living Theatre, Judith Malina and Julian Beck, who were sent the smuggled Artaud tape earlier in the decade and who were in the process of breaking down the fourth wall outside of the Théâtre de l'Odéon with their first productions of *Paradise Now*.[18]

Lest the only line of flight raised by the article be a preconceived negative – forcing de Gaulle's flight so that a positive assemblage could be built of his absence – Lebel's "French Diary" is at all times in the process of characterizing the movement according to its many lines of flight. From lines of fight in battles with police (led by a Vietnamese man hoisting a red flag [11]), to lines of flight from a generalized "Government" (not – as iterated by an eighteen-year-old woman, representing the black flag of anarchy – just de Gaulle or Pompidou [11]), to those that reassert that the movement was already there in the first place before running someplace else, spreading its assertions across the space of the city ("This rue Gay Lussac was ours all night till about 4:30 or 5 A.M. OURS. I ask a student for a piece of his dirty red shirt. We tie it to a stick, put it back on our barricade and run." [11]), the lines of flight that Lebel describes are negative and positive at once, a relay of flight and assertion, lines that turn away to assert themselves elsewhere (refusing to become trapped in the confines of any given assertion). Lebel is always in the process of relating a movement that is both constituted by, and constitutive of, movement.

Lebel not only wrote scenarios that resembled "lines of flight" in *RAT*; he was with one of the theorists who would go on to coin the term during the Parisian uprisings. He first met and became friends with Guattari in 1966 (by way of Jean-Pierre Muyard, who would introduce Guattari to Deleuze in 1969),[19] and the two men would reunite in the context of the Parisian uprisings in 1968, brought together, this time, not by Muyard, but by the intensities that the March 22nd movement was creating. Told that what he was writing about and practising under the rubric of schizoanalysis at La Borde was happening at

---

for the *Drama Review*. See Lebel, "On the Necessity of Violation" and "Notes on Political Street Theatre"). Lebel was also cited for his involvement in French street theatre in articles in *Yale French Studies*. See, in particular, Simon and Panici, and Shank and Powell.

18 For a discussion of the writing, politics, and first performances of *Paradise Now*, including the performance at the Théâtre de l'Odéon, see Martin 66–77.

19 Muyard invited Lebel to an installation that Guattari was orchestrating at the Musée d'art moderne at the Palais de Tokyo in 1966. The exhibit involved patients from the La Borde clinic and was organized by Lacan. So began a lasting friendship, which saw Lebel visiting, and being inspired by, La Borde. See Dosse *Gilles Deleuze* 210–11.

Nanterre, Guattari left the clinic for the suburban university (and later went to the Sorbonne, where the uprisings continued), enlisting Jean Oury and some of his patients for the occupation and standoff in the process. When the occupation of the Sorbonne dwindled, Guattari left the university for the Théâtre de l'Odéon, which Lebel, in the company of Beck and Malina and others, had liberated (Dosse, *Gilles Deleuze et Félix Guattari* 210–12). In this sense, when Lebel, in his *RAT* article, speaks of the revolt in terms of its flight lines, Guattari is literally there, but the "line of flight" is out of Guattari's hands, not a product of his books with Deleuze but a set of intensities that these books to come – as well as Lebel's *RAT* dispatch – capture.

"Capture," however, is a misleading term, particularly when related to Lebel's "Diary," the movement of which is testament to the term's inadequacy. Towards the article's end, before ending the diary abruptly, Lebel describes the increasingly brutal tactics being used by the police against resolute students. The clashing of resolutes suspended, the article ends with a parenthetical editorial note: "(The letter ended here)" (11). Ending openly, the diary renders the goings on in Paris in process and *uncontainable* at the same time as they flow out from the opening that is left at the article's bottom and into the surrounding layout. The article is an open flask (turned upside down): a Parisian word virus emptied into a New York underground, spreading through the city via a *RAT*.[20] It is in this way that Lebel, in 1968, provided Paris with subterranean passage into New York. Moving through this history "with" Jean-Jacques Lebel produces a lot of "ands," a complex set of enfolded relationships marked by reciprocal implication.

### Deleuze/Guattari–French Workers–Hoffman–Sinclair–Woodstock–Up Against the Wall Motherfucker

We can see, by way of Lebel, the transmission of Burroughs, Deleuze, Guattari, and Artaud on both sides of the Atlantic. We can also – if we agree to recognize the movement of Deleuze and Guattari without remaining transfixed upon their flesh – place the French philosophers at Woodstock, which Lebel attended with the group Up Against the Wall Motherfucker and Abbie Hoffman, opening the

---

20 Let loose in the context of the paper itself, a cartoon on the sixth page seems to be infected, a skeleton pointing the way onwards, carrying a torch burning the flame of anarchy, a sash proclaiming "Communism," carrying a sign that reads "PARIS BURNS / Henry Returns / Tonight St. Mark's Place." The cartoon was drawn by the Lower East Side group Up Against the Wall Motherfucker, with whom Lebel sympathized.

industry-orchestrated event up to its outside by cutting open the fences with UAW/MF and, with Abbie Hoffman, interrupting the music and drug-fest in order to draw attention to the need to mobilize around John Sinclair, the White Panther leader and singer/guitarist for MC5 who had just been arrested and jailed for the possession of two joints (Sloman 175–9). On the other side of the Atlantic, Lebel introduced Hoffman to French revolutionaries in Paris in 1968, providing Hoffman with a venue to deliver a speech to the French movement.

These are by no means examples that mark significant victories or success-es. At Woodstock, Hoffman, too far gone on an acid trip, fumbled his Sinclair statement (and Lebel would therefore never make it on the stage to translate the statement into French and Italian, giving it the "international flavour" that was proper to the movement). On the other side of the Atlantic, when Lebel brought Hoffman to France to give speeches to a number of the participants in the French uprisings, Hoffman, not recognizing that the majority of people at cen-tre of the French uprisings and in attendance were middle-aged workers, deliv-ered a similarly incoherent and inconsequential speech, preaching to them, in celebratory tones, on the wonders and importance of sex and drugs (Sloman 241–2).[21] Along these lines, we might be tempted to conclude that the opening of Woodstock's gates – liberating the "festival" to its outside – is certainly closer to what would conventionally be recognized as a "successful" act: the private space of the industry-oriented event is cracked open, given to the peo-ple. Using success as a dominant criterion for inclusion of this or that event, however, imposes stringent limits upon the drawing of an assemblage whose effects are often neither immediately effective nor discernible.

What I want to point out here are the subtle ways that currents are crossed in exchanges, which remind us that there is such a thing as a Deleuze/Guattari–French worker–Hoffman–Sinclair–Woodstock–Up Against the Wall Mother-fucker assemblage, brought together by way of Lebel. What I am arguing, in pulling such an assemblage together – by making note of a general mixing of elements rather than a particular selection of key texts that were concretely exchanged – is that it is not really all that important (or even possible or desir-able) to trace what came first and to place all elements exchanged along a linear

---

21  Abbie Hoffman's work in general was irreverent to the extreme. Published in 1968, *Revolu-tion for the Hell of It* chronicles Hoffman's late-sixties escapades in the movement, from the wonders of LSD as existential revolution to the levitation of the Pentagon, from the founding of the Youth International Party (the "yippies") to his participation in the Chicago Democratic National Convention. Published in 1970, *Steal This Book* documents how to live free in the most literal sense, providing advice on dining and dashing, hitchhiking, living in communes, getting social assistance, conducting credit card scams, and so on.

trajectory. We often ask questions like who had the most impact upon whom, and in what way exactly, but the fact of the matter is that what Burroughs, Deleuze, Guattari, Foucault, & Co. represent are ideas and acts that are *in circulation*, not unlike the editions of *RAT* by which Lebel is circulated in New York. It is in this sense that the sanitized narratives of historicity – lines of best fit – are insufficient. Such is also the case with the "post-structuralist" designation of French theory that looks to particular collections and presses in its consecration and development of a particular configuration of knowledge. From the example of Jean-Jacques Lebel's writings and interventions, we learn that the process of assemblage building is a far subtler affair than we often allow: subterranean routes between French theory and America were everywhere scattered years before the rhizome was theorized, and the rhizome was simply a way of trying to capture the exchanges that produced the powerful global events of the '68 years.

Lebel was not simply a go-between who brought Deleuze and Guattari to the American counterculture and vice versa; Lebel was himself marked by complex foldings and unfoldings of the French and American individuals and groups that he encountered through the '50s, '60s, and '70s, and these complex relationships are themselves folded into, and retrievable in, New York's underground newspaper *RAT Subterranean News*. This paper is one of the ways in which Deleuze and Guattari were translated for Anglo-American consumption (enfolded, unfolded, refolded, and so on),[22] and "the movement" that Lebel was writing for and about in *RAT* was the very phenomenon that Deleuze and Guattari were attempting to translate in *Anti-Oedipus* and *A Thousand Plateaus*.

---

22  Consider as well Barbara Godard's translation of Nicole Brossard's poetry. The translation of Deleuze (and Guattari) does not follow the trajectory that Godard includes as an appendix to "Deleuze and Translation" (76–8). Brossard was herself a reader/translator of Deleuze, whom Godard translated into English in turn. Although *Différence et repetition* (1968) and *Logique du sens* (1969) were translated only in the early 1990s, Godard's translation of Brossard's *L'Amer* (*These Our Mothers*) made these books available in translation in 1983. Words like "multiplicities" and "ramify" were being deployed in *These Our Mothers* a decade before they were released as Deleuzian terms. This is translation by association. Attention to association lines involves thinking metonymically, not metaphorically: *L'Amer* does not stand in for *Différence et repetition* but extends it by association. And Godard's translation is an extension of *L'Amer*. Brossard *and* Godard *and* Deleuze. In this associative configuration – with Godard taking Brossard and Deleuze in the middle – we witness the "and" as both transcreative extension and fold in the event of translation: Brossard and Deleuze are enfolded, unfolded, and refolded in Godard's *These Our Mothers*. *L'Amer* enacts a becoming-Deleuze of Brossard and a becoming-Brossard of Deleuze, a relationship that Godard unfolds while reading *L'Amer* and refolds into her translation.

As Kristine Stiles puts it in her introduction to a 2003 exhibit of Lebel's art at the Mayor Gallery in London, Lebel acted as a "radar scout" for Deleuze and Guattari "in terms of his associations, activities, and very life style, which covered territories unknown to them" (5). With not only Deleuze, Guattari, and Beat writers, but also Marcel Duchamp, Guy Debord, Abbie Hoffman, the New York anarchist group Up Against the Wall Motherfucker, Julian Beck and Judith Malina of the Living Theatre, Carolee Schneemann – and the list goes on – among Lebel's relations, his writing, art, and activism took several contingents from either side of the French-American divide down an intensive, middle line.

## II. For the Movement of Columbia
## (from the Movement in Columbia)

Although Lebel is an exemplary case, in that he explicitly embodies the crossing of contingents that are of central concern to this book, *RAT* itself, an energetic and engaged underground publication, was always in the process of collecting and projecting the movement; the UPS, in this sense, is the medium that bridges one event to the next (without neglecting the events in between) and acts as a sounding board for the laying out of issues and the development of strategies. This is not to say that the movement was a smooth space completely devoid of striation (something we will tackle below in the context of women's liberation), but it was certainly "transcreative."

Rather than sticking with the fetishized subjects of French theory and the American counterculture, it is ultimately more productive to follow the circulation of intensities that their writings celebrate and (in certain respects, and at certain times) represent. Over the course of 1968, *RAT* represented the collection and dissemination of this sort of potential and manifested itself in the form of a line from Columbia to Chicago. I began the previous section by relating Lebel's June '68 diary of the Paris barricades; I now step back a month in order to relate the way that *RAT* collected the intensities of Columbia, and how these intensities were projected into Chicago: this section explores the translation of issues into events, and of events into transcreative becomings.

### Collecting the Event

Deleuze and Guattari analyse events according to their collection and projection. In order for an event to be projected, it has to first be collected. In terms of Columbia, *RAT* plays a significant part not only in collecting the event from its midst (publishing smuggled documents) but also in reining the event into a context (What does Columbia mean in the context of global struggle?) *and* reining other contexts into the event (What do other struggles mean in the context of Columbia?). *RAT* orchestrates the convergence of several fields of struggle at once, laying bare the process of assemblage building.

The process of plugging an event into movement is illustrated in the layout of the *RAT* issue that was published from the midst of the Columbia revolt in spring 1968. For its 3–16 May issue, *RAT*'s cover carries a massive swastika-branded helmet roosting on the top of Columbia's Low Library while blood flows down the library steps. The machine gun–wielding rat that always occupies the top inside corner of the second page – but always with a different dialogue balloon – proclaims "Up against the wall, GRAYSON KIRK!" designating the Columbia president as the main target of the newspaper.[23] The issue includes articles on the tactics used to occupy several buildings on campus, from Fayerweather Hall to Low Library and the Math building (Shero "Blockade and Siege"), and it details the eventual police bust, where police broke into and cleared the many buildings that had been "liberated" across the campus (Moore "The Bust Comes"). The newspaper provides insider chronicling of the Columbia events, the accounts of the barricades and bust coming from within the buildings, from participant-reporters speaking about the ebb and flow of emotions, the way that decisions were made, the messages that were written on blackboards, and even an impromptu wedding that dissipated the nervous tension that had built in anticipation of the impending police raid (Shero). The centrefold of the paper pushes the insider status even further, devoting the entire spread to statements of injured students. The four most prominently displayed pages in the newspaper – advertised as "Liberated Documents" on the cover – are devoted to printing several documents that *RAT* editor Jeff Shero helped smuggle from Kirk's office,[24] documents that probe Columbia's involvement with the Institute for Defense Analyses (IDA) and reveal the corporate interests behind the Morningside Heights expansion that I detailed in the preceding chapter.[25]

---

23  Images from *RAT Subterranean News* were provided by Jeff Shero Nightbyrd. For more images from and information about *RAT*, see his forthcoming book *RAT Subterannean News, 1968–1970* and the YouTube channel RAT Subterranean News, https://www.youtube.com/channel/UC8yNZHuyCHMby2BzIReuMAQ.

24  Shero (who has since changed his name to Jeff Nightbyrd) describes his role in "liberating" the incriminating documents from Kirk's office in Helen Garvey's 2003 documentary *Rebels with a Cause*.

25  The three pages devoted to photocopied documents are titled "Columbia U: Company Store" (Embree), "Morningside Confidential," and "The Five Month Run-Around." The first page includes an article by Alice Embree alongside a document disclosing Columbia's ties to Socony Mobil and a letter from an undisclosed sender that presses President Kirk for the name

2.1. Front cover of Columbia issue of *RAT Subterranean News*,
3–16 May 1968 © Jeffrey Shero.

of his successor, boldly stating that "every tough minded corporate donor wants to know who's going to be running the store in five years. That's the question which is asked of each company head about his own corporation" (7). The page entitled "Morningside Confidential" provides excerpts from a fifteen-page report regarding Columbia's planned expansion, intended for the eyes of "trustees and persons specifically designated by the president" only (8). Finally, "The Five Month Run-Around" reproduces a set of xeroxed communications between the Morningside Tenants Committee expressing concern over Columbia's extreme neglect of the apartments that it owned in Harlem and for the university's failure to hold a meeting between itself and community members who were uniformly upset by its plans for expansion (9). Further on in the paper is a page entitled "IDA: Cold War Think-Tank" (Klare), which includes an article by Michael Klare alongside which a letter addressed to presidents of IDA-member universities is reprinted. The letter states that the presidents should do what they can to "allow the work of the IDA to continue without interruption" (15). This particular statement is underlined in *RAT*'s reproduction, and stamped across the document is an oppositional imperative: "Students and faculty of Columbia have interrupted. Now we must stop the IDA for good" (15).

2.2. Rat inset on the second page of the Columbia issue of *RAT Subterranean News,* 3–16 May 1968 © Jeffrey Shero.

If the documents seized from Kirk's office disclose the corporate ties and interests that motivated his (and Columbia's) decisions, the mainstream media's coverage of the uprisings, *RAT* points out, was tied to those same corporate interests, spreading the core of bias to a mass audience. Alongside *RAT*'s first set of liberated documents, the editors include the following disclaimer:

> Grayson Kirk is not, as the *New York Times* portrays him, the beleaguered administrator solely concerned with the unrest on his campus. And the *New York Times* is not the disinterested observer of revolt at Columbia University that it parades as. The reporting and editorial stance of the *Times* is influenced by the fact that its Chairman of the Board, Arthur H. Sulzberger, also sits on the Board of Trustees at the University of Columbia. (7)

At the same time as *RAT* provides an "insider" account of the Columbia events, the newspaper reveals how the establishment press is driven by its associations (which reveal why and how it is biased). If, in *RAT*'s estimation, the *Times* paints Columbia's president into the role of the well-intentioned victim, *RAT* plays the same card in return, painting the stairs of Columbia blood red, including the testimonials of the meek (injured students) that would – with persistence, and for a limited time – inherit the university. Though rhetorically overblown in its tone, *RAT* plays an important role in collecting and articulating the student masses.

The strength of UPS papers lay not only in their ability to report the local news with insider authority, creating local subjects; it was also built of the papers' coordination of struggles, of their ability to universalize the local, giving local struggles to common causes. Although the "Heil Columbia" issue of *RAT* was centred around the Columbia uprisings, exposés and articles regarding the revolts did not occupy the entirety of the issue. It also included an interview with Rudi Dutschke on the German SDS's parallel uprising in Berlin ("Berlin: A Struggle and a Leader"),[26] and, as was the case in every issue of *RAT*, it printed a column entitled "Blows Against the Empire," a full-page spread that included briefs on global struggles against capitalism. In this particular issue, the week's briefs included paragraphs on a solidarity strike – with Columbia – at the State University of New York at Stony Brook; the presentation of a 10,000-signature petition to the governor of Massachusetts that urged reform of the state's birth control laws;[27] a mass report-card burning by high school and university students in Berlin; a white radical march in memory of Martin Luther King Jr in Chicago;[28] and a Liberation News Service item that announced the shooting by the Oakland police of seventeen-year-old Black Panther Bobby Hutton.[29]

The reason that I think it important to list these diverse struggles is to demonstrate the process of assemblage building that is at play in the pages of *RAT*. To list a series of semi-colon-separated struggles is necessarily to provide a surface recording of the network captured by, and embodied in, underground newspapers. It is my desire herein to capture this network as best I can. In

---

26  On the German SDS, see Timothy Scott Brown.

27  On the importance of the birth control pill to the sexual revolution and women's liberation in the 1960s, see Eig; Allyn 30–40; and Bailey. While Betty Friedan's *The Feminist Mystique* does not explicitly deal with the question of contraception, it sparked the conversations and movements that would eventually catapult demand for access to contraception and abortion to centre stage. Friedan's *It Changed My Life* collects the reports and stories about the political campaigns that were sparked by her book and her continuing activism, including work that she did under the auspices of the National Organization for Women (NOW), which she cofounded in 1966. Friedan also cofounded the National Association for the Repeal of Abortion Laws (NARAL) in 1969.

28  On the unrest that followed the assassination of Martin Luther King Jr, see Risen; Elfenbein, Nix, and Holloway; and Ben W. Gilbert.

29  The account is provided by Kathleen Cleaver, communications secretary for the Black Panthers, whose husband, Eldridge Cleaver, was with Sutton when he was shot. Eldridge Cleaver provides his own account of the incident in "Affidavit #2: Shootout in Oakland." See also Newton 196–7. Newton's *Revolutionary Suicide* opens with a "Tribute to Li'l Bobby," naming him "the very first member of the Black Panther Party."

doing so, I hope that I am capturing something like the underground as body without organs: a recording surface upon which the movement is transcribed. Just as it was up to hippies, yippies, feminists, students, workers, and black, brown, and gay and lesbian activists of every stripe to determine which causes and directions they might pursue, every struggle that appears on a list in this chapter has a complicated history that can, or has been, further pursued via careful research. The fact that I am trying to illustrate is that in every issue of *RAT*, local struggles were given to an international context that represented a broad base of diverse and pressing concerns. If the mainstream press was caught up in a corporate web – as *RAT*'s disclosure of the Kirk-*Times* connection makes clear – the underground was enmeshed in a web of internationally networked struggles. While the "body without organs" is a cumbersome metaphor, the idea of a network of possibility where pathways are not predetermined, or overdetermined, is not only liberating, it is politically potent.

*RAT* is a particularly interesting resource because of the way that it plugs Columbia into other issues; in *RAT*'s hands, Columbia is a *featured* blow against the empire; it is always part of a larger movement and should not be considered in isolation. The strength of *RAT*'s snapshots of both the Columbia event and surrounding struggles was that they caused the movement to converge. *RAT* was responsible for situating Columbia alongside a simultaneous set of "blows against the empire," but, in its pages, Columbia is also given to film, music, and comics:[30] the issue ends with a review of Luis Buñuel's *Belle de jour*, columns on student films and theatre, a page devoted to the rock music scene, and a feature on Stevie Wonder. In this manner, the Columbia uprising is given to the larger context of the movement: in the layout of the UPS, the event is immersed into the movement (to which it already belongs), lines (that were already there) are drawn between it and other micro-events, and preparations are made for impending eruptions (which are already everywhere happening).

If we look at the specific targets of the Columbia protests, the more general set of issues that underlie them are readily discernible. Opposition to the IDA affiliation had to do with the Vietnam War and, even more generally, America's ruthless brand of imperialism; opposition to the proposed gym was part of the larger question of race relations in the United States and was another piece in the puzzle regarding the movement's complicated history of supporting black

---

30  On the place of film, music, and comics in the movement, see Comiskey; Doggert; Lipsitz; James; J. Miller, *Flowers in the Dustbin* 235–96; Rosenkranz; and Estren. For an excellent sampling of primary documents, see A. Bloom and Breines 227–86.

struggles; and, at base, opposition to the corporate structure of Columbia – its financial ties and the interests of its board of governors – had to do with the generally felt sentiment that it was appalling to see decisions being made with regard to capital rather than equality and justice.

## Projecting the Event: From (Paris X) New York → Chicago

Every assemblage is territorial, but it is also built of lines of flight that deterritorialize the assemblage. The Columbia assemblage is territorialized as the multiplicitous event that brings together a number of intensities, but it also traverses its connections; it is not in-itself a static entity. What is evident in the *RAT* run that follows the Columbia event is the way in which these connections continue to be brought together, for the purpose not of resolving the struggles at Columbia but of taking the energies articulated at and around the Columbia event elsewhere. I proceed, in this section, by demonstrating how the event is plugged into other struggles, moving away from New York, and becoming movement in the process. This is translation as transcreation: the diachronic development of movement by associations.

Containing a requisite article on the aftermath of the Columbia uprisings (Millman, "Aftermath(ematics)") as well as two more liberated documents and articles – one regarding a doctored story for the *New York Times* ("Shucking with the Times") and the other concerning the corporate ties that lay behind Columbia's expansion (Embree, "The Urban Removal Masquerade") – Columbia is pushed forward by the post-Columbia issue of *RAT*. It is not just that *RAT* provides more information regarding the uprisings (their causes, their persistence, their effects), but Columbia, as centralized event, is already and all of a sudden unfettered in *RAT*'s *current* edition; it is made part of a larger mix.

Covering the issue that followed the Columbia exposé, *RAT* sported a cartoon of a hooded, axe-wielding, and bikini brief–clad executioner. The entire cover, including the muscular executioner, is painted over with dozens of corporate logos. Among the blizzard of logos appear three that will also appear on the letterhead of liberated documents inside (the *New York Times*, Mobil Oil, and Western Union). If the tattooed and airborne logos represent the swarm of corporate interests and the inscription of these interests upon the body, the resolute and branded executioner stands in for what would become the movement's generalized enemy over the course of the next number of years: not Kirk and Columbia's board of governors operating in the interests of New York's elite, but the American Empire operating in the interests of capital.

Over the course of the summer, *RAT* brought uprisings together by linking events to each other *and* to the struggles that would inevitably follow: *RAT* was all about gathering under and rising up. Between the mid-May '68 "Heil

2.3. Front cover of first post-Columbia issue of *RAT Subterranean News*,
17–30 May 1968 © Jeffrey Shero.

Columbia" issue, marking the shutdown of the university, through to the "Back
to School" issue at the end of September 1968, marking Columbia's reopening,
*RAT* ran through the summer as a storehouse of struggles. The aftermath of the
Columbia uprising stretched through the summer, with *RAT* detailing apartment building occupations in Harlem ("Community Takeover")[31] and plans
for the creation of a "liberation school" in which, as an inset in a June issue
of *RAT* explained, all activities and classes – including high school organizing,

31  In *Harlem vs. Columbia University*, Stefan M. Bradley discusses a history of opposition to
the "renewal" of Harlem (27–38), a euphemism for developer-led gentrification that leads
to neighbourhood evictions of the local community. Neil Smith includes a chapter on the
gentrification of Harlem in his classic book on gentrification, *The New Urban Frontier*
(see 136–62). For a discussion of Urban Deadline, a collective of Columbia students with

underground newspapers, U.S. imperialism in Latin America – would be related to the movement ("Columbia Liberation School").[32] Surrounding this coverage on the continuing saga of Columbia were articles on high school revolts; an interview with Daniel Cohn-Bendit (Cohn-Bendit, "Danny the Red: Prohibiting Is Forbidden"); an article from an anonymous American G.I. outlining the racist motivations for crowd-control training, including racist comments made by high-ranking officers throughout the training process ("Your National Guard: Riot Control or Nigger Control");[33] an article describing confrontations between the Black Panthers and the police (Gerth, "Pigs vs. Panthers"); and a regular feature called "How to Make It in the Jungle" (which in itself documents the radicalization of the movement, from the first instalment on scamming one's way through subway turnstiles without paying to, in the latter months of 1968, diagrams of police formations in riot situations). Pictures of political figures such as Mao Tse-Tung and Che Guevara and symbols like the BPP logo were peppered throughout the issues, giving the movement its various icons. Furthermore, movement politics were not separated from movement culture. In the summer months that followed the Columbia uprisings, there were articles on, and reviews of, the Beatles, Jimi Hendrix, the Temptations, Cream, Ravi

---

backgrounds and interest in architecture and design that grew out of the Columbia protests aiming to work with communities under threat of displacement, see Richards 41–75; and Grant 137–8. Struggles to gentrify Harlem both preceded the proposed gym and intensified after it was temporarily stopped by the Columbia protests. For discussion of a similar wave of rent strikes and squats in the Parisian suburbs – a product of student-worker alliances – following the events of May–June 1968, see Ross 97–8.

32 The Liberation School was started with the dual purposes of demonstrating what a relevant education could look like and politicizing students. The school was organized by the Strike Education Committee, with courses taught by faculty, graduate students, and community members (Grant 138–9). On the radicalization of high school students, see Birmingham, *Our Time Is Now*, a collection of articles from high school papers inspired by the underground press and the politicization of university students.

33 Jordan T. Camp explains how special weapons and tactics (SWAT) teams marked the militarization of police forces and were developed by Daryl Gates in the wake of Watts riots, marking a two-pronged domestic counterinsurgency effort (coupled with COINTELPRO) that was predominantly focused on black protest. The first use of a SWAT team in Los Angeles was against the Black Panther Party. Camp argues that "aggressive policing as a strategy of racialized crisis management ... marked a critical moment in the development of the neoliberal carceral state" (41–2). See also Parenti, 111–38; Alexander 73–7; and the work of Pete Kraska. The American Civil Liberties Union recently produced a major study on the problematic, traumatizing, and heavily racialized use of SWAT teams, entitled *War Comes Home: The Excessive Militarization of American Policing.*

Shankar, Jean-Luc Godard,[34] Stanley Kubrick, François Truffaut, and Andy Warhol; there was a constant supply of political and psychedelic comics (including an interview with political cartoonist Ron Cobb); and there was a handful of articles on growing pot and acid trips.[35] Because there is never a single *one* issue, icon, or strategy, what the UPS achieves is something greater: mass mobilization on various fronts. These are the many "ands" of the movement.

If we see, in these examples, the way that *RAT* was involved in a perpetual process of collecting the movement's culture, politics, and events, the paper was also, in collecting them *as movement*, projecting this collection of events onwards; *RAT* never endeavoured to draw a definitive assemblage, because that would cut the events off from their transcreative outward/onward potential. That indefinite politics are often accused of displaying an impotent relativism is challenged by *RAT*: while the assemblages it drew were certainly indefinite, this did not preclude the determined drawing of lines, from one event to the next (with hundreds of points in between, and the promise of events to come). The summer run of *RAT* culminated in an issue that was devoted to the events that transpired at the Democratic National Convention in Chicago; the Chicago issue of *RAT* slipped in just before *RAT*'s "Back to School" issue. Such was the subterranean line that was drawn between the forced end of a school year and the beginning of another, burrowing under before popping up again, collecting intensities along the way.

If the focal points towards which the event reached were diverse, the Chicago event was adamantly without centre (a condition that is worth exploring because this intangibility, in part, renders the event ripe for projection in the first place).[36] The Chicago action had long been considered a protest against President Lyndon Johnson, who was expected to seek re-election; when Johnson announced that he would not be running, many young people started to

---

34 It is worth noting that Jean-Luc Godard's film *La Chinoise* – which depicted a small group of Maoist students from the Université de Nanterre discussing Marxism-Leninism in a bourgeois parent's apartment over the summer, contemplating how their discussions and guerrilla theatre would be brought to the university once its doors reopened – played in French theatres during the summer of 1967, framing Nanterre students' entry into the '67–8 academic year. Coincidentally, the film was reviewed in the *RAT* issue that directly preceded the Columbia events and that would therefore have been the issue in circulation at the outset of the New York uprisings (see Heins and Gassow).

35 Within the New York UPS scene, drug culture was mostly the terrain of the *East Village Other*.

36 Many book-length accounts and studies have been published on the 1968 Democratic National Convention in Chicago in 1968, including David Farber, *Chicago '68*; Hayden, *The Whole World Was Watching*; Lane, *Chicago Eyewitness*; Schneir, *Telling It Like It Was*; Schultz, *No One Was Killed*; and Stein, *Living the Revolution*.

question whether the demonstrations should proceed as planned. The action, Abbie Hoffman points out, had been planned a year in advance, and was to be the first Yippie gathering, an event that would send the press squabbling, a media myth-making event inspired by Marshall McLuhan ("Why We're Going" 12).[37] Speaking to the importance of going ahead with the Chicago action, Hoffman lays out the argument as follows:

> The point is, you can use Chicago as a means of pulling your local community together. It can serve to open a dialogue between political radicals and those who might be considered hippies. The radical will say to the hippie: "Get together and fight, you are going to get the shit kicked out of you." The hippie will say to the radical: "Your protest is so narrow, your rhetoric so boring, your ideological power plays so old-fashioned."
>
> Each can help the other, and Chicago – like the Pentagon demonstration before it – might well offer the medium to put forth that message. (17)

Not only was Hoffman's statement aimed at uniting the countercultural and political fronts in the movement, it was also about uniting local communities. What is most interesting about Hoffman's description in this regard is that the aim of Chicago sounds a lot like the layout of the UPS's most strategically sophisticated and best-laid-out newspapers at the time: culture and politics, local and global, side by side and in dialogue.[38]

The organization of unorganized action comes at a specific moment: in the aftermath of failed mass demonstrations and the beginnings of more militant

---

37 Abbie Hoffman, Timothy Leary, and Jerry Rubin were all very much taken by McLuhan's work, including the design of his collaborations with Quentin Fiore, *The Medium Is the Massage* and *War and Peace in the Global Village* (see J. Abbott Miller). Rubin commissioned Quentin Fiore to design his Yippie Manifesto *Do It!* and in that work invokes McLuhan's famous dictum, "the medium is the message," in a chapter on people's addiction to money: "People see each other not as human beings, but as financial transactions. The medium is the message. Money corrupts every relationship it touches" (121).

38 Hoffman's essay originally appeared in the underground newspaper *The Realist*. Toward the essay's end he flags Chicago's underground paper *The Seed* as an organizational hub for the demonstrations, asking people to write to organizers with their own plans and telling them to "watch the underground papers for the latest developments" ("Why We're Going to Chicago" 17). The UPS was an integral part of the movement, providing multiple sites for the movement's capture and redeployment. While the movement's message was much more complicated than, as Hoffman puts it, "each can help the other," the UPS, akin to the Chicago demonstrations' aspirations, "offer[ed] the medium to put forth [the movement's] message" ("Why We're Going" 17).

revolts like the uprisings at Columbia. Beyond the withdrawal of Johnson's bid for another term, a difficulty regarding the planned Chicago action was that mass protests – like the 70,000-large demonstration where protestors gathered to levitate the Pentagon in 1967 – did not seem to make much sense following the series of local protests that had taken place over the course of 1968.[39] Because of the increasingly pointed nature of protest, the lack of a focal point in LBJ made collecting in Chicago particularly precarious.

In this context, the *RAT* issue that preceded the Chicago convention issue features an article whose title asks the very question that was, at that moment – going into Chicago – on many young people's lips: "Has the Time for Demonstrations Passed?"[40] Recognizing that mass demonstrations of immense proportions had had no effect on America's foreign or domestic policy, many movement activists were beginning to recognize that it was crucial to take a next step, to adopt a new set of strategies. Beyond being up in the air due to the convention's lack of an LBJ (or, following his June '68 assassination, a Robert Kennedy, for that matter), the planned action was without centre because, at this point, there was no consensus among young people as to what protest was supposed to look like. Rather than being a pointed protest against something, the convention was treated as an opportunity to collect energies, ideas, groups, and tactics, bridging the gap between contingents by engaging one another in dialogue regarding – and building, in the process – the movement's future.

Strategies for collection, including debates on the question of scale, hovered around the convention, and it is at this juncture that New York's Lower East Side anarchist group – with whom Lebel sympathized – reappears. Where Hoffman promoted Chicago as an opportunity to bring "local communities" together, in the pre-convention issue of *RAT* – directly following Jennifer Wolf's ponderings on the passing of the time for demonstration – UAW/MF propose the concept of the "affinity group," giving the concept of the local community to a much smaller scale and giving this reduced scale to a sophisticated set of questions regarding strategy. Noting that mass demonstrations "fail to advance the nature and the forms of our struggle," UAW/MF propose

---

39  As Hoffman puts it, "Everybody began the tough task of developing a new tactic of new battlegrounds. Columbia, the Lower East Side, Free City in San Francisco. Local action became the focus and by the end of May we decided to disband Yippie and cancel Chicago" ("Why We're Going" 14).

40  See Wolf's article "Has the Time for Demonstration Passed?" about a protest against Hubert Humphrey's campaign. Frustrated by the campaign's indecision and ineffectiveness, the protest turned into a battle with police.

the advancement of struggle via "small group[s] executing 'small' actions in concert with other small groups" (Up Against the Wall 11). In order to successfully engage this form of strategy – which was, the article points out, already engaged in "Columbia's Communes, Berkeley's Revolutionary Gangs, [and] France's Committees of Action" – it was necessary that small groups look two ways at once, towards the "internal development and security" of groups and the development of "external relationship with similar groups" (11). These overlapping procedures are precisely the categories that are being considered in the context of this chapter: on the one hand, collection, on the other, projection, *always overlapping*. This is the "and" as disjunctive synthesis: the middle as a site of intermingling and exchange. As UAW/MF announces, it is a "network" that emerges on the other side of their proposed strategy, and not a net result.

The overlap with Deleuze and Guattari's theories on capitalism and schizophrenia are tangible. We cannot help but think of the rhizome when the Lower East Side group states that the affinity group is an "active minority" that "plays the role of a permanent fermenting agent, encouraging action without claiming to lead" (11). Furthermore, Guattari takes on the topic of anarchist movements in the United States (with Weatherman – for whom affinity-group theory was crucial – taking the emblematic lead of undertaking formations that undermine the hierarchical structures of family and state) in a crucial 1970 essay on groupuscules (*Psychoanalysis and Transversality* 368).[41] Against the verticalizing tendencies of the state and family, the UAW/MF article stresses that "[i]t is spontaneity which permits the thrust forward, and not the slogans or directives of leaders. The affinity group is the source of both spontaneity and new forms of struggle" (11). If we could mistake this passage as having been produced in *A Thousand Plateaus*, it is because Deleuze and Guattari's rhizome book is part of a complexly knotted UAW/MF assemblage noted above. That Lebel lingered among UAW/MF's loosely collected ranks reminds us, yet again, that correspondences between groups are never clean-cut or either uni- or bi-directional. *A Thousand Plateaus*, in this sense, is not at all unique in its constitution – it never claims to be – but continues a type of movement that surfaced, in the social field, at the turn of the seventies, one that compelled

---

41 For analyses of Deleuze and Guattari's relationship with anarchist philosophies, see May, *The Political Philosophy of Poststructuralist Anarchism*; Ferguson, "Becoming Anarchism, Feminism, Indigeneity"; Jun, "Deleuze, Derrida, and Anarchism"; and Newman, "War on the State."

writers and philosophers to do what they always do – imagine other worlds – but with greater purpose, conviction, and a host of fellow travellers.

Commissioned to cover the convention for *Esquire* along with Jean Genet, Allen Ginsberg, and Terry Southern, William Burroughs returned to America in 1968 after a long absence. He brought along a tape recorder and used the event as an opportunity to practise tape recorder experiments, an extension of the cut-up that he was theorizing at the time. He recorded speeches on the convention floor alongside the noises on the streets and played them back in order to incite chaos and confusion. Although Burroughs never speculates upon the results of these experiments, in an October edition of *RAT*, he notes that his experiences in Chicago compelled him "to move his apartment from London to New York so he [could] directly involve himself in the movement" ("William Burroughs Interview," 4–17 Oct., 11). In the two-part interview in which Burroughs admits this intention,[42] he and Jeff Shero converse about the changing nature of the movement, the education system, what transpired in Chicago, and the necessity for writers to commit themselves to movement causes. In response to Shero's suggestion that the literary scene is detached in America, Burroughs, just returned from London, notes: "I feel it's time for every writer who's worth a salt to put his ass where his mouth is. If he is standing for freedom, get out there and stand for it. I'm willing to do this" (4–17 Oct., 11). Even though the event did not exactly, in the end, project Burroughs from writing to activism,[43] the terms that he uses in the process of promoting a

---

42  See Burroughs, "William Burroughs Interview."

43  For a discussion of Burroughs's status in the movement, see Miles. Hippies and radicals found a sympathetic worldview in his rejection of straight society and his condemnation of the Nova Mob and its desire to control. He wrote about these issues, including his rejection of government and police violence – and his rejection of pacifism as tactic, the placement flowers in the barrels of guns – in the *London Guardian*, London's underground newspaper *International Times*, *RAT Subterannean News*, and *Rolling Stone*. While Burroughs's rhetoric became increasingly radical, Miles describes a failed tape recorder experiment wherein Burroughs unsuccessfully tried to rid London of Scientology by stationing himself outside of their building and conducting recordings and playbacks. Burroughs tried a similar tactic on an establishment called Moka Bar that had served him bad cheesecake; they eventually went out of business (Miles 171–6). While Burroughs may not have been particularly remarkable at "put[ting] his ass where his mouth [was]" ("William Burroughs Interview" 11), Olivier Harris's introductions to the newly "restored" editions of the Nova books productively point to Burroughs's identification of his writing with "assymetrical warfare," his citation of Mao's formula for guerilla tactics ('Enemy advance we retreat')" in *The Ticket that Exploded* as he manipulated words and images to produce effects (Harris Introduction to *The Ticket That Exploded* xxi). Similarly, in his introduction to *Nova Express*, Harris draws a parallel between the discovery and strategic use of the cut-up with the situationist

re-attachment of the literary scene to "America" are intriguing: the conjunction between ass and mouth, that same intensive BwO that Deleuze celebrated in Burroughs above, but this time in the context of a literary scene *attached* to America, not suffering from a drug-induced catatonic collapse.

### The Walker Report: Capturing the (Anti-)war Machine

We can see the synthesis of diverse forces in an event. It is intensive. It is a plateau, or middle ground in that it is part of a continuity (it doesn't come out of nowhere). But it is also a marker of discontinuity: the event is linked into transcreation because the event isn't a singular, capturable state of being. While Deleuze and Guattari recognize continuity and rupture, in their anti-representational philosophy, states of being are tied to the encoding and inscription practices of the state. As Kristin Ross's book on May '68 demonstrates, even the event par excellence can become an apparatus of capture, an enclosed metaphor that cuts off all of the lines that were drawn into, and emerged out of, that intensive month. The types of narrative histories that Ross is writing against in *May '68 and Its Afterlives* have managed to translate most of that event into oblivion. Columbia's '68's translation into liberation schools is linked into global revolt and is part of a line of intensifying revolt leading from Columbia to Chicago, demonstrating a complex network of translation and folds. Ultimately, what we see in '68 is a network of interconnected singularities in revolt against various states of being (from the exclusions and injunctions of "the establishment" to those of the movement itself). This is what Deleuze and Guattari would eventually term the "war machine," and with the help of this concept, the strategic impulses behind the Chicago cacophony can come into sharper relief.

The "war machine" is given its most extensive development in the "Nomadology" chapter of *A Thousand Plateaus*, but Guattari first used the term in passing in an essay entitled "Machine and Structure" in 1970. Deleuze extracts and begins to play with the term in his introduction to Guattari's *Psychoanalysis and Transversality*, and employs it again in his paper "Nomadic Thought," presented at a July 1972 meeting at Cerisy-la-Salle on "Nietzsche today." While the focus of this latter paper is Nietzsche – a Nietzsche that

---

concept of media détournement, and labels *The Third Mind, Electronic Revolution*, and "The Revised Boyscout Manual" as "handbooks to inspire future generations of media guerillas, culture jammers, computer hackers, and pop-up subversives" (xlvii–xlviii).

will always fare badly in philosophy because, "in our regimes," Deleuze states, "we use any means necessary to pin [nomadic thinkers] down" (259) – Deleuze closes it by characterizing "revolutionaries today" as similar kinds of nomads (259). For Deleuze, Nietzsche's thought forms a type of "counter-philosophy" and is nomadic because Nietzsche's utterances are not put to work in service of "a rational administrative machine," where philosophers are the "bureaucrats of pure reason" (259). Instead, Nietzsche's thought moves as "a mobile war machine" (259). Nietzsche's work compels not simply because it is antagonistic towards the canon, but because its very form presents problems: his aphorisms are a "battering ram," a "nomadic force" (259). If the problem for Nietzsche was that philosophy wanted to settle him, to translate him into its code, the same was true of contemporary revolutionaries in struggle against the state.

The war machine is, somewhat confusingly, not bound to the concept or practice of war. It is a difficult term because, among Deleuze and Guattari's concepts, it is particularly mobile. As Paul Patton argues quite well, that Deleuze's philosophy is a metaphysics of process, stressing becoming rather than being (which, generally speaking, is the traditional property of metaphysics), means that he and his cowriters produce "mobile concepts" (19). First and foremost, nomadism and the war machine are external to the state form. As Guillaume Sibertin-Blanc puts it, "a given group forms a war machine ... when it becomes heterogeneous to the state apparatuses, to their procedures of administration and of control over the social field, as well as to their particular modes of territorialization." For Deleuze, representationalism in philosophy – pinning down concepts, capturing their essence – is analogous to the state form that captures and territorializes according to its mode of organization. Deleuze and Guattari's chapter on the war machine therefore traces the flow of assemblages that operate, or have operated, external to the state. Whereas state space is striated – which is to say, heavily coded – as Patton remarks, "it is the active relation to smooth space that defines the fundamental nature of the nomad, as well as that of the war machine" (38).

The tag line for Chicago '68 was "the whole world is watching," a gesture towards the presence of television cameras outside the convention, a technology consciously being exploited by protestors to expose the hypocrisies and excesses of the state. While Daniel Walker's state-commissioned report on the convention denounces the police violence that undeniably took place during the event, the ultimate effect of the report is that it captures the excesses of protestors and police alike and renews the legitimacy of the state in the aftermath of a messy event. The report reproduces state authority and asks that a minority of officers who behaved badly – with respect to "sound police procedures and common decency" – be publically condemned so as to strength-en the weakened bond "between police and community" (xxviii). In other words, the problem is not the state, but a minority who acted outside of its normal operating procedures. Even if official condemnation of police violence by the police commissioner or Mayor Richard Daley did not occur, the offi-cially sanctioned and submitted report plays the part of proxy denouncer and apologist: a minority of those entrusted to serve and protect the state acted outside of law and are captured and encoded by the very sentences that encode their indecent behaviours. The report is a part of the grammar of the state; it is a state-commissioned apparatus of capture.

The conservative grammar of the report goes beyond simply reinforcing the soundness and decency of state institutions; it articulates, as well, the limits of permissible protest and public demeanor. While the first sentence of the report unequivocally states that "[t]he right to dissent is fundamental to democracy," the statement is immediately qualified in the following sentence: "But the ex-pression of that right has become one of the most serious problems in contem-porary democratic government" (xiii). This is not to say that policing dissent has become problematic, but that the very exercise of that democratic right has increasingly become a thorn in the side of those who govern. The report sum-mary proceeds by separating the wheat from the chaff: the shock of "crowd-police battles" was "intensified by the presence in the crowds (which included some anarchists and revolutionaries) of large numbers of *innocent* dissenting citizens" (xiii, emphasis added). Among the 10,000 demonstrators gathered in Chicago were the easy-to-spot "hippies – the long hair and love beads, the calculated unwashedness, the flagrant banners, the open lovemaking and dis-dain for the constraints of conventional society" (xxi), but these visually and vocally loud hippies merely stood out of an otherwise diverse crowd intent on expressing its dissent peacefully (xxi–xxii).

The report's summary collects an array of innocent victims of police mis-conduct. The more protracted stories see a young man saving his girlfriend from police attack (xxiii), and "a well-dressed woman" and "a priest" describ-ing a "'boy, about fourteen or fifteen, white,'" being clubbed by police and then carted off by a police van (xxvii). The report's summary spends no time dis-cussing the protest itself. It is instead filled with accounts of bystanders being clubbed and carted off, people who "weren't demonstrators at all, but were just pedestrians who didn't know how to react to the charging officers yelling 'Police!'" (xxvii). Although dissent may be "fundamental to democracy," so too is its suppression. What is entirely unacceptable in a democracy, however, is when "innocent" people – with respectable attire, vocations, haircuts, hygiene, sexuality, gender roles, and skin colour – are subject to violence at the hands of state agents who are supposed to be preserving the order, not upsetting it. Nowhere in this report is there any mention of the fact that the violent suppression of assembly, whether such assembly is intentional or accidental, might have a stifling effect on dissent and, therefore, democracy. This was nothing new to those who had already been politicized; the *Port Huron Statement*, which founded the SDS, was written precisely to address the paradoxes and hypocrisies of democracy (Hayden *Port Huron Statement* 45–8).

While the report summary can be read as a conduct manual for state agents and citizens alike, the report's first section, "The Gathering Forces," provides an excellent account of the year of organizing work that led into the convention, and it provides a solid account of the war machine that the state was trying to capture. Walker notes that the confrontation was blamed on "outside agitators" (3), and he describes the various contingents that constituted this "outside": from "Negroes" who "demanded, and took control, of their own movement"; to students who didn't want a place in a system that excluded them, but rather "wanted to replace the system"; to various alienated "students, nonstudents, [and] ex-students" who "turned their backs on [the system] and became hippies." Given the participation of such activists, "conventional behavior and traditional values," Walker notes, "were under attack at every level" (3). Walker not only makes note of how this mass disillusionment with society was leading to outside agitation, but he also observes that those who had "forsaken electoral politics" were "becoming concerned with their relationship with the 'other society,'" and that "a few of the more deliberate and creative of these invented an acronym, YIPPIE! and a 'non-organization' to go with it" (5). The impulse to create new spaces for living together unhindered by the blockages, hierarchies, and strata that constitute contemporary society was a complex experiment. That Walker's description of this turning away is dripping with condescension and disdain – a disposition shared by the administrators and police with respect to these "outside agitators" – illustrates the manner in which the war machine, which doesn't seek war, ends up in conflict with the state: the war machine is incommensurable with the striated space of the state; it seeks to deterritorialize its rigid fixities. Of the various ways in which the state can capture these outside agitators who threaten the very constitution and unquestioned legitimacy of the state, violent force is perhaps the least effective, as it must be legitimized. It was, after all, the intent of demonstrators to provoke and thereby "expose the inhumanity, injustice, prejudice, hypocrisy, or militaristic repression" of the state (Walker 5). Making agitators the subject of unsavoury sentences is a much more effective means of maintaining the state's grammar.

To be a "non-organization" was the main creative motor of the movement, and this is precisely what Guattari was trying to capture in his theory when he met Deleuze. In his preface to Guattari's *Psychoanalysis and Transversality*, Deleuze makes note of Guattari's distinction between two types of groups: "subjugated groups and group subjects" ("Three Group-Related Problems" 13). Deleuze explains that groups are subjugated by the installation of leaders and the institution of hierarchies, structures, and a tendency towards centralization that acts to ward off creativity, rupture, the participation of other groups, and "genuine collective 'enunciation'" (14). Group subjects operate differently. They are "defined by coefficients of transversality that ward off totalities and hierarchies" (14). Revolutionary unification – the act of bringing together a multiplicity without crushing or verticalizing it – must occur as *"the unification of a war machine and not a state apparatus ... [I]t must play the role of an analyzer* with respect to the desire of the group and the masses, and not the role of the synthesizer operating through rationalization, totalization, exclusion, etc." (16, emphasis in original). In other words, the desires and struggles of individuals and groups must be taken seriously, understood, respected, and worked through. The group subject is not a synthesizer because struggles, though taken seriously by the group, remain autonomous, and no struggle or desire can be subordinated to the others. To oppose the work of the state, groups must also avoid working like states, as stratification comes as much from modes of organization as from state policy.

The national mobilization that brought people to Chicago was conceived analogously. Walker's chapter on "gathering forces" documents the mobilization strategy. Activists had learned from the McCarthy years. So as to evade capture, membership was not required: all meetings were open. The resulting coalition comprised pacifists, revolutionaries, and anarchists of every stripe (10), and the challenge that the non-member group sought to work out was how to build a national coalition that could accommodate the "desire for local, decentralized action" (13). The answer was to create "movement centers" that would act as a kind of information-sharing hub and gathering space that could lead a mass march while privileging local planning and decentralized demonstrations (13–14). Not only was this a strategic manner for organizing a movement and event, it was consciously built as an alternative to the state form on display at the convention: rather than deciding between two candidates, or seeking to reform the Democratic Party, the committee sought to demonstrate how alternative modes of organization – organizations that were "under the control of the actual people with grievances" – were ultimately more desirable, accommodating, and effective (Davis and Hayden qtd. in Walker 14).

While more theatrical in its intervention, Yippie was similarly conceived. As alluded to above, Hoffman encouraged a synthesis of hippies and radicals. In a statement, published in the satirical underground paper *The Realist* a month before the convention and reprinted in the Walker report, Hoffman – using botanical metaphors that recall Deleuze on the orchid and the wasp – calls for "[t]he blending of pot and politics ... a cross-fertilization of the hippie and New Left philosophy" (qtd. in Walker 31). "Yippie" was conceived as a "connecting link" that would tie together willing constituencies from the underground at the "national get-together" in order to develop "a model for an alternative society" and "make some statement, especially in revolutionary action-theater terms about LBJ, the Democratic Party, electoral politics, and the state of the nation" (31). Paul Krassner, editor of *The Realist*, explains that Yippie is a "national disorganization" meant to disrupt (Walker 31). When one thinks about the "state of the nation," it becomes possible to separate the two: while the state organizes the nation and its citizens, the nation can be disorganized: striated space can be rendered smooth.

The point is, however, that this type of organized disorganization was not exclusive to the Yippies or the national mobilization. It was also present in the March 22nd Movement (which Deleuze points to as an example of a war machine / group subject alongside Guattari's work at La Borde in his preface to *Psychoanalysis and Transversality* ["Three Group-Related Problems" 17, 19–21]); it was theorized as "affinity groups" by UAW/MF, the street gang with analysis frequented by Deleuze and Guattari's radar scout Lebel; and affinity group theory had a profound impact, alongside Régis Debray's theory of focoism, on the development of the Weather Underground Organization,[44] the American group that emerged on the other side of Chicago and that is folded into the final paragraphs of Guattari's *Psychoanalysis and Transversality*: "Then anarchy! No coordination, no centralization, no headquarters ... Just the opposite! Take the Weathermen in the USA. They are organized in tribes, gangs, etc., but it doesn't prevent them from coordinating and doing it well" (368). In the discussion that follows Deleuze's 1972 presentation "Nomadic Thought," Deleuze says that he's not interested in textual commentary; instead, he wants to explore "what one can do with an extra-textual practice that extends the text" ("Nomadic Thought" 260). If Deleuze was a lightning rod who

---

44 On the importance of UAW/MF to the development of the WUO, see Morea 18. On the importance of Régis Debray's *Revolution in the Revolution* and his theory of focoism, see David Gilbert 98–101; and Rudd 144.

grounded Guattari's brainstorms (Deleuze "Letter to Uno" 239), what Deleuze reined in as the "war machine" was not simply a concept, but all of these groups that were folded into Guattari as activist and analyst, and it is these extra-textual war machines that extended the text of philosophy. Deleuze and Guattari do not try to fit within the dominant frame of philosophy; instead, with the help of actual, extra-textual war machines, they create concepts to map new social relations and ways of becoming.

While *Anti-Oedipus*, produced in the immediate wake of '68, is more directly militant than Deleuze and Guattari's later collaborations, *A Thousand Plateaus*, with its autonomous yet interlinked chapters, is a kind of philosophical equivalent to the movement. Deleuze and Guattari's theory of the war machine helps us to recognize that the movements that developed in the '60s and '70s were not opposed only to the state; they were also, at their most sophisticated, opposed to statist ways of thinking. As Andrew Robinson points out, the theory of the war machine is a strategic reminder that "autonomous activists need to be prepared to 'ward off' the state, both within movements (by challenging statist ways of thinking and acting) and in relation to the wider context (by resisting state repression)." Even when the sole goal of a movement is to "defend or express its own difference," antagonism between movements and states is inevitable (Robinson n.p.). This is precisely what we witness when we look back to the struggles of the sixties, as youth worked to organize around expressing their difference in creative ways. While events like May '68, Columbia's '68, or the 1968 Democratic National Convention are artificially isolated and treated as failures, the interconnection of these events – their enfoldedness, their transcreation and becomings – links them all to an outside, to experimentation with alternate states and modes of (dis)organization. On the one hand, Deleuze and Guattari's work is an effort to capture the essence of thought and politics in motion (a metaphysics of process, becoming over being), but, on the other, in translating the movement into their book, they have translated the state of the book itself: whereas activists interrogate the state of the nation and conceive new ways of being, philosophers interrogate the state of the book and conceive new ways of writing. *A Thousand Plateaus* as rhizome book – with its autonomous, decentralized chapters and interrelated, yet distinct and ready-to-deploy concepts – is their philosophical expression of the '68 years.

## III. Becoming Allies. Becoming Women's LibeRATion

I have followed the thought of Deleuze and Guattari thus far by demonstrating how it and the international movement are immanent; the '68 years are folded into them, just as they are folded into the '68 years. Their excursions through history, philosophy, and politics are protracted negotiations that identify despotic, verticalizing forces and seek, in every overcoded corner, alternative ways of living, thinking, writing, and doing politics. This is not something that they were doing on their own, nor were they seeking to lead a new philosophical movement. As they say in an interview conducted after their publication of *Anti-Oedipus*:

> We're writing for unconsciousnesses that have had enough. We're looking for allies. We need allies. And we think these allies are already out there, that they've gone ahead without us, that there's lots of people who have had enough and are thinking, feeling, and working in similar directions. ("On *Anti-Oedipus*" 22)

What types of alliances might be forged between Deleuze, Guattari, and those who are working in similar directions? While an analysis of Deleuze and Guattari's resonance with contemporary social justice theories on the role of the "ally" is beyond the scope of this chapter, I think it is worth taking note of a very real privilege rooted in the practice of being an ally to those engaged in struggle. As African-American poet and activist Ewuare Osayande argues in an article on the popularity of white anti-racist activist Tim Wise within liberal white and black communities alike, being a non-oppressed ally provides one with the privilege to paraphrase, appropriate, and claim the arguments and analyses of the oppressed without being accused of being overly invested and emotional. Adapted to the context of this study, Osayande's observation raises the question of the relationship between philosophy and its "others."

Deleuze, Guattari, and Derrida converge on non-representational grounds that guard against certain tendencies in philosophical thought. As we saw with "The Ends of Man," Derrida was wary of the imperialist tendencies of philosophy: conceiving itself as universal, it was content to write others into a particular vision of enlightenment that, while universal in its reach, did not in fact include the vast majority of people on the planet. In "The Ends of Man," Derrida had more sense than to translate the marginalized into philosophy proper. Deleuze and Guattari's philosophy is similarly non-representational. They see the tendency to use concepts as metaphors that pin down, or capture, states of being as a type of despotic work that fixes or stops flows or movements of becoming.

The line of becoming that I have traced herein, with the help of *RAT*'s accumulation of networks, is the line that I will continue to follow to the end, a line that takes us to the combinatory space of feminist writing and activism. To follow *RAT* to the end is to end by making Deleuze and Guattari ramify with a network of American feminists, a combination of non-intrinsically related women in struggle for a better world who make a festering *RAT* – a newspaper that was becoming irrelevant in its irreverence, pinning women to particular roles and relations – become *Women's LibeRATion*. Significantly, this is also the site of a productive regime change where the distinction between metaphor and metonymy itself becomes troubled and must be revisited.

## Up Against the Wall, RAT!

In 1970, *RAT Subterranean News* was taken over by an all-women's collective that recognized, challenged, and overcame statist ways of thinking and acting that had stratified the movement along gender lines from the start. The takeover of *RAT* was catalysed by a last-minute editorial decision to turn the preceding issue of *RAT* into a sex and porn special. The issue was so uncritically objectifying that Jane Alpert, the only woman who was official staff, decided, after an initial leaf-through, that she would resign. A friend that she was with when she encountered the issue convinced her otherwise: it would be more effective to have the all-male editorial board relinquish power for a week, leaving the content, layout, and printing to an all-women's collective for the next issue. The takeover would prove permanent. The problem, as Alpert relates in *Growing Up Underground*, was not only that the newspaper "was deteriorating from a lively radical journal to a sophomoric joke sheet" but that women were treated with the same systematic condescension at *RAT* as they were encountering elsewhere: their ideas were ignored, and their positions on staff were subordinate (242).

The takeover of *RAT* was by no means an originary moment – that is, the issue that brought the women's liberation movement into being. In *Sisterhood Is Powerful*, Robin Morgan's anthology of writings from the movement (like *Women's LibeRATion*, entirely produced by women, published in 1970), Morgan situates the beginnings of the turn of the seventies women's liberation movement in 1966, when, surrounding the formation of the National organization for Women (NOW), women's caucuses started to convene, demanding representation – and the representation of women's struggles – in and around various groups like SDS and forming independent radical groups devoted to the elaboration of theories and practices of radical feminisms ("The Women's Revolution" xx–xxiv).[45] Guilty of dismissing and ridiculing the concerns of

---

45 While Morgan's *Sisterhood Is Powerful* is indeed an important compendium of the women's liberation struggle, its elision of racialized women's struggles is readily apparent, with less than 10 per cent of the book devoted to work by people of colour. See note 50 for collections and studies that tackle the issue of second-wave feminism and women of colour.

women were not only the movement's Abbie Hoffmans, countercultural celebrities who read the objectification and mistreatment of women into free
love, but also the politically engaged, who argued that women's struggles
were secondary and distracted the movement from the important causes at
hand.[46] Whereas *RAT* was becoming insignificant under the direction of men,
its takeover by women marked its reinvigoration; retitled *Women's LibeRATion*
by the beginning of 1970, it became a venue within which women could articulate their concerns as an integral part of an always complex and multifaceted movement.

The reductive and unfounded concerns of the movement's most obstinate
men were challenged by the front cover of the liberated issue. *RAT*, a 17" x 11"
paper, was often printed with a half-page front and back cover on its flipside.
By folding the paper over backwards, it became an 8½" x 11" booklet for distribution whose centerfold, once opened, would be the full-size cover page of
the newspaper. Although the issue proclaims that the paper has been taken over
by women on its folded cover page – which announces the newspaper's inclusion of three features: "panther 21 interview p.1," "women take over rat
p.2," and "weatherwomen p.5." – it is an interview with imprisoned BPP member Afeni Shakur that is printed on the full front-page cover that emerges when
the paper is opened to be read. That the Panther 21 interview is given to this
first page means that it is, in effect, the cover story (the breaking story of the
newspaper's liberation could itself wait until the second page). In effect, Shakur
is women's liberation and women's liberation is Shakur. They are in immanent
relation. This issue-engendering use of the fold – the fold as reciprocal implication – is tangible throughout the liberated paper.

Shakur, interviewed by Alpert, was the most prominent spokesperson
among twenty-one Panthers who had been arrested in an early morning raid on
2 April 1969 in New York, allegedly for plotting to bomb department stores
and the New York Botanical Gardens. (All twenty-one Panthers were acquitted
after only forty-five minutes of jury deliberation two years later.[47]) The day
after the first issue of liberated *RAT* hit the streets, the trial was set to begin.
That the paper features an interview with Shakur on the eve of the trial's

---

46  As Morgan recounts, when women proposed a women's liberation plank for SDS in 1966,
the women who presented the resolution "were pelted with tomatoes and thrown out of the
convention" ("The Women's Revolution" xxi).

47  For definitive accounts of the trial, see Kempton, *The Briar Patch*, and Kioni-Sadiki and
Meyer, *Look for Me in the Whirlwind* (a recent release by PM Press that reprints the collective
autobiography of the Panther 21, which has long been out of print).

commencement suggests that the paper continued to be committed to reporting on, and rallying around, the gravest of the establishment's contrivances. Beyond discussing the immediate situation of the Panthers going to trial – how trials against the BPP members and black people in general were invariably infused with a racism that overrode fundamental rights and freedoms that were constitutionally "guaranteed"[48] – Alpert and Shakur discuss the respect and excitement that Shakur inspired among inmates in the women's house of detention, a phenomenon that Alpert was able to witness first hand during her overlapping incarceration there (Shakur 1, 24).[49] Although a large grey fist superimposed upon the last page of the interview has the unfortunate effect of obscuring some of the text at the centre of the interview, the gesture is one of solidarity with Shakur, the prisoners in the women's house of detention, and the Panther 21. Solidarity among an array of oppressed individuals and groups was inherent in the women's liberation movement: issues of race, class, and gender were intertwined.[50]

---

48  An extremely enlightening historical document in this respect is a five-page letter by the Panther 21 entitled "To: Judge Murtagh, From: The Panther 21" which *RAT* printed in its 7–21 March issue. The powerful letter draws on a history that extends from the seventeenth century to their present case to detail the ways in which racism is built into the legal system. The letter is reprinted in Philip S. Foner's *The Black Panthers Speak*. See also Davis, "Notes for Arguments in Court." Davis's notes, which she drew up as she prepared for her own trial, survey legal issues surrounding the trials of Bobby Seale and the Panther 21. Indeed, a number of texts publicized court proceedings during this time, from the Black Panther Party's underground newspaper, to mass-market paperbacks. See Bond et al., *The Trial of Bobby Seale*; Keating, *Free Huey!*; and Levine, McNamee, and Greenberg, *The Tales of Hoffman*.

49  Alpert, charged with conspiracy to bomb eight government and commercial buildings, was out on bail. When her trial was about to start at the end of the spring, she jumped bail, going underground until 1974.

50  I say that issues of race, class, and gender are intertwined in *RAT* following its takeover, to allude to the "intersectionality" coined in Kimberlé Crenshaw's "Mapping the Margins," an article that describes the shared experiences of black women along various overlapping axes of oppression. Not only would use of the term "intersectionality" be anachronistic, but the relationship between white, black, and Chicana feminists during the second wave was a complicated one that often left racialized women in the margins, a phenomenon infamously explored in bell hooks's *Feminist Theory: From Margin to Center*, which points to the appeal to "sisterhood" as a universalist move that masked the racism and classism inherent in the movement. In *Ain't I a Woman?*, hooks traces the overlap of racism and sexism back to the antebellum South and examines the marginalization of black women within black struggles and feminist struggles alike. Angela Davis's *Women, Race, and Class* traces a similar trajectory. For works that dissect and correct the phenomenon of racialized exclusions of the second wave, see Collins, *Black Feminist Thought*; Valk, *Radical Sisters*; Roth, *Separate*

On the second page of the newspaper, news of the *RAT* takeover is rendered in full. In the top right corner of the page, always reserved for the same machine gun-wielding rat, but always carrying an updated caption that relegates the most current and despicable enemy to the wall, the rat appears as usual, but feminized. The caption "Up against the wall, RAT!" is given to the Rat woman who, rather than stone-facedly standing, is jumping victoriously over top of the headline "women take over rat." As the italicized column that runs beneath, signed by "the rat women" explains, "*RAT* is supposed to be a paper about revolution. Our revolution." In the Rat women's estimation, the paper no longer seemed to be up to this task:

> More than ever in the last couple of months, *RAT* has given the impression that we regard politics as that thing the Black Panthers and the Young Lords are into. White youth, and non-Panthers/Lords (one would think after reading recent back *RAT*s) just lie back and groove on pornography, dope, rock, movies. *RAT* has been moving no one into action, has failed to even suggest directions for action. It labors along with humorous pretensions, which most of us can't even find funny anymore (particularly those of us who bear the brunt of its jokes) about the cultural revolution. Can we still be under the illusion that the cultural revolution, in this time of heavy repression, of mounting police power and courtroom insanity, is going to pull down the state with its dope and music and its so-called liberated sex? ... This is not to say that our culture isn't an integral part of the way we fight the system. But the culture has got to be revolutionary as surely as the revolution has got to be cultural. (Rat Women 2)

If the Rat women were arguing for a revolutionary culture, exploitative culture was certainly not it; if women were objectified by *RAT*'s old ideas about the cultural revolution (including the printing of pornographic pictures and cartoons that were run in order to sell papers), the drawings and photographs depicting women in the liberated run of *RAT* were the exact opposite: women in these images were strong, racially diverse, active, and resolute.

Acting as a corrective to *RAT*'s irresponsible turn away from politics and its headlong dive into revolutionary culture, the issue is brimming with political

---

*Roads to Feminism*; Moraga and Anzaldúa, *This Bridge Called My Back*; Hull, Bell-Scott, and Smith, *All the Women Are White, All the Blacks Are Men, But Some of Us Are Brave*; Guy-Sheftal, *Words of Fire*; Garcia, *Chicana Feminist Thought*; and Thompson, "Multiracial Feminism."

2.4. Women take over *RAT*, 9–23 February 1970 © Jeffrey Shero.

articles (a turn towards politics peopled by everywhere already active women). Where the BPP is concerned, the issue carries not only the cover interview with Shakur of New York's Panther 21 but also a further statement from her and a Liberation News Service (LNS) item featuring Kathleen Cleaver, an active Panther who was persistently relegated to the shadow of her husband. The item, titled "Kathleen," sees Cleaver giving a reporter a powerful and matter-of-fact answer to his question regarding the place of women in the revolution: "No one ever asks what a man's place in the revolution is." The problem at the heart of all such questions, Cleaver points out, is that, regardless of women's demonstrated capability to perform the same labour as men during wartime (evicted from the factories upon their return), everything that they do continues to be considered secondary – including the labour of giving birth – by capitalist society ("Kathleen" 8). If the voices of BPP women were stifled not only by white radical newspapers but by the BPP's own organizational deficiencies (a problem that was recognized but was not substantially remedied until Elaine Brown took over the party in 1974, appointing several women to the BPP central committee in the process[51]), in the pages of liberated *RAT*, the struggles and positions of Shakur and Cleaver are *featured*. The perpetually ignored and often derided matter of fact that this particular issue of *RAT* lays bare (from an examination of the Panthers through Shakur and Cleaver; to the recognition, among Palestinian women and men, that women were not only caregivers but equal participants in the Palestinian revolution (Ryan "Refugee Revolution"); to a focus by Anna Louise Stronger on the Chinese Revolution that looks beyond Chairman Mao and Lin Piao, introducing the waves being made by Ciang Ch'ing under the title "Are Women Seizing Power in China?"[52]) is that women are entrenched within the movement. Women did not depoliticize the movement by introducing questions regarding their oppression into the movement's already vast, varied, and networked catalogue of struggles (as the male-dominated Left was fond of arguing); they were themselves depoliticized when they were ignored or relegated to secondary positions within the movement. How could it be argued that women were imposing themselves upon the revolution when their own complex and multifaceted political positions were already everywhere inherent in the movement?

If struggle was meant to be a collective endeavour, was it not counterintuitive to kick out *RAT*'s men? The Rat women, arguing for unity in the revolution, were understandably sceptical about whether their own paper's men and women, at that point, could "function together as a revolutionary unit" (Rat Women 2). If women writers were being relegated to secretarial duties, and entire issues were being published in complete disregard for the politics of its staff (the pornography issue),[53] it was clear that the paper was operating and structured in such a way that women were being excluded from positions of influence. The Rat women planned to render the paper truly *collective* by

---

51  Brown's autobiography, *A Taste of Power*, provides an important – and sobering – account of gender divisions within the party. Regarding her assuming the leadership of the party and her appointment of women to the central committee, see 356–76. On gender dynamics within the BPP, see Jennings; Matthews; Leblanc-Ernest; Cleaver; J. Bloom and Martin, 302–8; and Heynan 412–15.

52  The article on Chiang Ch'ing occupies the folded back cover of the issue, a particularly biting choice considering the centrality of Maoism to the movement. In the midst of Maoist China, women were rising.

53  As Alpert relates in her memoirs, her very first dealings with *RAT* were marked by the sexist demand that – as she entered and met editor Jeff Shero to offer an article on hijacking based on her recent experiences – she commit to the paper by becoming a secretary. Judging by the state of the office, Alpert noted, "it was obvious that the paper needed a housekeeper" (177–8).

breaking down editorial hierarchies ("Editor, Assistant Editor, etc. etc. ... divisions of labor that are dragging on both the men and women here" [2]).[54] Regarding the exclusion of men, one should in fact recognize the black nationalist and black power warnings about collaborations and alliances in the collective's decision to exclude men at this juncture: inclusion can amount to infiltration and a concomitant taming and redirection of energies (especially when one considers historical power imbalances).[55] To work separately did not amount to separatism: the liberated *RAT* operated as an affinity group that was plugged into, and whose activism coursed through, the movement.

Once divorced from the uncritical stagnancy of the newspaper's editorial board, *RAT* opened itself up to several outside contingents. Among those responsible for the first liberated issue of *RAT* were "more than a dozen unaffiliated women and sisters from WITCH, Redstockings, the Gay Liberation Front, LNS and Weatherman" (the Rat women). The collective planned, wrote, illustrated, and laid out the paper in an eight-day stretch between takeover and printing. Political objectives were most effectively realized by *collectivization*, and coming together did not mean that autonomous struggles ceased to develop or to be recognized as such. A synthesized Left could not be articulated by an organization in isolation; it involved the collection of a variety of voices: internal synthesis via relations of exteriority.

An example of how this seemingly complicated internal/external relationship works – a marker of *RAT*'s collective approach – is that authorship virtually disappears once *RAT* is liberated. Authorship was renounced by the liberated newspaper because it was considered to be a signifier of bourgeois individualism. Although this decision has the unfortunate effect of blurring agential lines, the positive effect of the lack of individual indicators (and this, I would argue, is precisely the effect that the paper intended) is that, regardless of apparent differences, all of the issues produced – and all of the positions covered in those issues – are the manifestation of a collective voice, and they

---

54 At the bottom of the page, in a space reserved for the standard rundown of "Rat Staff" is the same box, but this time headed by the title "Rat Collective." The box lists all of the women who worked on the first liberated issue of the newspaper, without hierarchical designations appended: "Jill Bosky – valiant typesetter for *RAT* for unheralded decades, Jane Alpert, Lorelei B., Ruth Beller, Pam Booth, Valerie Bouvier, Naomi Glauberman, Carol Goldberg, Sharon Krebs, Robin Morgan, Joyce Plecha, Daria Price, Judy Robinson, Miriam Rosen, Barbara Rothcrug, Judy Russell, Liz Schneider, Martha Shelley, Sue Siminsky, Brenda Smiley, Christina Sweet, Laura Tillem, Judy Walenta, Cathy Werner, AND Mark, Jan, Anton, Neil, IN SPIRIT: ALICE EMBREE and PAT SWINTON."

55 See, in particular, Malcolm X, "Message to the Grassroots."

therefore represent a women's liberation movement that is capable of accommodating singularities but that is itself in no way singular.[56]

## "Goodbye Male-Dominated Left," or Presenting Futurity

Divided between doing away with the past and ushering in the future, the *Manifesto* seeks to produce the arrival of the "modern revolution" through an act of self-foundation and self-creation: we, standing here and now, must act!

Martin Puchner, *Poetry of the Revolution*

Robin Morgan's "Goodbye to All That" is something of a centrepiece to a newspaper without centre, a manifesto situated in the moment of takeover. More important than its specific criticisms of *RAT* staffers, Morgan's essay let loose on the entire "male-dominated left" (the name stenciled onto the side of a cruise ship, drawn into the second page of the article, that is sinking while, onshore, four women watch, dance, wave, and sing "bye bye baby bye bye"). According to Morgan, the takeover of certain "pornzines" might have been more obvious, but taking over was "reserved for something at least *worth* taking over," and she noted that the most obviously vile publications "should just be helped not to exist – by any means necessary" (6, emphasis in original). Morgan's essay is direct in its condemnation of *RAT* staff and other movement leaders because *RAT* was part of an entire movement worth saving, oozing with potential but fundamentally stratified. To label Morgan's piece as a "manifesto" is to recognize that it is marked by forward orientation in a moment of suspension.

If the Left was merited in its championing of race, why did it turn a blind eye to gender? As Morgan puts it, "two evils pre-date capitalism and have been clearly able to survive and post-date socialism: sexism and racism." Using Mao's well-known terminology regarding the primacy of anti-imperialist struggle, Morgan remarks that "Women were the first property when the *Primary Contradiction* occurred: when one half of the human species decided to subjugate the other half because it was 'different,' alien, the Other" (7, emphasis added). How could the movement's men wave their red books and champion racial struggles while not only ignoring women but perpetuating their

---

56  Consider Deleuze and Guattari's renunciation of authorship, here: "The two of us wrote *Anti-Oedipus* together. Since each of us was several, there was already quite a crowd" (*A Thousand Plateaus* 3).

subjugation? Morgan makes use of Mao and appropriates other New Left and countercultural discourse in the process of staking a claim from within the movement (lashing out at John Sinclair's atrociously misogynistic comments while at the same time using the title of an MC5 album to point out that, "this time, we're going to kick out all the jams, and the boys will have to hustle just to keep up" [7]). If manifestoes are about both establishing a present/presence and a future, what Morgan's "Goodbye" makes clear is that women are already there, leftist discourses are already theirs, and they are moving on.

It would be misleading to consider the women's movement that the paper represented as being something of a catch-all for a Left that was without internal antagonisms; "Goodbye to All That" both takes on and embodies these divisions. Although women from Weatherman (as it was still called at the beginning of 1970) were part of the RAT collective that put the issue together, Morgan did not spare the group in her critique of the emergent New Left.[57] Evaluating the group in which many movement women found themselves, Morgan disparages the women who joined the group for renouncing "their own radical feminism for that last grab at male approval," offering an important public criticism of the female-saturated but, as personal and public accounts had revealed, male-dominated group. Morgan was particularly sceptical of the group's adoption of the policy of smashing monogamy as a cornerstone for practical solidarity. As women had learned from experience, Morgan argues, the "theory of free sexuality" tended to translate into the "practice of sex on demand for males" (6). At the conclusion of Morgan's paragraph on Weatherman, the group is forcefully swept aside, given the same treatment as the other perpetrators and perpetuators of the counterfeit male-dominated Left: "Goodbye to the illusion of strength when you run hand in hand with your oppressors; goodbye to the dream that being in the leadership collective will get you anything but gonorrhea" (6). Though Morgan's warning is an important reminder that Weather women should do

---

57 One of the most remarkable things about *RAT* over the course a five-month post-takeover stretch is the dialogue that persists between Weatherman (written, for the most part, by an anonymous "Weatherwoman," meaning that it was via the organization's women that the WUO's positions were reported) and its detractors, either side representing diametric opposites within the dispersed collective. Without erasing their differences, the paper conveys a synthesis of sorts. The manner in which Bernadine Dohrn's "Declaration of a State of War" appears in *RAT* makes for a good representative example. Announcing the impending attack on "a symbol or institution of Amerikan injustice," the first official communiqué of the "Weatherman Underground," published under the "Weather Report" headline that had

everything they can to ensure that their newfound positions on the Left are more than tokenistic, it also, in effect, expresses something of a lack of faith, or, in any case, a belief that statements made by Weather women were either disingenuous or naive.

The placement of Morgan's article within the issue is in itself an interesting and instructive matter. That her article is placed just after a testimonial from "Inside the weather machine" – written by "A Weatherwoman" – that celebrates and affirms the Weather practice of "smashing monogamy" does not mean that the Rat collective had decided to lay the paper out in such a fashion that Morgan was to get the last word (and do away with Weatherman once and for all). What it *did* mean was that women in the movement, regardless of their respective commitments and constituencies, would be recognized in the pages of *RAT*, given the space that they had been denied pre-liberation. On the other side of Morgan's article are the items regarding Kathleen Cleaver and Afeni Shakur, a reminder to the dullest of feminism's critics that writing a feminist manifesto did not mean an end to all other political subjects. Where the article before Morgan's is signed by a "Weatherwoman," and the items on the proceeding page are devoted to Panthers, Morgan signs her manifesto WITCH (in this instance of the acronym that was given various configurations at the turn

---

become a virtual staple in *RAT*, is immediately followed by an unsigned "Weather Retort," an italically rendered response to the statement that critiques both the sexism of its references and its stated decision that violence was the way to advance the movement's interests. See Dohrn "WAR: Weather Report," a reprint of "Declaration of a State of War," and the anonymous "Weather Retort." On gender relations and the question of male supremacy in the Weather Underground, see also R. Jacobs 90–126. Edited collections of original communiqués, like Harold Jacobs, *Weatherman*, and Dohrn, Ayers, and Jones, *Sing a Battle Song*, demonstrate how the issue of women's positions within the collective, and women's struggles within the movement, was often at the forefront of the Weather Underground's concerns. While the volume of work produced by women within the collective is notable, and while self-awareness and self-criticism – a Maoist inflection – give the impression that the group was not as male-dominated as its most vocal movement critics alleged, recent memoirs suggest otherwise. In *Flying Too Close to the Sun*, Cathy Wilkerson notes that some of her harshest criticisms of the group were edited out, unbeknownst to her, before they appeared in SDS's *New Left Notes* (260). She also discusses how self-criticism, including the antimonogamy approach, often warped into "the men of the Weather Bureau dictating 'women's liberation' to a woman against her wishes" (269) and she addresses physically abusive relationships (308). Jane Alpert uses the last chapter of *Growing Up Underground* to discuss her renunciation of the Weather Underground in favour of longtime friend Robin Morgan and the feminist movement (341–69).

of the seventies, Women Inspired to Commit Herstory[58]). That so many organizations were involved in assembling the issue was an indication that, from the beginning, multiple feminist positions were welcome in the collective.

While ideological and personal gaps were never entirely bridged – arguments between politicos and feminists, a major divide used to characterize a rift at the core of women's liberation, were a constant in liberated *RAT* – the biweekly product did go some distance towards achieving this feat in print. In some ways, this is simply to say that the pages of *RAT* made it glaringly obvious that "politicos" had as much a stake in feminism as the "feminists" did in politics, or, in other words, that it was as reductive to consider the former as anti-feminism as it was to argue that the latter was apolitical. Women's liberated *RAT* is a remarkable demonstration of how the "and" and "with" that constitute assemblages are markers of disjunctive syntheses: they bring together different elements without erasing the differences that reside on either side. The line of articles that continued to pour into *RAT* over the next number of months stood as juxtaposed testaments to the fact that the positions were in no way mutually exclusive. Important articles on abortion, midwifery, and lesbianism mobilized readers around protests, shared information regarding access to services, and fostered the creation of communities.[59] Alongside these articles

---

58  As Morgan notes, "Goodbye" marked "the debut of the word 'herstory'" (*Word of a Woman* 51). WITCH was subject to a number of configurations starting in 1968. While the original WITCH title was Women's International Conspiracy from Hell, Morgan notes that

> on Mother's Day one coven became Women Infuriated at Taking Care of Hoodlums; another group, working at a major Eastern insurance corporation, became Women Indentured to Traveler's Corporate Hell; still another set of infiltrators, working at Bell Telephone, manifested themselves disruptively as Women Incensed at Telephone Company Harassment. When hexing inflationary prices at supermarkets, a Midwest coven appeared as Women's Independent Taxpayers, Consumers, and Homemakers; Women Interested in Toppling Consumption Holidays was another transfigutory appellation – and the latest heard at this writing is Women Inspired to Commit Herstory. ("WITCH Documents" 538–9)

59  Regarding abortion, see, in particular, "Abortion," an article that announces a march concerning impending legalization legislation in New York and and carries eye-opening statistics regarding the prevalence of illegal abortions in New York and the economics involved in access; and "Women Unite," a map that documents the abortion laws in each state with a legend that indicates the only circumstances under which access is granted (the categories included are life, health, physical health, mental health, physical deformity, forcible rape, statutory rape, incest, time limit, m.d. approval, residency) and that provides dates when each of the states' present abortion laws were passed. Regarding midwifery, see "Modern

was a constant stream of coverage regarding the Panthers, the Vietnamese National Liberation Front, the Front de Libération du Québec, and the Weather Underground. Beyond simple juxtaposition, the items are interwoven on a more profound level: an imprisoned member of the WUO is given coverage because she is 3 ½ months pregnant and does not have enough money to make bail to get an abortion;[60] interviews are run with women in the New York women's house of detention in order to expose the lack of important women's health services available to them;[61] and women's work in Cuban fields is attributed to the creation of a national daycare program that was "crucial to women's ability to become active in production" (while the persistence of machismo in Latin American media and in the fields was subject to sharp criticism).[62] Rather than articulating a specific *RAT* ideology, or printing the perspectives that would suggest that there was one, articles appeared from each of the many constituencies that had a stake in "the movement." What the paper made clear was that each of these fronts had everything to do with women, but that contextualizing the women's liberation movement as being a movement in and for itself would be counterintuitive and counterproductive: if feminism were bracketed, women

---

Midwifery," which explains the procedures and options associated with the practice. *RAT* also printed a questionnaire entitled "Are Doctors Pigs," headed with information regarding the importance of gynecology to the sustained health of women and the preponderance of bad gynecologists. The questionnaire was meant to weed out bad offices and doctors, and the results were to be collated and published in *RAT* and in pamphlet form and distributed to women's liberation groups.

Regarding lesbianism, there were articles by women in the Gay Liberation Front (GLF) in almost every liberated issue. See, in particular, "Out of the Closets into the Streets," an article regarding systemic persecution of lesbians by police, at workplaces, and in high schools and universities; "Women Are the Revolution" comprising four pages of coming out stories, meant to humanize the process and to encourage others to follow suit; and "Women's Liberation Is a Lesbian Plot," a report from a woman who was part of the Lavender Menace group, explaining how they intervened during the Congress to Unite Women in order to put lesbianism on a women's liberation map that had, until that point, been ignoring its existence in the movement.

60  See "Free Dionne and Joan." Beyond raising awareness of the issues, the article announces the establishment a bail fund for Dionne Donghi.

61  See, in particular, "Bail Fund" and "Tear Down the Walls!"

62  See New York Area Venceremos Brigade, "Women in Cuba" and "Women in Cuba ..." See also "Revolutionaries Are Unfit Mothers," a letter regarding tactics being used against movement women, like denial of prenatal care in prison. In particular, the letter attempts to mobilize around the case of Robin Gish, who was deemed an unfit mother and had her daughters taken away when she went to Cuba with the New York Area Venceremos Brigade. The letter argues that the case is part of a norm dissuading women from engaging in the movement.

would continue to be excluded from "the movement," but, in this case, by women, not men, and this involved an immediate and difficult negotiation of identity politics.

In many ways, the question at the heart of liberated *RAT* was "what does the revolutionary subject look like?" As Martha Shelley argued in an article entitled "Making the Revolution," articulating just what the revolution is involves "a process of finding out who you are, and what you can do. Sometimes it means running dances, or selling papers, or saying NO to the Mafia. Sometimes it means bombing pig stations. To me it always means being what I want to be and not a thing – worker, baby-factory, consumer – to be used by somebody else" (24). That *RAT* did not define itself meant that it refused to "liberate" women into a mould that would set the parameters of what it was to be a woman in the movement, but this also meant that those who were more decided about the particulars of this position were very critical of the newspaper; it left itself open to criticism from all sides, making it a tricky space to defend. In the face of such attacks, a letter signed by "a rat worker" described the collective's editorial structure and the procedures that constituted the compilation of all issues:

Our structure is like this – we do all of the work and no men work on the paper. That is, all of us take a day in the office, write articles, make editorial decisions, hawk the papers, do layout, do distribution, go to the printer, do mailing, etc., etc. No one is in charge of any major function. Our meetings are unchaired and cha- otic. Every Friday night we have open collective meetings at 6 where we decide on policy and select articles to be printed. These meetings are held in the office and any woman wishing to work with us is welcome. Welcome also are any arti- cles women want to submit. The decisions about whether or not to print any article are made in the open Friday collective meetings and any woman wishing to dis- cuss an article should come .... We honestly don't think ourselves to be *the* paper that meets the needs of all women. To the extent that we are failing to meet the needs of many women, we are trying to improve the content of the paper and welcome suggestions. We really have worked hard on the process of evolving a work collective that is genuinely open, non-elitist, and non leader-oriented. The paper is a place for each of us to start to live out as much of our potential as this whole endeavor can extract from us. (Rat Worker 2)

The revolutionary subject is the *collective*, free from strata in both constitu- tion and speech: *RAT* articulated itself according to collective will, not the will of a centralized and closed editorial group. Frustrated by the request that she tone down the identifiable style of her writing, Morgan left *RAT* within months of the takeover, pursuing other projects. When Morgan reflects that *RAT*'s feminism was foiled because the collective "had to keep covering issues that were interesting to [men], to win their approval" (*Word of a Woman* 52), she is, in effect, becoming complicit in the act of denying women access to the political issues that the liberated newspaper covered, arguing that they are somehow "men's" issues, when the real problem was that they were considered as such in the first place.[63] Women had been present in the movement since its very beginnings and, as such, they were inherent in, and co-producers of, all of the movement's more particular facets and constituencies. That being said, that she felt that her departure from *Women's LibeRATion* was necessary is worth pause, especially as it did not signify her departure from the women's liberation movement at large.

### *Women's LibeRATion* and the Disjunctive Synthesis: On Metaphor and Metonymy

If men doubted women's leadership capabilities and excluded women from positions of leadership within the movement in general, the all-female *RAT* collective, during this time, did not simply prove themselves capable of occupying

---

63  As Gary Thiher pointed out in an editorial that appeared in the third issue after the paper had been taken over:

> The whole situation became even more confused when the two camps turned out to be divided not only along lines of sex, but also on matters of political outlook and journalistic style. The first women's issue had projected an exaggerated militance, a somewhat apolitical moralism and total lack of humor. (The second mellowed a bit.) While many male staffers were willing to see female editorship, they did not want *RAT* to espouse a line that they could not support. The women – understandably, and in some cases correctly – considered this argument as no more than a means of dodging the issue of sexism. And, of course, it would have defeated the whole purpose of female editorship if the women had agreed to hew to those views which the men approved. (2)

> Thiher's editorial is, in many ways, as condescending about the liberated issues as it is candid about the necessity for the takeover (the editorial staff's decision to twice "accede" to the women's collective – first for a week and then, the next week, indefinitely – is brandished as what he hopes will be a "first step" in grinding away "one of the pillars in this oppressive culture"). Particularly notable is the counterpoint that Thiher's account provides when read against Morgan's account of the run. Rather than being radical for the sake of male approval, Thiher's account makes clear that the politics that were avowed in *RAT* pages were written *in spite of* men, without concern for male approval, and, in fact, in terms that ran completely counter to the political positions of many of the men who had been involved in the running of the paper.

roles that had traditionally been reserved for men – never the point – but took hold of the reins of a widely distributed newspaper in order to articulate the significant issues that were not being covered by male-dominated leftist media. They did not do this on their own as a closed collective. Rather, the collective remained open to all willing participants and to whatever issues they brought to bear on the liberated newspaper. Beyond being open, they inspired other women to follow suit: letters poured in, there were takeovers of other underground newspapers, and the paper became, in part, a medium that linked women's collectives together across the entire country without missing a beat in keeping up with other movement news and politics. Here, one might think of Guattari's first use of the term "war machine": "Every new discovery – in the sphere of scientific research, for example – moves across the structural field of theory like a war machine, upsetting and rearranging everything so as to change it radically" (*Psychoanalysis and Transversality* 321). The second wave of feminism ran through *RAT* like a war machine, ousting chauvinism from the editorial board and newspaper alike and ushering in a politics of affirmation. By ousting chauvinism, women were no longer forced into defensive, subordinate positions, but were able to affirm who they were and what women's liberation, as a positive, affirmative force, looked like.

The movement was characterized as such – that is, it had momentum – because, at its best, it recognized that assemblages are characterized by relations of exteriority. At the turn of the seventies, *RAT*'s becoming-sophomoric (as Alpert put it) marked a process by which it was beginning to favour the interiority of its relations, the closing off of its concerns. The sex and porn issue of *RAT* – conceived according to the uncritical executive decision of a couple of male editors at the helm of the celebrity underground paper – was simply a catalytic example of what was becoming typical of *RAT*/movement behaviour towards women: women, in spite of their numbers in, and contributions to, the movement, were always treated as secondary, as operating in relation to the movement, which was "male." Men were assumed to be the centre of the movement, and women (as secretary, as object of the male gaze, as activist) were relegated to the periphery. To argue that the movement was characterized by relations of interiority at this juncture is to argue that it was phallocentric (which is not to say that it was instrinsically male but that it was being *organized* as such). If phallocentrism is the product of an assemblage reduced to its relations of interiority, as Manuel Delanda points out in his book on assemblage theory, what "relations of *exteriority* guarantee [is] that assemblages may be taken apart while at the same time allowing that the interactions between parts may result in a true synthesis" (*A New Philosophy* 11). Men's fear that the women's liberation movement would somehow highjack the movement as no other group had (the inclusion of one group's struggle being so saturating that it would distract the movement from all other struggles) was rendered unfounded by the paper that the open collective of Rat women produced. Rather than subjectifying struggle, women's liberation included women's struggle *within* the movement, arguing the existent and important link between women and revolution while continuing to reach out to the movement's other constituencies. As such, post-liberation, week-to-week, the paper's layout laid bare a complex set of internal syntheses forged of relations of exteriority.

Thinking about phallocentrism provides analytic insight into the structural relations that characterized pre and post-liberated *RAT,* but the horizontal and vertical axes that I mobilize in this chapter help us to understand how the Rat collective conceived a solution, and to rethink what has been in this chapter an exclusive emphasis on metonymy as the associative motor of movements. As Deleuze and Guattari point out, "Whenever desire climbs a tree, internal repercussions trip it up and it falls to its death" (*A Thousand Plateaus* 14). What we see in *RAT*'s trajectory is enormous potential becoming rooted in a vertically coded counterculture: women are freely objectified by men who consider themselves to be the rightful speaking subjects of the movement. We could certainly read this as the metaphorization of movement – from the contiguity of transcreation to the erection of a paradigm: what was once *becoming* is solidified into a state. In line with Deleuze and Guattari – but all the while taking them in the middle – I think it's important to revise my thesis here, or to put it more comfortably in line with the language I use to distinguish between metaphor and metonymy in the introduction to this book. While we can and should identify aphasic *tendencies* in translation, we can't let metonymy climb a tree. The movement of translation is the movement of metonymy *and* metaphor.

Before moving ahead, it might be useful at this juncture to gather our bearings. In keeping with Jakobson's association of metonymy with the axis of combination, and metaphor with the axis of selection, in this chapter I have mobilized contiguity via the translative movement of transcreation or becoming (hence the narrative flow of this chapter). We need to rethink the distinction between metaphor and metonymy, however, because a problem arises at the moment of takeover. While the takeover of *RAT* was enacted so as to overcome the strata that came to divide and hierarchize the paper, what is a takeover but an act of substitution, a new paradigm – in this case, replacing male authors with female ones? What does it mean to accept takeover as an integral part of a movement's becoming?

The distinction between metaphor and metonymy is not absolute.[64] Rather than *either* metaphor *or* metonymy, it is certainly more fitting to think about metaphor *and* metonymy at every juncture: a disjunctive synthesis. To rethink metaphor and metonymy via the disjunctive synthesis is to suggest that our *selection* of terms has an effect on the *association* between terms within a system, and vice versa. Not only does the unfolding of a sentence imply a movement of selection *and* combination at one and the same time, but, if we think about the takeover of *RAT*, every substitution (on the axis of selection) is also a succession (and succession is a word that itself has both syntagmatic and paradigmatic connotations: sequence or progression *and* accession or elevation). To *select* between a male-dominated *RAT* or *Women's LibeRATion* determines the nature of *associations* that are carried in the underground: one is arborified while the other has "connect[ed] the roots or trees back up with a rhizome" (*A Thousand Plateaus* 14).

Lest it look like I'm putting Deleuze and Guatari up in a tree, I should note that significant middling is required to make them take this position. That Deleuze and Guattari are non-representational philosophers means that they are as wary of metonymy as they are of metaphor:

> The importance some have accorded to metaphor and metonymy proves disastrous for the study of language ... [T]he translative movement proper to language is that of indirect discourse ... Language is not content to go from a first party to a second party, from one who has seen to one who has not, but necessarily goes from a second party to a third party, neither of whom has seen ... Language is a map, not a tracing. (*A Thousand Plateaus* 77)

Deleuze and Guattari subscribe to a discursive and performative linguistic model rather than a representational one. Language does not capture the world or, for the most part, even try to; instead, language responds to other language. It is in this sense that language is indirect discourse, and that translation moves laterally and immanently within language; translation is not a bridge between reality and its linguistic representation. That this sounds a lot like metonymy

---

64 Consider the quibbles between Paul de Man and Marcel Proust (that what Proust was calling metaphor was actually metonymy [de Man 13–18]), or Umberto Eco's reversal of the conventional langue/parole distinction (the system of language is itself metonymic; metaphor arises from metonymy and not the way around [*A Theory of Semiotics* 279–83; *The Role of the Reader* 68–78]).

means that, at the very least, metonymy might not be so difficult a tropical pill for them to swallow. So why not leave it at that?

In the end, the issue isn't really with metaphor or metonymy, the issue is with their usage. When Deleuze and Guattari reject metaphor and metonymy, the implicit target is Jacques Lacan, who, in arguing that the unconscious is structured like a language, adapts Jakobson's axes of combination (metonymy) and selection (metaphor), associating metaphor with condensation and metonymy with displacement.[65] Deleuze and Guattari are troubled by the Lacanian system in general, but it is what Lacan carries over from Freud, the Oedipal mommy-daddy-me, that they find so objectionable. Somewhat akin to Irigaray, who subverts Freudian metaphors (male phallus / feminine lack) by introducing slippages into the signifying chain, Guattari brought Deleuze a theory of a machinic unconscious, the unconscious as desiring machine, where the question was – as per the rhizome – the plugging together of machines to promote unobstructed flow. To think machinically is to forge linkages and encourage flow rather than to subjugate desire to a particular mode of interpretation. For Guattari, psychoanalysis is "the best of all capitalist drugs" because, rather than challenging social structures and relations produced by the school, the family, and the army, it reduces these problems to a coded, structural logic and it works to remedy these recoded problems by harnessing desire to a confined and private space: desire is assigned to "the small, secret domain of the couch" ("Best Capitalist Drug" 216). While Guattari's critique is productive, his coinage of "transversality," "group subjects," "desiring machines," and a whole slew of other concepts with or without Deleuze in order to modify the way we think about desire and analysis is nothing but the mobilization of alternative metaphors (coded and deployed as mobile concepts). *And* one might *select* theirs and/or Irigaray's and/or Cixous's, and/or Kristeva's, when pursuing a line of flight from the Freudian system.

If we want to bring another thinker into the fold here, we could consider Derrida, who not only establishes, in "White Mythology," that metaphor is the basis of all philosophical language, but who also associates metaphor with movement – connecting the roots or trees back up with a rhizome – in "The *Retrait* of Metaphor," a later debate with Paul Ricœur. As per its conventional definition, a metaphor is a vehicle, and the vehicle does not only carry the tenor, it also carries us (48). We inhabit metaphor. We are carried over in its carrying over. Metaphor is movement, and this movement, the essence of movement itself, is "circulating in translation" (48). Concepts atrophy when

---

65  See Lacan "The Instance of the Letter in the Unconscious."

associated with particular systems (metaphor and metonymy in Lacanian psychoanalysis), but that doesn't mean that they can't be reinvigorated in another milieu. To situate Deleuze and Guattari squarely in between the thinkers that fall on either side of them in this book, consider, as well, Foucault, revising his own oeuvre – as he perpetually did – in "Nietzsche, Genealogy, History": "The isolation of different points of emergence does not conform to the successive configurations of an identical meaning; rather, they result from *substitutions, displacements, disguised conquests, and systematic reversals*" (378, emphasis added). The genealogist wears the mask of objectivity while affirming a perspectival slant, deploying and redeploying anew that mobile army of metaphors and metonymies that we all have at our disposal.[66] There is no origin. There is no end. There is just a perpetual battle to maintain a smooth space in the middle.

And this is where we should return to the becoming of women's liberation. Just as metaphor atrophies within the psychoanalytic system, so too does "women's liberation" – a metaphor used to describe a movement – when it is reduced to a newspaper takeover where the particularity of style can lead to banishment. Women's liberation is of course a liberated underground newspaper *and* Robin Morgan (and … and … and …). The women who inhabited *RAT*, pre-liberation, were translated by it, and they translated *RAT* in turn. *Women's LibeRATion*, as the signifier of an event, describes a carrying over, or a transfer (*metaphero*); the reaching out of something that was building, but stifled, within both the newspaper and the movement at large. The same is true of Robin Morgan, who inhabited *Women's LibeRATion* before her own departure became necessary. While *Women's LibeRATion* is something to celebrate, it is *Women's LibeRATion and* Robin Morgan that more properly capture the women's liberation movement, not just as transcreation but as reciprocal implication. Just as *RAT* is in *Women's LiberRATion* and *Women's LibeRATion* was in *RAT* (a substitution *and* a becoming), Morgan and the Rat collective are profoundly enfolded, and the unfolding of Morgan's politics and style – and we can think here of her affinities with *écriture feminine*, and of the importance of women's autobiography and life writing – was and is an important part of the folding and unfolding of feminism's waves.[67]

---

66  See Nietzsche "*From* On Truth" 46–7.

67  In "The *Retrait* of Metaphor," Derrida discusses the process whereby metaphors repeat and beget new traits, like the ebb and flow of waves on a shoreline, associating this movement with a folding and refolding, and an accumulation of "internal multiplicit[ies]" (66). Affinities with Deleuze and Guattari are strong.

## Conclusion: Reassembling Post-structuralism

Underground newspapers, state-commissioned reports, and philosophy books are sites where local struggles are redistributed, and they are also sites where groupings are collected and rendered visible for researchers whose project is to collect connections that destabilize traditional boundaries. To map Deleuze and Guattari's enfoldedness within the events of '68 makes them become something other, productively transforming them by expanding the networks within which they are typically kept. This is a way of doing translation by contiguity (accumulating networks, building assemblages, Deleuze and Guattari as nomads, part of the anti-statist war machine of the '68 years) rather than as instrumental communication (from French to English, an abyss in need of a bridge, the substitution of a term with its equivalent in another language, or the substitution of concrete meaning in the place of abstract philosophy).

In the context of this study, where translation is the motor for exploring the relation between French philosophers and American liberationists movements, I must emphasize that considering Deleuze and Guattari as philosophers whose work is immanent in the movement also means that they do not have any kind of privileged explanatory power. On the contrary, it means that they are inseparable from a constellation that was continuously remaking itself in the attempt to secure alternative ways of living devoid of the strata that constituted life within the modern, capitalist state. Following the logic of the fold within assemblages, the various facets of the movement were, could have been, and can still be, translators of philosophy, as much as philosophy can translate movements into its concepts and books. Deleuze and Guattari are dependent on the company in which they are kept. Good books and concepts can be corrupted in the wrong hands, or they can be given new life, but there is nothing like an essence to any book or concept unless it is artificially severed from other worlds altogether.

More often than not, chronicles of the sixties render the decade as the accumulation of energies that, in the seventies, collapsed: SDS, whose ranks swelled exponentially throughout 1968 and at the beginning of 1969, would be no more by the beginning of 1970, and, perhaps most emblematic, the Kent and Jackson State shootings in the spring of 1970 effectively put an end to an era of university protest (after a final spike in response to the shootings themselves). What the lines that I am drawing have in common are various intensities that, before being struck down, carried vast amounts of potential. Rather than chasing the origins and ends of lines, I focus on their various crossings; these are sites where the possibility of new assemblages arises. Rather than lamenting the death of the left to COINTELPRO, corporations, fatigue, and bad decisions – or the Anglo-American consecration of French thought as post-structuralism – it is certainly more appealing, and I would argue more useful, to explore the moments when the potential for things to turn out otherwise ran deep, and in many directions. If re-assembling the social is about the accumulation of prematurely severed, assemblage-forming points, *RAT Subterranean News* is worth following because of the groups that it permits us to collect along the way.

And herein lies an important qualification: while it is tempting to get swept up in the associative movement of narrative accounts, selection is most definitely at play in both movements (women's liberated *RAT*) and their retelling (this chapter). While Kristin Ross's warning about the reduction (read: metaphorization) of May '68 is spot on, metaphors are powerful and necessary mobilizers. If my own project is to plug "French theory" back into the contiguous relations of a globally networked '68, I too have made selections and severed countless associations in the process. It is productive to identify aphasic *tendencies* in translation, but it is never a matter of choosing either metaphor or metonymy, it is always a question of both (and of mobilizing an army of them to affirm a perspectival slant).

If part of my desire is to locate allies for "French theory" in America, these allies, as Deleuze and Guattari had predicted, were already there and were already active at the time that they were writing *Anti-Oedipus*. One of the important lessons that we can extract from *Women's LibeRATion* is that locating allies is not as simple as arguing for a regime change (from a male editorial board to a female editorial collective or, in our case, out from the academy and into the streets). The systematic pursuit of a common world involves perpetual negotiation, the forging of external relations, and a delicate negotiation of (externally oriented) internal syntheses. To put it more simply, perhaps, what a search for allies involves is the bringing together of groups that are themselves characterized by their reaching out. French theory, post-structuralism, May '68, the movement, and even the names of philosophers operate like metaphors; they are the names we select to denote the borrowing and reassignment of concepts, they challenge conventional boundaries, and they demand that new relations be forged. While these intensive signifiers can transport us to unthought of places, they can also atrophy. And so we repeat the mantra, which is a mantra about translation: "Plug the tracings back into the map, connect the roots or trees back up with the rhizome" (*A Thousand Plateaus* 14).

# 3 Prison Liberation by Association: Michel Foucault and the George Jackson Atlantic

From 1970 to 1972, Michel Foucault was involved in a prison activist project called the Groupe d'information sur les prisons (GIP). This group proposed to produce the speech of prisoners at a time when prisons were not only one of the most secretive regions in French society but were also teeming with activists rounded up in the tumultuous years following the May '68 uprisings. While this activist project has only recently begun to generate discussion in Anglo-American circles, the GIP itself looked across the Atlantic to learn about and mobilize prison resistance after prominent political prisoner George Jackson was killed during an alleged escape attempt from San Quentin prison in August 1971. This chapter discusses the pertinence of this Franco-American relation to the politics of the GIP. Central to the political practice of the GIP was its functioning as a group: it was not the work of a morally inspired, engaged intellectual, it was a product – and process – of its associations.

Discussions of the GIP are teeming with binaries and dyads: Cecile Brich considers whether the GIP's discourse on prisons is "the voice of prisoners or Foucault's"; Marcelo Hoffman discusses "intolerance" as resistance to the "intolerable" ("Foucault and the 'Lesson'" 24–30); Michael Welch contemplates GIP "counterveillance" as a "reversal of [pan]optics" that sees the watchers being watched ("Counterveillance"); Thomas Biebricher notes that Foucault's activist work to incite prison speech is diametrically opposed to his invocation, in the *History of Sexuality*, of silence as a cultural ethos to evade power (725); Grégory Salle proposes the term "statactivism" to describe the group's production of statistics that countered official figures; and Perry Zurn argues that the GIP mobilized a "positive publicity" campaign to counter the "negative publicity" that the state produced about prisoners. While discussions of the GIP's oppositional work have helped to explain some of the strategic resistances that the group mounted to combat the carceral system in France, one cannot overemphasize the ways in which relays and networks informed and animated its group work.

The pervasiveness of binaries and dyads, and the ways that they distract from otherwise well-conceived positions, is perhaps best illustrated in Zurn's paper on GIP publicity. While Zurn makes the important point that the GIP acted as a multi-directional relay station, combating "cellularization" with boundary-crossing "transmigration" (9), his overreliance on dyads (power/resistance, cellularization/transmigration, positive publicity/negative publicity, intolerable/intolerance) makes his theorization of "radical publicity" appear more as a vector than, as Foucault describes resistance in *History of Sexuality*, a "dense web" or "swarm of points" strategically codified (96). To become a relay station, the GIP abandoned the French tradition where the public intellectual acted as a moral compass for society in order to think about how the intellectual might more effectively function within a group. As a "web" and a "swarm," the GIP was strategically constituted as a network that could penetrate prisons and produce prison speech. Beyond the local, it collected not simply inspiration, but *force* from the prison liberation movement that was gaining substantial momentum across the Atlantic. Every point in the GIP was part of a mobile relay network.

The word "relay" is twice mentioned regarding the work that the GIP did for inmates, once by Deleuze in conversation with Foucault, and once by Foucault scholar Philippe Artières. In each case, it has a slightly distinct, yet related meaning: on the one hand, "relay" is a subject position for transmitting the speech of others while, on the other, the term is used to describe the networked relationship between theory and practice. Most recently, Artières proclaimed that one of the defining characteristics of Foucault's participation in the GIP experience was that he played the part of "third-party relay":

> Foucault is no longer a teacher; instead of lecturing, he reads a text written by others. He does the job not of production, but of transmission. Foucault speaks and yet it is someone else who is speaking, the person who was previously not entitled to speak. The philosopher is not being philanthropic; he simply wishes to take the prisoners' statement seriously, using his symbolic power as a professor at the Collège de France to make it heard outside prison walls. (49–50)

In this context, "relay" denotes an ethical practice that makes strategic use of intellectual status. That intellectual discourse has currency does not mean that it should overwrite the concerns of others; instead, it means that its charge should be used to plug otherwise neglected voices into the information system. One might think of André Lefevere's work on translation as a system of patronage, where individuals and institutions (which Lefevere, with a nod to Foucault, calls "powers") "can further or hinder the reading, writing, and re-writing of literature" with their selection of texts (*Translation, Rewriting* 15). The patron, Lefevere points out, "delegates authority" (15). Whereas the prison is generally translated by government representatives or workers whose title, salary, and pension are provided by the state, incarcerated persons are those who sit on the other side of the law. Recognizing these supports and sanctions, as well as his own position, Foucault is the patron who makes the reading, writing, and rewriting of prison speech possible.

While Artières uses the word "relay" to describe Foucault's participation at demonstrations, in Foucault and Deleuze's 1972 conversation "Intellectuals and Power," Deleuze uses "relay" to describe an active and fluid network rather than a singular disposition. He describes GIP activity as a "system of relays" and rejects the concept of the "theorizing intellectual" as "representing or representative." Instead of representation, Deleuze argues that "there's only action – theoretical action and practical action which serve as relays and form networks" (206–7). In other words, theory and practice are interdependent. If each worked exclusively, they would reach an impasse, whereas together, each works as a relay for the other. The representing or representative intellectual is useless in an activist context because there is no such thing as a static situation to represent. Similarly, if one acts consistently, one is predictable and vulnerable to capture. To be effective, theory and practice must be fluid and interrelated.[1]

What we see here is a shift in translation paradigm: from metaphor, or the axis of selection (one selects the theoretical terms to appropriately describe the practices, or selects certain practices to enact the theory), to metonymy, or the axis of combination (theory and practice develop as a movement over time, like a sentence, or narrative).

As a concept, "relay" demands more careful attention and development because it not only characterizes the GIP approach to inmate speech, but it entails a powerful and ethical approach to supporting the struggles of others. "Relay" speaks to the larger practice of developing activist networks: assembling the constituent parts of a discourse that incorporates not only prison speech but

---

1 While Marcelo Hoffman and Michael Welch, respectively, discuss the impact of Foucault's GIP activism on *Discipline and Punish* and his theorization of pastoral power – a theory-practice dialectic – this chapter is more invested in this interdependent, on-the-ground fluidity of theory and practice. See Hoffman, "Foucault and the 'Lesson" 32–6 and Welch, "Pastoral Power" 49–52.

the testimony of insiders; the participation of intellectuals, families, and social workers; alternative statistical analyses; correspondent struggles from across the Atlantic; and voices from beyond the grave.

Fundamentally, "relay" is a practice of translation that, due to its operational privileging of transmission over representation, continues to demonstrate the political potential of thinking translation contiguously.[2]

## On Authorship, Committed Intellectuals, and Group Subjectivity

On 2 December 1970, Foucault delivered his inaugural lecture as the chair in the History of Systems of Thought at the Collège de France, one of the most prestigious institutions in France. For the inaugural lecture, "L'ordre du discours," he provided an outline of the larger project that he planned to undertake over the course of his career as chair. The governing hypothesis: "[I]n every society the production of discourse is at once controlled, selected, organized and redistributed according to a certain number of procedures, whose role is to avert its powers and its dangers, to cope with chance events, to evade its ponderous, awesome materiality" ("Discourse on Language" 216). This ordering of discourse is achieved via exclusions, rules, and operations that, taken together, characterize the will to knowledge in any given era. While it would be wrong to mark "L'ordre du discours" a definitive text – the schematic that Foucault provides for analysing the circulation of discourse would be elaborated in many different ways over the course of the next fourteen years – it is certainly a useful and important speech that provides a good general outline of the project that Foucault would pursue over the course of his career.

On 8 February 1971, just two months later, Foucault performed yet another inaugural address. While the first address was a scheduled lecture at the

---

2  Although she doesn't invoke "relay" as a concept, Kristin Ross makes similar use of the word throughout a section on the centrality of the Vietnam War to the politics of the '68 years in *May '68 and Its Afterlives* (80–90). Vietnam was at the centre of a nexus of struggles, linking the Third Word-ist, anti-colonialist politics of early 1960s with the workers struggle in 1968, linking external and internal stakes: "In the years immediately preceding 1968 ... it was the Vietnamese peasant, and not the auto worker at Billancourt, who had become, for many French militants, the figure of the working class ... The Vietnamese fighter provided the transitional figure, the *relay* between the 'intimate' colonial other, the Algerian of the early 1960s, and the French worker during '68" (81, emphasis added). In this usage, "relay" describes the transmission of struggle through a network via nodes that carry a certain significance or charge; this is a type of translation that is distinguishable from simple representation. The Vietnamese fighter, as transitional figure / relay is a translator.

venerable Collège de France, the latter consisted of a two-page statement read at a press conference in the cavernous Chapelle Saint-Bernard, where a hunger strike was underway. The strike was being conducted in solidarity with imprisoned activists who had been rounded up in the increasingly repressive months following the events of May '68. A group of prisoners was on hunger strike for a second time since September 1970. The prisoners demanded acknowledgment of their status as political prisoners, which would afford them access to books, newspapers, and each other. The February press conference, held by lawyers representing the imprisoned activists, announced that the latest, thirty-four-day strike was over: representatives of the strikers had been granted a meeting with Minister of Justice René Pleven, and a working group regarding obtention of special regime status was established. On the surface, the majority of the inmates' demands seemed met. Following the lawyers' address regarding the end of the hunger strike, Foucault was passed the microphone to read a brief statement. While the group of political prisoners had argued for recognition of their political status, they argued from the beginning that this did not mean that they thought they merited special treatment; the ultimate aim of the imprisoned activists was to obtain better conditions for all prisoners. In order to pursue this larger cause, Foucault inaugurated the GIP. The GIP, Foucault announced at the February news conference, was a group of magistrates, lawyers, journalists, doctors, and psychologists whose purpose would be to collect and publish information regarding prisons, one of the most hidden and secretive regions in the French social system. The group would circulate questionnaires and publish the results of their findings.

While Foucault's inaugural lecture at the Collège de France was translated, the statement at the press conference at which Foucault inaugurated the GIP remains untranslated.[3] The valorization of certain types of texts over others has a profound impact on the way that thinkers appear and circulate in translation. The texts that are most likely to be translated are those that answer questions being asked in the target language field. This means that the most

---

3 The text, written and spoken by Foucault, was co-signed by Pierre Vidal-Naquet, a historian of ancient Greece who gained notoriety for his denunciation of French torture during the Algerian War, and Jean-Marie Domenach, editor of the Catholic review *Esprit*. The statement was printed in full in *Esprit* and *La cause du peuple*, and the first paragraph was printed in *Le Monde*. The statement is collected as the "Manifeste du G.I.P." in Foucault's *Dits et écrits*.

context-bound interventions – interventions that are of the moment and/or of their location – are unlikely candidates for translation, particularly early on. Target-language audience is a determining factor in decisions made regarding translation, as are medium and genre. When considering, in "What Is an Author?," the parameters of Nietzsche's oeuvre, Foucault raises the problem of meeting reminders, addresses, and laundry lists. Why are certain texts considered part of an oeuvre while others are not? While I would not suggest that we dig up such scribblings to reconstitute a more complete Foucauldian oeuvre, I do think that it is important to think about the effects of overlooking certain types of texts upon the profile of a thinker in translation. The Anglo-American Foucault is constituted of his books, journal articles by or about Foucault, collections of essays and interviews, and, more recently, his lectures at the Collège de France. Although there are significant exceptions, what tends to be left out in English translation are the press conferences, demonstrations, political pamphlets, newspaper articles, questionnaires, and posters that constituted the circulation of Foucault in France in the early 1970s.[4] In many ways, it is among these media that Foucault was writing the history of the present for which his books and public lectures sketched out a broader context. Over the course of its less than two years in existence, the prison information group that Foucault co-constituted published dozens of articles in mainstream and alternative newspapers, mobilized targeted protests outside of prisons, and published five pamphlets. The pamphlets that the GIP produced, and most of the articles that the group penned, have not been translated.

---

4 Fragments of Foucault's activist work have been translated, not only in the thematically organized, three-volume *Essential Works of Michel Foucault* series edited by Paul Rabinow between 1997 and 2000, but in the 1970s, so, relatively early on. Donald F. Bouchard, for example, devotes an entire section in his three-pronged edited collection *Language, Counter-Memory, Practice* (1977) to "practice." The section includes two interviews that explicitly discuss the GIP: an interview that Foucault conducted with the French Underground Press Syndicate magazine *Actuel* in 1971 ("Revolutionary Action: 'Until Now'"), and Foucault's well-known conversation with Deleuze, "Intellectuals and Power" (1972). That "Revolutionary Action" was culled from an underground magazine for translation is notable, but, as per convention, original sources are bibliographically acknowledged in the translated text, but there is no discussion or indication of the position of publishers and publication venues in the academic/cultural economy at point of source. While *Actuel* is an irreverent French countercultural magazine, in translation the interview appears equivalent to all of the other texts collected in a book put out by an American university press. Translated texts are framed by the journals and book covers within which they appear in translation.

If "L'ordre du discours" provided a hypothesis regarding the way in which discourse is ordered, the GIP was a project that provided a practical and timely example regarding the way in which Foucault's thought could be, and was being, operationalized: How might the excluded be brought into discourse? This movement between Foucault's Collège de France hypothesis and the GIP's activism is a relay between theory and practice. This is not to say that the GIP represents an application of Foucault's theory; instead, this is a juncture where the networked relationship between theoretical and practical action is particularly clear. Although Foucault articulated his theoretical concerns with originality and lucidity, they were by no means original: Foucault's work occupies a space in the history of ideas and, although he increasingly distanced himself from the structuralist label that had been applied to his work, his thought was heavily influenced by contemporary trends in French thought (structuralism, Marxism, psychoanalysis). The GIP was simply a point where an aggregation of contemporary and historical theoretical concerns were articulated – and transformed – in practical action. On the other side of this relay point, Foucauldian theory was certainly not the sole or primary beneficiary of the GIP project. To treat this historical moment dialectically would be to privilege subsequent Foucauldian texts at the expense of the prison speech that this relay was orchestrated to produce. Both the point of theory/GIP contact and the effects of GIP relay are multiplicities.

That being said, Foucault's discussion of a single subject-position – the author – is a good place to begin analysing the constitution of the relay network. When he published *The Order of Things*, Foucault was accused by critics that he invoked authors' names ambiguously and with haphazard attention to the totality of their works. Instead of returning to the texts of the authors in question (Buffon, Cuvier, Ricardo, Marx), Foucault took the criticisms as a prompt to analyse why it was important to employ authors in a specific manner in the first place ("What Is an Author?" 113–16). In "What Is an Author?," Foucault's 1969 response to his critics and Beckett's rhetorical "what matter who speaks?," Foucault proposes that we think about authorship as a function and not a subject position. The author, Foucault argues, is not the person behind the text, the author is a function in discourse. Foucault's position on authorship fit with the structuralists among whom he had been grouped in that his position was, crudely speaking, anti-humanist, but it was certainly not, as per the criticism levelled at structuralism by Sartre, ahistorical. Foucault's argument was that authorship operates in different ways, at different times, and in different cultures. It is tied to questions of property and to institutions that determine the meaning and limits of the discourse whose circulation the "author" not only makes possible but authorizes. Analysis of the position, capacities, and function of particular subjects in discourse – those imbued with authority and those that were cordoned off – was essential to GIP strategy.

The French intellectual practice of taking political positions publically, as Foucault did when he announced the formation of the GIP at a press conference, was not novel in France; the post-1968 period marked a continuation and intensification of the practice of using intellectual status as a buffer against state repression. Jean-Paul Sartre was the model against which intellectual intervention into political matters was measured during the postwar period. Alongside Simone de Beauvoir, Maurice Merleau-Ponty, and Raymond Aron, Sartre was co-founding editor in 1945 of *Les temps modernes*, the infamous postwar review of philosophy and political engagement where Sartre developed a political existentialism and argued about social responsibility of intellectuals and writers to produce and speak a *littérature engagé* – a committed literature whereby the author was responsible for taking a moral stance regarding contemporary events. In line with the committed prose that he championed, Sartre was a committed intellectual; he spoke as a conscience for the masses, famously opposing the state regarding its role in the Algerian and Vietnam Wars.

It was Sartre, and not Foucault, who was first to take up the issue of imprisonment in post-May '68 France. When the French Maoist group the Gauche prolétarienne (GP) was banned in May 1970, and GP leader Alain Geismar was arrested under a new *"anti-casseurs"* law that effectively outlawed protest (establishing that the organizations and organizers behind demonstrations could be prosecuted for anything that happened at a demonstration), Sartre provided immediate and prominent assistance to the embattled group, reconstituting the French branch of the Secours Rouge International (SRI) alongside a who's who of representatives from three generations of the French Left (Artières et al. 29–30). The SRI, originally conceived by Bolsheviks in the Soviet Union in 1922, was an international movement in solidarity with imprisoned revolutionaries. The French branch of the SRI was originally founded alongside eighteen other branches in 1924, but it dissipated and was dissolved by the end of the 1930s. Beyond spearheading the resurrection of this high-profile advocacy group for political prisoners, Sartre took over the editorship of the GP newspaper *La cause du peuple* when its editors were imprisoned in 1970, and Simone de Beauvoir founded the Association des amis de *La cause du peuple* to make sure that the banned paper would receive wide and visible distribution. Sartre's postwar political turn is often attributed to his detention as a prisoner of war in Germany in 1940–1; it is therefore not surprising that he was one of the first to provide assistance to the political prisoners being rounded up in the aftermath of May 1968. While these post-1968 interventions are part of a longer trajectory of Sartrean intellectual intervention in the political arena, it is worth noting that the Maoist position that Sartre supported in this case promoted collective action and decentralization, tenets that were somewhat at odds with Sartre's postwar position-taking as an engaged intellectual. It is in this context of decentralization and collective political action that Foucault explored the question of authorship and intellectual status, differentiating himself and the GIP from the era of intellectual engagement led by Sartre.

Foucault played a prominent part in the GIP project, but it would neither have existed nor worked if not for its constitution and functioning as a group. Foucault was able to assume the role that he did in the GIP because of his new appointment at the Collège de France. Absolved of most of the administrative responsibilities associated with being an academic when he was appointed to the collège chair, Foucault filled this void by administering the GIP. The academic position was important because it provided Foucault not only with the prestige that was necessary to raise the profile of others, but also, in very material terms, with the time that was necessary to administer an activist project. The address of the group was Foucault's apartment, meaning that it was the mailing address for completed questionnaires, a place where frequent meetings were held, and an open door for former prisoners and prisoners' families to discuss their grievances regarding the prison system in France. We can understand Foucault's decision to do administrative work to make space for the articulation of others' concerns rather than to speak in their place through his work on the history of systems of thought, which involved thinking about the intellectual's role in the production of knowledge.

While "The Discourse on Language" and "What Is an Author?" were penned just prior to the GIP project, Foucault's thoughts on the status of the intellectual are more directly addressed in the 1976 interview "Truth and Power." In that interview, he discusses the difference between the "universal" and "specific" intellectual. The universal intellectual was the consciousness and conscience of the masses. Due to the spectrum of concerns covered by this general position, he or she often invoked scientific knowledge without understanding it, and the universality of his or her position necessarily implied distance between a general conscience and the many specific conditions it encompassed. The specific intellectual, on the other hand, is the expert or savant whose pursuit of a subject is scientific, whose analysis of specific problems is not only honed, it is material, and whose knowledge, though specific, has wide applicability. While Foucault invokes Zola and Oppenheimer as examples of the universal and specific intellectual, respectively (127–9), the trend he describes in "Truth and Power" was more immediately manifest as a move beyond Sartrean political engagement in post-1968 France. If Foucault was a specific intellectual, it was not due to his expert knowledge on prisons. As Foucault put it in a late interview, "My own work is not a history of institutions or a history of ideas, but the history of rationality as it works in institutions and in the behavior of people" ("Truth Is in the Future" 299). This is why Foucault is regarded not so much as an expert on the asylum, the clinic, or the prison, but as a theorist of power, knowledge, truth, and subjectivity.

According to Foucault, the intellectual occupies a specific position within a society's apparatus of truth. This is not only to say only that the intellectual has specialized knowledge about specific domains; the intellectual also occupies a privileged position within a political economy of truth because truth is produced and transmitted through a select number of privileged sites and activities like the university, the media, and writing. Rather than discounting the specific intellectual as one whose work is detached from the masses, or as one who conducts his or her work in service of the state, Foucault argues that specific knowledge – drawing on the example of Oppenheimer – can benefit or destroy life ("Truth and Power" 129). The specific intellectual's position in relation to the state and capital (the university, research funding) does not mean that he or she is a relay for state-sanctioned ideology; on the contrary, this relationship makes the position of the specific intellectual a strategic one within the political economy of truth.

Foucault used his privileged position within this political economy of truth to act as the general conscience of the masses and to relay messages about the everyday life experience of inmates. Recognizing that the regime of truth in any given society involves a politics of supports and sanctions that enable or prevent speech and deem it to be true or false, Foucault and the GIP's approach to the French penal problem was to mobilize a group of specialists (current and former inmates, family members, social workers, nurses, magistrates, judges, lawyers, journalists, intellectuals) who could function as a network that relayed the truth of prison. The GIP approach to penal struggle was not simply about the ethics of privileging an individual conscience or mobilizing a horizontalized group, it was a highly strategic approach that took into account the networked politics of truth that Foucault had been studying in earnest since his late-fifties work on mental illness.

Foucault recognized "truth" as a battleground, and the GIP was engaged in a battle over the truth of the prison. To draw upon the Clausewitz quote that Foucault famously inverted at the Collège de France lectures the same year that he gave his interview on "Truth and Power," "Politics is the continuation of war by other means" (*Society Must Be Defended* 48). When Foucault discusses truth as a battleground, he is not of course speaking of a battle "'on behalf' of the truth," as this would assume the existence of essential truth in political affairs. Instead, the battle over or around truth was "a battle about the status of truth and the economic and political role it plays" ("Truth and Power" 132). One can clearly see the objectives of such regimented battles over truth when activists are interned and incapacitated via a declaration of war on protest (the passing of the *anti-casseurs* law in April 1970), or when "sexual deviants" and a disproportionate number of racialized bodies are those that are not only confined but dominate the list of prison's casualties at the beginning of the GIP pamphlet on prison suicides (*Suicides de prison* 7–12). Such is precisely the sort of indirect killing – "increasing the risk of death for some people, or, quite simply, political death" (*Society Must Be Defended* 256) – that biopower is built upon While Foucault failed to articulate the direct linkage between racism and prison in his work, the GIP produced discourse that rendered this battle visible. The work of the GIP was not to produce an analysis of the prison or to direct the activism of inmates; instead, the knowledge of its resident theoreticians was mobilized to "relay" the prison speech that constituted a significant and formerly unsupported discourse.

Alongside the names of Hélène Cixous, Daniel Defert, Gilles Deleuze, Jean-Marie Domenach, Alain Geismar, Jean Genet, Jacques-Alain Miller, Jean-Paul Sartre, Pierre Vidal-Naquet, and so on, Michel Foucault's name lent the project a status that ensured that the voices of the prisoners who had otherwise been denied access to speech would be disseminated and heard. Most GIP texts were written by prisoners, and, save for a few exceptions, the remainder were either anonymous or group-signed. While certain individuals were more visible or invested in the workings of the group than others, the GIP was not a member group but a network that made the relay of prison speech possible.

That the group was much larger than the core of public figures who are typically considered to constitute the GIP is elucidated when the groupwork necessary to collect information is taken into consideration. Distributing questionnaires was not a simple feat: access to prisons was restricted to family members and those that worked inside the prison. In order to penetrate prison walls, the GIP targeted prisoners' families and social workers. As a means to distribute questionnaires, the group split up into small teams assigned to prisons around Paris in order to make contact with family members waiting in line to visit prisoners. In order to create a wider network, the GIP then printed one of the first completed questionnaires in full in the journal *Esprit*, edited by GIP co-founder Domenach.[5] Because the journal was widely read by social

---

5 See "Des détenus parlent."

workers, it was a means to distribute the survey to members of this profession, who in turn became a network for distributing the survey to inmates in the French provinces beyond the Paris area. With the help of this network, the GIP was able to gather information from twenty prisons rather than the initial six at which individuals associated with the project were stationed.

Relay is present at every juncture here, from the distribution of surveys to those who had access to prisoners, to the distribution of information from the inside out. The GIP was not simply Foucault as a general intellectual conscience for the masses or Foucault as singular relay point: the GIP involved the participation of recognized public figures, but it also coordinated itself around a network of social workers linked by a professional society and its journal, social worker and family visits to inmates, the testimony of inmates and specialists (a later pamphlet was based around the testimony of an unnamed social worker and psychiatrist Dr Edith Rose), and the publication and distribution of findings among alternative and underground media networks associated with public intellectuals and the internationally developing New Left. As Deleuze later reflected about this activity, "The goal of the GIP was less to make [prisoners] talk than to design a place where people would be forced to listen to them, a place that was not reduced to a riot on the prison roof, but would ensure that what they had to say came through" ("Foucault and Prison" 277). Riots, though visible and uncommon, are susceptible to capture (the authorities need only re-articulate what they have already said about the contemptible behaviour of prisoners). As Deleuze adds, prisoners and GIP activists "knew how to make speeches about prison"; the problem was that, until the GIP set up an apparatus for this precise purpose, "neither the prisoners nor the people outside prison had been able to produce any themselves" (278). The problem, in other words, was fundamentally a problem of relay. While prisoners, loved ones, and activists might learn and be able to exchange the truths of prison among themselves, only certain people – Minister of Justice René Pleven, in particular – were sanctioned to produce statements about the institution.

Amidst a regular stream of underground and mainstream newspaper and magazine articles, the major texts published by the GIP consisted of five booklets, four of them published under the series title "Intolérable," which collected and distributed prison speech. A statement of purpose-like blurb printed on the back of the first two booklets foregrounds the issue of authorship and the GIP: the newly formed prison information group did not have reform in mind, nor did it envision some sort of ideal prison. The objective of the GIP was to act as a conduit, making prison-speech possible:

**The G.I.P. (Prison Information Group)**
does not propose to speak
for prisoners from different prisons:
it proposes
on the contrary
to give them the possibility to speak
themselves,
and to say what is happening in prisons.
The goal of the G.I.P. is not reformist,
we do not dream of an ideal prison:
we hope
that prisoners can relate
what is **intolerable**
in the repressive penal system.
We will spread
as quick as possible
and as widely as possible
the revelations
made by the prisoners themselves.
The only way to unify
in a common struggle
inside and outside the prison.
    (GIP, *Enquête dans 20 prisons*, back cover, my translation; emphasis in original)[6]

Fundamentally, information needed to find passage through prison walls so that the public could learn about prison conditions. The booklets were printed not only to provide information on the intolerable conditions to which prisoners were subject, but also to report the voices behind a rash of uprisings that would otherwise be reducible to transgressive behaviour on the part of a population already on the other side of the law. The purpose of the GIP was to "give [prisoners] the possibility to speak themselves." The first two booklets

---

6 Le G.I.P. (Groupe d'Information Prisons) / ne se propose pas de parler / pour les détenus
  des différentes prisons: / il se propose / au contraire / de leur donner la possibilité de parler /
  eux-même, / et de dire ce qui se passe dans les prisons. / Le but du GIP n'est pas réformiste,
  / nous ne rêvons pas d'une prison idéale: / nous souhaitons / que les prisonniers puissent dire
  / ce qui est **intolérable** / dans le système de la répression pénale. / Nous devons répandre /
  le plus vite possible / et le plus largement possible / ces révélations / faites par les prisonniers
  mêmes. / Seul moyen pour unifier / dans une même lutte / l'intérieur et l'extérieur de la prison.

accomplished this task: they liberated prison speech by organizing the channels via which it could be heard outside prison walls, even as the bodies of prisoners remained confined.

When the GIP published its first booklet in 1971, the markings of individual authorship were nowhere to be found: committed intellectuals were absorbed into the larger group, and the group itself disappeared in a booklet devoted to relaying prison speech. Rather than providing a solution to, or even commentary on, the French prison system, the GIP's first booklet, entitled *Enquête dans 20 prisons*, made available prisoners' responses to surveys distributed at the end of May 1971. After a brief introduction – which restates the by then well-known purpose of the project to provide prisoners with access to speech and explains the means through which this was being achieved – the booklet consists of two questionnaires completed in full (from La Santé and Province), two prisoner narratives (from La Santé and Nevers), and a section, broken down into twelve categories, that collects the most typical responses to questions regarding visits, cells, rights, work, medical care, surveillance, and so on. The categories correspond to those included on the survey, which was drafted with input from former prisoners and modified when initial responses were received. The names of GIP members are nowhere to be found in the text; the brief introduction is signed "Le Groupe d'Information sur les Prisons." Sweeping across twenty prisons, the pamphlet served as a general introduction to what was happening in prisons without visible intervention by the personalities who made the publication and dissemination of this information possible. While the status of affiliated intellectuals was used to publicize the GIP and the work that it was doing, when it came to publishing the results of their group efforts, the names that were used to garner the attention of the press were suppressed. While the removal of names is certainly related to the desire to transmit the unadulterated speech of the prison, editing, as well as the solicitation of speech via survey questions, is itself a form of rewriting and is concealed when member-group names are omitted. We are reminded here, perhaps, of the invisibility of the translator, that figure who, as Susan Bassnett points out, has the power "to change texts and so change the world" ("The Meek or the Mighty" 23). While archival holdings exist to dispel the potential accusation of tampering, the selection and sequencing of texts involve their splicing into relations that do, in fact, change them. The solicited effect, however – having the public listen to and take seriously the speech of prisoners – is certainly shared in this instance by writers and patron/rewriters alike.

For their second booklet, the GIP liberated and distributed the speech of prisoners who were literally confined under a mandate of silence. *Le GIP enquête dans une prison-modèle: Fleury-Mérogis* was devoted to the newest and most "modern" prison in France, a prison that graced television screens with its spotless and shiny interior but that, beyond the shine, was at the forefront in experimenting with new penal techniques, keeping many of its inmates solitarily confined for twenty-three hours per day. While general conditions were established in the first booklet via the publication of broad-based survey results, the second booklet, published in June, relayed a site-specific prison struggle and therefore relied on the work being done by one of the small splinter groups deployed to a specific site.[7] The prison was being built to replace La Santé, an old and deteriorating prison in Paris, but La Santé remained at three times capacity, and the wings of Fleury-Mérogis were filling up as they were being built. The booklet has neither introduction nor conclusion but instead consists of a series of narratives and statements that flow from one to the next almost seamlessly, relating what it is to be confined at Fleury Mérogis. Treatment is related from entry point to lockdown: when a prisoner entered Fleury-Mérogis, he was held in the "reception" area for eight to ten days, housed with another inmate in a cell that had been made for one. During this "assessment," a dossier was established. He appeared before a tribunal. As if by lottery, the prisoner was assigned cell- or yard-work or was solitarily confined for all but an hour a day. Among these cells there was a mandate of silence. Valium was distributed. If pills were refused, a needle was administered (10–32). Two of the wings at Fleury-Mérogis consisted of eighteen- to twenty-year-olds from Paris and the suburbs (7). In a single year, there were seventy-five attempted suicides among the 1,500 youth that constituted one of these wings (7). The second GIP booklet was an exposé of the most contemporary penal practices, and it relayed the speech of some of the most deeply buried and secluded inmates in the French penitentiary system.

Conditions in French prisons did not immediately improve with the publication of the GIP's first two booklets; what the booklets, interviews, demonstrations, and general presence of the GIP ensured was that discourse from and about prison continued to circulate in the press at a time when tensions were running high inside. That prisoners were beginning to air grievances did not translate into immediate action by prison administrators or the minister of justice. Protest in French prisons was by no means new, but its visibility meant that the public and press were now scrutinizing events taking place in prison, where guards, administrators, and ministers could before rely on a cloak of

---

7 While the introduction to the first pamphlet is attributed to Foucault, assembly of the second pamphlet is attributed to Jacques-Alain Miller and François Régnaut.

invisibility over day-to-day operations. That information about conditions and protests was being made public meant that they would have to be addressed.

Considering the prominent place of the committed intellectual in French culture, the provision of raw materials with little to no editorial gloss was a statement in itself. The GIP was a strategically constituted group within which Foucault was a "specific intellectual" who specialized in the scientific study of discourse and the production of truth. Foucault's understanding of regimes of truth – in this context, that the problem of the penal system is not singular, but is the amalgam of heterogenous elements in a network of mechanisms, procedures, and sanctions that produce and police subjects – was crucial to the efficacy of the GIP as a political project. By identifying the mechanisms and procedures through which people who engage in deviant behaviour are made into delinquents, and by understanding how inmates were made inaccessible, Foucault and the GIP were able to devise a strategy for accessing inmates and producing alternate truths.

The concept of the investigation (*enquête*) is itself a product of cultural translation and an indication of the GIP's Maoist inflection. The *enquête* came straight out of Mao – "No investigation, no right to speak" ("Oppose Book Worship" 28, "Preface and Postscript" 13) – and was among a set of methods widely adopted by Maoists during the '68 years, all of which centred on the principle of "going to the people."[8] Just as Mao identified social classes in need of investigation – from peasants, to farm labourers, to the urban poor – French Maoists were embedding themselves in suburban factories and prisons to participate in, probe, and make notes on the actual living conditions of populations who had no access to speech and who would otherwise be overwritten by the idealist projections of intellectuals taking theoretical approaches to the problem of class struggle. As Marcelo Hoffman puts it, "[T]he GIP adopted and

---

8  While Richard Wolin's *The Wind from the East* makes note of the Maoist origins of the GIP's *enquêtes* (18, 307), Marcelo Hoffman's essay "Investigations from Marx to Foucault" endeavours to explain the Marxist underpinnings of the *enquête* to dispel the misconception that the GIP's interventions aspired to be neutral. Kristin Ross's account of the *enquête* in a section of *May '68 and Its Afterlives* that is entirely unrelated to the GIP is particularly useful because it situates the investigation alongside other practices, including the practice of *établissement*, whereby students were taking factory jobs to learn about working conditions from workers (99–113). As Hoffman puts it, "Ross enables us to begin to situate and appreciate the magnitude of a practice whose genealogy has yet to be fully written" ("Investigations from Marx to Foucault" 169). See also Bosteels 578–83, which not only contextualizes Badiou's philosophy in the politics of the Maoist *enquête* but also explains how and why the investigation was a central tenet of French Maoism.

adapted investigations *as* weapons of struggle from the Marxist tradition," and Marxism "inhabited Foucault's political practices and propelled them in unique directions" ("Investigations" 182, emphasis in original). In other words, at the same time as the voices of incarcerated people are being relayed via the GIP's investigations, Marxism was also being relayed and translated with each *enquête*, a series of relays at the heart of changing ideas about the role of the intellectual in France. Indeed, the GIP's investigations can be situated among a set of relays going back not just to Mao, but to Marx's "A Workers' Inquiry," which was distributed as a questionnaire published in *La revue socialiste* – recall the publication of the GIP survey in *Esprit* – and the production of 25,000 pamphlets meant to distribute the questionnaire through France so that Marx could compare working conditions within continental Europe (M. Hoffman "Investigations" 171). As we continue to broaden our scope, it becomes increasingly clear that relay is not simply an a-to-b affair, but an entire network of interrelated points and projections: from prison to public, from Marx to Mao, from China to France, from GP to GIP, from committed to specific intellectual, from theory to practice, from America to France (as we will see in the next section), all bundled together into a network of causes and concerns that changed the political landscape for intellectuals and marginalized people alike during the '68 years in France.

## The George Jackson Atlantic

Although Foucault's commitment to the burgeoning prison liberation movement and his "scientific" expertise in the operation of discourse made him a valuable part of the GIP network, it must be stated that prisoners were revolting as a result of widespread conditions, not GIP instruction or provocation. Furthermore, Foucault and the GIP were not alone in joining the prison movement on the outside: police, the courts, and the prison were tools for crushing the black liberation movement in the United States. The 1960s and 1970s claimed many political prisoners who remain incarcerated to this day.[9] The GIP

---

9  Mumia Abu-Jamal, sentenced to death in 1981 following a trial that had millions around the world proclaiming his innocence, is perhaps the most widely known political prisoner currently incarcerated in the United States. Other prominent political prisoners from the era include Jamil Abdullah Al-Amin (H. Rap Brown), Sundiata Acoli, Herman Bell, Veronza Bowers, Romaine "Chip" Fitzgerald, Kenny "Zulu" Whitmore, Jalil Muntaqim, Ruchell Cinque Magee, Pete O'Neal, Ed Pointdexter, Mutulu Shakur, Russell Maroon Shoatz, Leonard Peltier, Kamau Sidiki (Freddie Hilton), and Seth Ben Ysaac Ben Ysrael (Robert 'Seth'

network extended beyond a local set of actors and struggles; it gleaned tactics and force from this similarly networked American struggle.

In "Foucault and the Black Panthers," Brady Thomas Heiner boldly states that, if Foucault had not been exposed to the writings of the American black liberation movement in general and the writings of the Black Panther Party in particular, "it is quite reasonable to assume that there would be no 'Nietzsche, Genealogy, History,' no *Discipline and Punish* and no theory of biopolitics; he would not have set out to theorize the institution of the prison, discourse as power-knowledge or sought after the historical sources that he did in 'writing a history of the present'" (337). To recognize the overlap between the work of Foucault and the Black Panther Party from the perspective of Foucault studies is to reopen a field that has been closed to others that it had always already included. Foucault was certainly aware of much of the movement writing that was being produced in the United States, and he was particularly excited by the BPP. That being said, it is impossible to pin down just who had an influence on Foucault, when, how, inflected by whom, and so on. From what we know about Foucault and the context he was writing in, there was already significant interest in Nietzsche when he wrote "Nietzsche, Genealogy, History" in 1971. The creative Nietzschean philosophy of Maurice Blanchot and Georges Bataille and the work of Pierre Klossowski were of major influence on Foucault, and his contemporaries Deleuze, Roland Barthes, Jean-François Lyotard, and Jacques Derrida turned to Nietzsche as a serious philosopher with important insights regarding questions of metaphysics and truth. Foucault's infamous genealogy essay itself was collected in a book paying homage to Jean Hyppolite. Furthermore, Mads Peter Karlsen and Kaspar Villadsen analyse the influence of GIP experience on Foucault's development of the concepts of genealogy, power, and critique, arguing that French Maoism provided the main thrust in this new theoretical direction.

While Heiner's argument is a bit heavy-handed, Cornel West's contention – based on conversation with Foucault's life partner and fellow GIP activist Daniel Defert – that the turn towards the "strategic and tactical" in Foucault's genealogical work comes from his reading of the BPP is more balanced. Further, the GIP's strategic use of the American prison liberation movement is certainly evidence of the presence of the BPP at this juncture in the early

---

Hayes). Oscar Lopez Rivera, Marshall "Eddie" Conway, Robert Hillary King, Albert Wood-fox, and Herman Wallace spent thirty to forty years in prison, mostly in solitary confinement, before having their convictions overturned or being released on humanitarian grounds.

seventies (270 n.27).[10] What we see in Foucault and the GIP's uptake of the American prison liberation movement at this point is above all a strategic use of names – Jean Genet and George Jackson in particular – for the connotations that they carry: the GIP-BPP connection is another point of relay.

The GIP's third booklet was devoted to George Jackson, the most renowned prisoner of Soledad State Prison in California. Jackson's transatlantic "travel" is not only an extremely significant piece in the international prison movement that was beginning to thrive at this juncture, but, considering his circumstances, it is also endlessly more remarkable than the transatlantic travel of a Collège de France-chaired French intellectual. Unlike Richard Wright, C.L.R. James, or Frantz Fanon, George Jackson never physically crossed the Atlantic. He spent his early youth in Chicago and Los Angeles, moving out to the west coast when he was fifteen. What is notable about Jackson's migration to France is his complete lack of physical mobility. Because *Soledad Brother* is a book of letters, the Jackson that readers encounter is fundamentally communicative. This is misleading. From the time that he was eighteen years old, Jackson spent much of his life in solitary confinement, with sporadic visitor privileges. There are few images of Jackson; photographs are either headshots or Jackson pictured in chains, shackled ankle-to-wrist in handcuffs and leg-irons. For the most part, the best he could do outside of his cell was shuffle. Not only was his movement restricted by holding cells and chains, it was painful for him to move: he suffered from untreated and debilitating ingrown toenails because the state shoes assigned to him were too small. Jackson did not have access to recreational facilities; to keep fit he did 1,000 push-ups each day – 10 sets of 100. Not only was Jackson confined to a prison, his mobility within the prison system was restricted to an absolute minimum and strictly policed. When the Soledad Brothers – Jackson, John Clutchette, and Fleeta Drumgo – attended their court dates, they were segregated from the rest of the courthouse by a plexiglass cage stamped – ironically – with "America – Bullet Resistant" ("The Glass Cage Must Come Down!" 11). The glass cage sent a message to the jurors: these particular convicts presented an exceptional danger to the court.

Although Jackson could not cross the Atlantic in the flesh, he most definitely crossed the Atlantic in search of writings that would help him understand and theorize the relationship between fascism and capitalism. Jackson was indeed a transnationalist, Atlantic thinker. Spending so much time in

---

10  Beyond this footnote from West, Daniel Defert (33) makes passing indication in a chronology in *Dits et écrits* that Foucault expressed interest in BPP writing in 1968.

solitary confinement meant that he was, for long stretches of time, without human contact. The closest thing approximating companionship was books, and he often found himself speaking aloud with authors (Armstrong xiv). He was a devoted student of Marxism and guerilla warfare, and his most frequent companions were Mao, Marx, Fanon, and Guevara. As Paul Gilroy argued when he proposed that we take the Atlantic as a unit of analysis, transatlantic travel does not occur only in the flesh: the Atlantic is a passage for books, ideas, music, newspapers, and so on (4). If we think about Jackson's travels in this way, we can see how he, although confined, crossed the Atlantic many times over and went elsewhere besides.

Jackson exceeded both his cell and national borders by reading literatures produced in western Europe, Latin America, and East Asia; moreover, his ideas were disseminated internationally via his books and the underground press. The *Black Panther Party Intercommunal News Service*, in particular, which published both Jackson's writing and a consistent stream of articles on the case of the Soledad Brothers, beginning in 1970, had international distribution. The first issue of the newspaper, dated 25 April 1967, was a very local production, devoted to covering the death of Denzil Dowell at the hands of Richmond, California, police on 1 April and publicizing and organizing around strategic response to the killing of black people by police in the North Richmond community. Within just a few short years, however, Sam Napier set up a national distribution network and arranged for international distribution, subscription, and sale of the paper throughout western Europe and in Africa, South America, Asia, and the Middle East (Hilliard Preface vii–viii; E. Brown "Significance of the Newspaper" ix–x). When Jackson's writing was published in the newspaper, it had international distribution.[11]

The Black Panther newspaper was made available in several American prison libraries and inmate mailboxes beginning in mid-1970 as a result of inmates at Soledad prison organizing work stoppages and hunger strikes to affirm the right of prisoners to receive all letters or publications allowed to pass through the mail. Lawyers from the BPP went to court on their behalf and won a court order that enabled inmates to receive the newspaper by mail (Kumasi xviii–xx).[12] The widespread arrest of black militants and party members filled the

---

11  The most effective way of understanding the international reach and scope of the newspaper is to read the intercommunal segment that appeared in the paper on a weekly basis.

12  Censorship in American prisons is by no means a problem of the past. New Jersey state prisons recently made the news when they decided to include Michelle Alexander's *The New Jim Crow* on banned book lists, a decision that was quickly reversed upon intervention by the American Civil Liberties Union (see Bromwich and Mueller). The continued battles to

prison system with black people who had been politically educated and were educating and organizing inmates on the inside. Setting up a communications network between inside and out was of crucial importance if imprisoned members and new recruits were to keep abreast of developments in party philosophy as well as in black and oppressed communities outside prison walls. The opposite, of course, was also true: the communications network linked prison struggle into the BPP news stream, which had widespread distribution in black and Leftist communities not only in prison but across the nation and around the globe. The ability of inmates to subscribe corresponds with increased communication with, and letters being published from, prison.[13]

As a result of GIP efforts, prisoners in France were permitted to subscribe to a daily newspaper or magazine beginning on 12 July 1971 – a year after the Soledad victory – provided that it had not been subject to ban or seizure in the past three months. Summer 1971 through to the beginning of 1972 marked a period of intensified revolt in French prisons, involving hunger strikes, work stoppages, and hostage takings. The generalized nature of prison revolt was indicative of the prisoners' awareness of what was happening elsewhere, in France and internationally. The GIP's concern with information flow had to do with the transmission of prison speech into the French public, but also with the reverse: to make the public available in prison. The combination of an increased population of political prisoners and an opening of the channels for information flow led to a continuation of prison activism.

My focus is on exchanges that occurred between the United States and France, including the particularly significant relationship between the countries regarding the movement of Jackson and the BPP. Although Sam Napier

---

make the invaluable prison newsletter *Prison Legal News* available in prison are illustrative (see Hudson). Even more insidious, however, is the vendor system that has swept through state systems, restricting loved ones to purchasing items through a list of approved vendors. For an account on how recent adoption of this system in New York has affected access to reading materials, see Gross).

13  Opening up a communications channel between incarcerated people and the underground press had a tangible effect on Jackson's writing. Consider, for example, his disclosure in an interview with underground newspaper *Berkeley Tribe* that a regular publication schedule had been planned to publish his theories on fascism: "I believe that pretty soon all these questions, as far as I'm concerned, will be cleared up. The Party paper is going to run a series of articles where I discuss the nature of fascism and in particular the form that it has taken in the United States" (Jackson, "Reflections" 4). The quote reveals the extent to which Jackson was familiar with the role that he was playing in the development of party philosophy in its primary communications organ.

was very successful in his efforts to set up an international distribution network for the BPP newspaper, this did not mean that the newspaper in all cases circulated openly. France was among a number of countries in which the newspaper was banned. As was the case in Soledad prison prior to the court order, the newspaper was distributed clandestinely, smuggled into the country by, among others, Jean Genet.[14] When it came to prison activism, Genet was a significant relay point, a go-between who facilitated the movement of writings – and social movements – across the Atlantic, between France and the United States.

It was Jean Genet who introduced Michel Foucault as well as the French and American public to the writing of George Jackson. Genet not only wrote the introduction to *Soledad Brother*, but he snuck into the United States without a visa (via the Canadian border) in early 1970 in order to give talks on behalf of BPP members on trial, living among the Black Panthers all the while. When he returned to France in May, he did so with the express intent to establish "Committees of Solidarity with the Black Panthers" in France and elsewhere (Genet "Interview with Michèle Manceaux" 302n). Genet's objective when intervening on behalf of the BPP was to extinguish false and damaging "truths" by introducing readers to the voices that are spoken for by these truths. The mainstream press put forth only certain facts, providing minute details in order to give an appearance of truth; what was always lacking, Genet observed, was "the *why* and not the *how* – behind these facts" ("Angela and Her Brothers" 56, emphasis in original). Genet wrote articles and conducted interviews (on the condition that he speak of the Panthers and not his creative work) in *Le nouvel observateur*, he gave public speeches and television addresses on the imprisonment of George Jackson and Angela Davis, and he circulated petitions in France that helped to build an international profile for their cases, demanding their immediate release. When Jackson was assassinated, and when the Attica massacre occurred shortly thereafter, Genet responded in both France and the United States, contributing articles to underground newspapers on either side of the Atlantic.

Although Genet never met Jackson, he was a logical candidate to introduce Jackson's prison letters. Using his status as an internationally recognized writer (and former thief and prisoner, deepening his affinities with Jackson), Genet introduced Jackson's book of prison letters as an epistolary narrative that was both combat weapon and love poem (Introduction 7). *Soledad Brother* was

---

14 In a letter to David Hilliard, Jean Genet describes his role in distributing the BPP newspaper: a member of the party sent him the newspapers, and he, in turn, made them available to the activist community in Paris.

resolutely modern, situated, by Genet, alongside the writing of the Marquis de Sade, Antonin Artaud, and Richard Wright. In Genet's estimation, Jackson's book was both an important literary work and an instruction manual on the American prison system and on fascism not only in America, but across the globe. Although Jackson's writing speaks for itself – and it reveals in Jackson a beautiful writer and powerful intellect – Genet's name bestows upon Jackson a status otherwise extremely difficult for a prisoner to attain. Similar to the way in which intellectual status was a vehicle for the transmission of prison speech in France, Genet's status was used to transmit Jackson's prison writing. Such is the power and prominence of association to the act of relay.

Genet was therefore also a fitting choice to write an introduction for the GIP's pamphlet on George Jackson. That Genet allegedly demanded that his name not be included under the banner of the GIP and was upset when he was told that the text he wrote would be included in one of their pamphlets tells us something about both Genet's association with the Panthers and the shortcomings, in Genet's eyes, of the GIP. According to Edmund White, Genet's reluctance to be associated with the GIP was not because he did not support the project, but because he did not want to be labelled a French intellectual (alongside the likes of Cixous, Deleuze, Foucault, and Sartre). While the "intellectual" label was riddled with a set of expectations, assumptions, and postures, Genet felt that this was not the case for the poet (568).[15] Even if prison speech was not obscured or overwritten by the names and projects of its GIP purveyors, to participate in the group, in Genet's estimation, said or required something of the purveyors themselves. It was as a poet that Genet lived among Black Panthers and Palestinians alike.[16] He was not constrained within a country of origin (France), nor was he bound to a certain manner of intervening, or thinking (as per the intellectual). The poet lived a nomadic life.

As a poet without borders, Genet had a nomadic lifestyle that was a particularly stark contrast to Jackson's time in solitary confinement, but that is what made the relationship between former thief and current prisoner all the more enabling and germane; it was through Genet, as well as through editors, publishers, and journalists, that Jackson was able to escape his confinement and,

---

15 The booklet opens with a notice that distinguishes between Genet and the group: "The Preface was written by Jean Genet. The other texts were prepared by the Prison Information Group" (GIP, *L'assassinat de George Jackson* 2, my translation).
16 For accounts of Genet's fellow travelling with the Black Panther Party and Palestinians, see, in particular, Genet, *Prisoner of Love*.

ultimately, his death. When Jackson died, Genet wrote Jackson onto a similarly nomadic path. Immediately following Jackson's death, Genet contributed a letter and an article to the Black Panther Party's newspaper. The letter, printed in a lengthy section devoted to "Letters for George Jackson from the People," exempts Jackson from the confines of the American nation: no man "'belongs' to a country in which ... he just happens to be born" ("Untitled" L), Genet asserts. Jackson's "countrymen [sic] ... [are] those of us who read, loved and admired his book ... entire peoples, whole countries of men for whom he wrote, deep in the bowels of Soledad prison" (L). Rather than isolating the murder of Jackson, Genet situates Jackson within the larger community that is affected by the loss, collecting for him the larger body that remains even after his own has perished. Lest Jackson's ideas be interred with his body, Genet's article speaks to the community that surrounds Jackson's work, and he gestures towards an indeterminate future ("one can expect anything" [L]), pregnant with possibility. The use of Jackson by Foucault and the GIP shortly after his assassination, the nature of which I discuss in the next section, represents just one of these futures: a French-American relay.

### Relaying Revolt, Desubjectifying Delinquency

Jackson was killed at a time of widespread revolt and increasing repression in French prisons. Prisoners staged hunger strikes and work stoppages, demanding better medical care and visitation rights. Inmate beatings by guards were on the rise, and reports of violence were circulated by the GIP and published in *Le Monde*: in July, a guard was injured and eventually died when an inmate set off fireworks received in a parcel at Saint-Paul Prison; in September, a guard and nurse were taken hostage and killed at Clairvaux dans l'Aube; on 14 October, an inmate at Baumettes was killed after he took a nurse hostage at knifepoint (Artières et al. 133–6).

Tensions in French prisons in summer 1971 were at an all-time high. When the GIP published the voice of a political prisoner killed in the United States, it was responding, in large part, to increased repression and an inmate killing by guards in France. Jackson was killed on 21 August, but the GIP did not publish their pamphlet on his assassination until 10 November. France was part of a larger international community concerned with the treatment of political prisoners such as Huey P. Newton, Angela Davis, and George Jackson and the Soledad Brothers in the United States. Although the GIP was certainly part of this concerned community, Jackson's death also presented the group with a unique opportunity to draw parallels with, and to relay attention to, the worsening situation in French prisons.

That the preface of the GIP's *L'assassinat de George Jackson* is authored by a renowned French writer known for his mobilization efforts on Jackson's behalf begins the work of connecting Jackson to France. Genet's preface – half of which is a long quote from *Soledad Brother*, making it a preface in which the prisoner is permitted to introduce himself – is an homage to Jackson as writer, brother (to his brother Jonathan), and revolutionary. Jackson would have needed little introduction in France at this point, particularly by Genet, who was responsible for introducing him to the French public in the first place (the translation of *Soledad Brother* was published by Gallimard in April 1970). Instead, the pamphlet's preface provides Genet with the opportunity to provide closing remarks, or to explain what the next chapter will be now that Jackson, in body, has perished. In this vein, Genet ends the preface by noting that his brief remarks simply cannot capture Jackson, who lived on for weeks beyond his death in uprisings at Attica, in Baltimore, and in New Orleans (11). Genet's interpretation of the situation follows the BPP line that, even in death, "George Jackson lives!" This exclamation captioned the artwork of BPP Minister of Culture Emory Douglas in the 28 August 1971 issue of the BPP newspaper, which was dedicated to Jackson from which one of the interviews translated for the GIP pamphlet was pulled. While the prison uprisings that Genet cites in closing are American, his preface opens with the claim that it has become rare to see a man in Europe accept that he will be killed for his beliefs (3). What, then, might Jackson's legacy be in Europe? How did French struggles and casualties stack up against these American examples?

If we keep in mind that the French situation would be the immediate frame of reference for the GIP's readership, the two Jackson interviews that make up the bulk of the pamphlet resonate in significant ways. When Jackson talks about the crucial, positive influence that the influx of Panthers has had on the prison population (which, prior to BPP entry might have been considered one of the most conservative enclaves in America) ("La lutte dans les prisons" 13), a French reader would surely think about the influx of post-May political prisoners in France, and particularly those culled from the ranks of the Gauche prolétarienne, who were behind much of the agitation in prison in recent months. Or, when Jackson goes on to point out that expressions of solidarity on the street have been a major source of inspiration and have provided an important sense of community ("La lutte dans les prisons" 14), the sentiments are a prompt for the pamphlet's readership to continue to participate in solidarity struggles outside, which offer, at the very least, an indirect remedy to the forced isolation that characterizes the daily lives of those that are imprisoned.

More potent than striking a parallel between the situations in French and American prisons, the booklet included supplementary essays that implicitly made connections between them, situating French prison struggles within the larger context of an international prison movement. In "L'assassinat camouflé," the GIP deems Jackson's assassination an act of war and argues that the mainstream media, by relying entirely on statements made by the prison administration, was effectively distributing war communiqués. Not only did the reports and statements made by the administration contain contradictions, but they were carefully constructed so as to destroy the credibility of prisoners, their lawyers, and the entire black community while simultaneously inspiring sympathy for the administrators of punishment – prison guards in particular – as the victims of unprovoked attacks (*L'assassinat de George Jackson* 41–52). The message is that one should be wary of accounts in the press, particularly those provided by "official" sources, which work to situate the civilized and the savage on either side of a war taking place in prisons. Administrative accounts of the events that took place at San Quentin are countered in the GIP pamphlet by a statement undersigned by twenty-six inmates whose testimony was barred from preliminary hearings but that was read by a defence lawyer to the public and the press outside the courtroom. The inmates had been witnesses to Jackson's assassination and were presently being tortured and were barred from providing their accounts of the events of 21 August.[17]

The deconstructed statement and prisoner-signed counterstatement are again illustrative of Foucault's 1976 reversal of the Clausewitz aphorism ("Politics is a continuation of war by other means"). Foucault's analysis of the manner in which authoritatively and institutionally sanctioned truths circulate is pertinent here: there are persons who have the credentials that allow them to tell "the truth" – or, put differently, to translate an event into a position in battle – while others are not permitted to speak. The pamphlet provided San Quentin's imprisoned witnesses with a platform in France; although their statements were barred from official channels, their "unofficial" eyewitness accounts of the events of 21 August and the torture that they had been facing since managed to breach San Quentin walls, via activist lawyers and an underground publication, and travel across the Atlantic. The GIP publication of these statements,

---

17 According to the San Quentin inmates who survived the assassination of George Jackson, the events were nothing short of a premeditated political assassination meant to stifle a prison movement that had been gaining momentum under Jackson's direction. See GIP, *L'assassinat de George Jackson* 54.

however, was more than a revelation of injustice; recognizing that "justice" was a political battleground, the prisoner-signed counterstatement was a weapon in the hands of the GIP. When the GIP relayed the inadmissible voices of San Quentin inmates post-assassination, it was not only advocating on their behalf, it was also, by extension, forcing readers to think about the unprinted voices facing unheard of repression following recent episodes of violence in French prisons. What were conditions like after the fireworks episode at Saint-Paul or the hostage takings at Clairvaux and Baumettes? What types of reprisals were taking place? The GIP – via independent presses and mimeograph machines – was engaged in asymmetrical warfare against the state and its interviews and press releases published in the mass media.

On the same day that the GIP published its booklet on the assassination of George Jackson, *Agence de presse libération* (*APL*) published the full list of demands made by prisoners in Attica prison during the standoff in September. On 11 November, the GIP held an assembly of thousands at the Salle de la Mutualité regarding the situation in prisons in France, Italy, and the United States. Attica and George Jackson were featured, and family members of French inmates were among those that spoke at the meeting.[18] To learn about Attica (as well as San Quentin and Soledad) was to learn something about the French penitentiary system, which, as mentioned earlier, operated in secrecy. Moreover, Attica was an event that contained a great deal of symbolic power, and it was, in this sense, a tremendous mobilizer. Understood in the immediate context of its publication – alongside the *APL* issue on Attica and the Mutualité meeting – the George Jackson pamphlet was not about advocacy on Jackson's behalf, it was part of a coordinated effort to mobilize the French branch of a

---

18 On the other side of the Atlantic, within months of the Attica massacre, we find Foucault on New York State soil, in Attica prison. In early 1972, he was giving a seminar as Melodia E. Jones Chair in the Department of French at SUNY-Buffalo, and he used his stay as an opportunity to visit the embattled prison. In an interview with John K. Simon, he provides a brief account of his impressions of Attica (which, due to restrictions on who could enter a prison in France – prisoners, guards, lawyers, family – was Foucault's first ever visit to a prison [Foucault, "On Attica" 113]). In the GIP archives, we find the announcements for a public meeting related to Jackson and Attica at the Mutualité and the issue of *Agence de presse libération* that translated the Attica demands for a French audience concerned with the functioning of prisons. We also find a copy of *Attica News*, addressed to the French group. That the newspaper was produced by the Attica Defense Committee with whom Foucault met within months of his visit to Attica is intriguing. The paper contains a list of indictments against Attica prisoners as a result of the uprising, the list of twenty-eight demands made during the uprising along with notes regarding their status, and a description of the brutality committed by guards after the state has re-asserted its control of the prison.

budding international prison movement. This is what the transatlantic relay of prison struggle was all about. Jackson and Attica are both metonyms for the suppression of inmate speech, and patrons for its production.

Just as public intellectuals, via their status, made the circulation of prison speech possible, George Jackson and the Attica demands "authorized" the communication of demands made from prison in France. From summer 1971 through 1972, prison uprisings in France continued to multiply and intensify. The GIP followed the movements, provided media outlets with inmate demands so that they would be more widely distributed, and published a pamphlet, outside of the *Intolérable* series, that compiled demands made from seven prisons. *Cahiers de revendications sortis des prisons lors des récentes révoltes* (Book of demands released from prison during recent revolts) includes tracts produced in Toul, Loos-lès-Lille, Melun, Nancy, Fresnes, Nîmes, and La Santé. Demands, including improvements to food, medical services, showers, and heating, were by no means outlandish and were most shocking when they revealed the inhumane conditions in which prisoners were being kept – for example, the use of 2 x 1.1 metre chicken cages at Nîmes. As L.D. Barkley powerfully stated from the midst of the Attica rebellion, "We are men, we are not beasts, and we do not intend to be driven or beaten as such."[19] It is only the releasing of the speech of prisoners that forces the public to confront the hidden, barbaric limit of societal prejudices.

The demands in *Cahiers de revendications* are authorized not by the status of a French intellectual conduit,[20] but by the corroborating testimony of two prison workers: an unnamed social worker and the psychiatrist Dr Edith Rose. The social worker relates his difficulties in gaining access to a prisoner who asked for his help after the prisoner was beaten by guards, and how his attempts to access and assist this prisoner led the administration to send a request to the Red Cross to have his licence revoked. He ends his contribution by asking whether social workers have a role in assisting prisoners or if they are simply an auxiliary for the exercise of power over inmates (GIP *Cahiers de revendications* 26–30). Dr Rose's testimony, an open letter to the inspector general of prisons, the president of the republic, and the minister of justice, provides accounts of the deplorable conditions at Toul, where a riot broke out before being brutally crushed by riot police in December 1972. Noting that

---

19 Interviews with inmates during and after the Attica events are available on compact disc from AK Press / Alternative Tentacles (see Freedom Archives).

20 Hélène Cixous has been credited with compiling the booklet, but her name does not appear inside.

none of the inmates in the Toul population were "hardened" criminals, Rose testifies that inmates were not allowed to participate in sports until they recorded a year of good behaviour and that limitations were placed on the number of photographs allowed in their cells (which caused great distress for a mentally ill inmate). She witnessed inmates being kept in restraints for more than a week (often due to attempted suicide, the rate of which was becoming alarmingly high), and, after the revolt, the director refused to allow her to see inmates to provide them with medical and psychiatric care (GIP *Cahiers de revendications* 31–40).[21]

When the GIP needed a spokesperson for the development of a prison movement, it turned to George Jackson; when inmate demands needed corroboration, the GIP turned to accredited prison workers; when suicide rates among prisoners hit an all-time high the next year in France, the GIP turned to the writing of a recent casualty of the French penitentiary to relate the tragic consequences of policing certain types of bodies in French prisons. Like the George Jackson pamphlet before it, *Suicides de prison* features as its centrepiece the voice of a single inmate: letters written by a prisoner in the months leading to his suicide in late 1972. In both the one page introduction to H.M.'s letters and the short essay that follows, H.M.'s sexuality is emphasized as the reason for his suicide. H.M. was solicited by a police officer in summer 1972 and was arrested and sentenced in court to six days in solitary for homosexuality. This was not the first time that he was arrested and incarcerated because of his sexual orientation. After having been through more than a dozen prisons, H.M. hung himself in solitary.

That this posthumous collection published by the GIP comes in epistolary form strikes a parallel between H.M. and George Jackson that is expressly invoked in the essay that follows the letters. In the short, unsigned essay, which has since been attributed to Deleuze,[22] snippets from H.M.'s letters from confinement are quoted in quick succession as lines of flight. When H.M. says that he does not have or want a lawyer because all they do is whine and he wants one who will storm, or when he proclaims that he will not demand mercy from the tribunal but will instead address them with proclamations against the fundamental injustice of the court and the corruption of police, his lines of flight are akin to Jackson's active and political flight, where one does not flee without looking for weapons, without attacking (GIP *Suicides de prison* 39). By

---

21 Before being published in the GIP pamphlet, excerpts of Rose's testimony were published in *La cause du peuple* and *Le nouvel observateur,* and as a paid advertisement in *Le Monde.*
22 See Deleuze, "H.M.'s Letters."

publishing and framing H.M.'s letters in this manner, the recently deceased inmate becomes both victim of and hero in the system rather than a buried and derided statistic. Like George Jackson, in death, H.M. lives.

While the pamphlet features H.M.'s letters, they are surrounded by supplementary essays and information regarding prison suicides. After a half-page GIP-signed introduction on the increasing rate of suicide in French prisons, the pamphlet provides a list of prison suicides that occurred in 1972 and a paragraph of narrative regarding the circumstances surrounding seven of these suicides (*Suicides de prison* 7–12). Lack of medical or psychiatric care, the profound psychological effects of being placed in isolation or physical constraint, and institutionalized homophobia play a prominent part in these narratives. The narratives desensationalize prison by pointing to the petty crimes for which many of these victims of the penitentiary were incarcerated in the first place, and they point to troubling trends: three of the seven suicides narrativized occurred in Fleury-Mérogis. That all three of these suicides were committed by Algerians points to the racism and class dynamics involved in policing the Parisian suburbs from which much of the inmate population at Fleury-Mérogis was constituted. The pamphlet places an emphasis on the racialized nature of suicide for a reason: as a preface to the list of suicides, the GIP notes that eight of thirty-two reported suicides were committed by immigrants (5). In prison, racism and homophobia have particularly fatal effects on the bodies of the condemned.

Beyond the simple movement of information across prison walls, the more complex operation that the liberation of prison speech performed was desubjectification: prison speech was the means whereby the "delinquent" could obliterate the reductive mould to which he or she was subject. Foucault argues in *Discipline and Punish* that the "delinquent" (characterized by his or her life) – the successor of the "offender" (characterized by his or her act) – appeared at the same time as the penitentiary technique, "the one extending from the other, as a technological ensemble that forms and fragments the object to which it applies its instruments" (255). Giving prisoners the possibility to speak themselves, as the GIP set out to do from the beginning, involved the obliteration of discursive categories such as these, categories that obscure the complexity and humanity that resides in every cell.

Although the desubjectification of delinquents was part of the GIP project from the beginning, the final two of the GIP's pamphlets were decidedly devoted to the project of allowing the categorically dismissed – and recent casualties of the penal system – to speak themselves. Thus, the intolerable-information coupling – it was intolerable that there were thirty-seven suicides in French prison in 1972 (GIP *Suicides de prison* 8), and it was intolerable that a black man who allegedly stole $70 from a gas station was assassinated after serving eleven years of a one-year-to-life sentence (GIP *L'assassinat de George Jackson* 3–4) – is deployed in such a fashion that reductive (tactically measured) discursive categories are shattered by the uncontainable complexity that characterizes the speech of these recently deceased "delinquents." While the GIP's first two pamphlets evidence the establishment of a network for relaying prison speech, the last three demonstrate the multidirectional work of establishing a transnational network for the relay of revolt.

## For the Relay of Prison Speech

From the prestigiously chaired subject as conduit, to explorations of group subjectivity and the transatlantic relay of revolt, Foucault's prison information project foregrounds the importance of associations. While it is tempting to reinscribe Foucault as a leader of the GIP, and as an intellect who was able to free the voices of inmates, if not their bodies, it would be a mistake – prompted by the discourses within which the names of great intellectuals circulate – to put more stake in a French intellectual's body of work than the bodies of those who are incarcerated. It would seem much more significant and productive to take strategic lessons from this project, to build upon the strategies that the GIP employed to relay prison speech, and to listen to and learn from the speech that was relayed by them. That the GIP was able to relay prison speech in France at this juncture was no small feat. Because only families, certain professionals, and certain publications were allowed into prisons, the GIP focused on these. To buffer against bias, the GIP was without mandate and was constituted of many different groups and professions. The status and connections of group members were certainly used to gain access to the information network, but status did not overwrite the prison speech for which it was ultimately a vehicle.

"What Is an Author?" is not only a widely anthologized answer to Barthes ("Death of the Author") and Beckett ("What Matter Who Speaks?") but a signpost essay that designates a time during which Foucault was working through the way that certain names authorized certain types of discourse, including that of the intellectual. Consider a comment that Foucault makes during an interview with a Renault worker in the French newspaper *Libération*:[23]

---

23 *Libération* is itself an interesting case. What has become a standard paper in France started as a new venture for a united Left, including Foucault among its ranks from the first meeting onwards. The paper was originally printed under the name *Agence de press libération* (*APL*)

The workers don't need intellectuals to tell them what they are doing; they know perfectly well what they are doing. In my view, the intellectual is the guy [sic] who is plugged into the information network, not the production network. He can make his voice heard. He can write in the newspapers, give his point of view. He is also plugged into an older information network. He has the knowledge acquired by reading a certain number of books, knowledge which other people do not have at their direct disposal. His role is therefore not to shape working-class consciousness, as that consciousness already exists, but to allow that consciousness, working-class consciousness, to enter the information system. (qtd. in Macey *Lives of Michel Foucault* 318–19)

In the process of making an argument against intellectual vanguardism, Foucault makes a pointed and fundamental distinction: industrial workers and intellectuals are plugged into different networks. Although the knowledge of workers extends far beyond the machinery of the plant, that they are plugged into the production network means that they have the power, in protest, to manipulate the rate at which the machinery of production produces goods. Industrial workers do not, however, have access to the information network that provides intellectuals with the power to produce public knowledge. The task of the intellectual, then, is to use her subject position as a point through which neglected consciousnesses can gain entry to the information network. This is the intellectual as translator in the system of political patronage. The role of the intellectual, for Foucault, is to collect neglected voices and their histories, and to project the past into the present, the neglected into the public eye. The role of the intellectual is to configure, and become part of, a relay network.

Relay is an associative translation practice. In the context of this book, relay is a practice that involves the facilitation of border crossings (and we should note that prison walls are much less penetrable than national and linguistic borders), the work of collection (the development and linkage of networks to overcome the stifling effects of those borders), and the work of projection (the strategic deployment of voices for the purpose of developing a movement). Relay, as translator (between incarcerated people and the public, and between theory and practice) is linked to the axis of combination rather than that of selection; it is linked to the development of networks with an emphasis on

---

and acted as a regular news bulletin for the Left. Foucault's original idea for a contribution to the project was to provide proletarian chronicles from the nineteenth century that would relate to current struggles in the factories in France. Although he never followed through, he made other contributions to the *APL*. See Macey 313–18.

movement. Relay is an associative translation practice because it is by association – with prominent intellectuals, with the demands of imprisoned activists, with high-profile prisoners, with high-profile internationally distributed revolts – that the lives and living conditions of locally situated prisoners, isolated from public view, have the potential to be redefined.

Foucault's answer to the contention that he was a historian who bent the truth was that he wrote "a kind of historical fiction," and that the purpose of his work was to "provoke an interference between our reality and the knowledge of our past history" ("Truth Is in the Future" 301). Foucault is not admitting to committing untruths to paper here, he is simply recognizing that all histories are necessarily selective, and that his histories were written not from some impossibly objective vantage of the present, but with the future of the present in mind. Recognizing the problems of over-incarceration that plague the North American present – warehousing; the overrepresentation of black, Indigenous, and mentally ill prisoners; the overuse and abuse of solitary confinement and of sedatives; the standardization of no-contact visits; the preponderance of prison profiteers; the scourge of immigrant detention; and the list goes on – what futures might our knowledge of this GIP history hold? Firsthand accounts of incarceration certainly trickle out of prison,[24] but the regime that brands not only inmates but entire racialized populations as delinquent is as insidious as ever. While the histories of slavery, colonialism, and the profit motive constitute a genealogy of the contemporary North American prison, there are tactical lessons to be gleaned from this history of the relay network – perhaps the truth of the GIP is in the future.

---

24  The podcasts and blogs that perhaps make inmates seem accessible are a product of dedicated relay efforts, not open channels. Mumia Abu-Jamal's radio work and podcasts are available due to the work of Noelle Hanrahan. As a result of rallying efforts of the Fraternal Order of Police, his first radio show was cancelled just as it was set to air, and, in a convoluted twist that illustrates the difficulty of relaying prison speech, some of his radio texts originated as "prison letters" mailed to Hanrahan because he could not bring paper with him to visits. Abu-Jamal mailed his texts to Hanrahan so that she could tape them to the glass for him to read into the microphone for the radio (Hanrahan 29). Similarly, writings from solitary confinement are part of the Prisoner Hunger Strike Solidarity blog (https:// prisonerhungerstrikesolidarity.wordpress.com/), thanks to the existence of an outside solidarity coalition that has been supporting a series of hunger strikes for more than four years. Blogs by individual inmates such as Toronto G20 activists Mandy Hisckocks (https:// boredbutnotbroken.tao.ca/) and Alex Hundert (https://alexhundert.wordpress.com/) were similarly online thanks to the relay efforts of friends and activist networks. Relay work done by individuals and coalitions remains the only means of enabling prison speech. The virtual invisibility of relay belies the difficulty of breaching prison walls to communicate the contemporary realities of American and Canadian prisons.

# 4 In Search of Common Ground: On Semiotext(e) and Schizo-Culture

The revolution will not be televised. But *The Coming Insurrection* was. Originally published in France in 2007, the small booklet, written by the anonymous Comité invisible, was denounced as a manual for terrorism by the French government. It became a key piece of evidence against nine activists arrested in a raid in the small commune of Tarnac. The "Tarnac 9" were allegedly planning to bomb train lines. Among them was one of the text's alleged authors, Julien Coupat. In July 2009, shortly after the English translation of the book was published by Semiotext(e),[1] it was "reviewed" by Glenn Beck on Fox News with video from the 2008 Greek protests running in the background. Beck's advice: that everyone should own a copy to keep abreast of the evil elements in America's midst. Sales went through the roof.[2] As if he had not yet given it enough of a plug, Beck picked up and wagged the book at Fox News cameras a second time in May 2010, this time against the backdrop of the massive May Day rallies across the United States and in Arizona in particular (in response to Senate Bill 1070, which targets migrant workers and their employers by requiring a show of documents on demand). Zeroing in on common protest slogans being chanted in the crowd, Beck scratches his chin and ponders: he's read that somewhere before. Beck resumes his little blue book wagging and asks how on earth it was possible for so many protestors to gather in such a short time. With a plug from Beck to his twenty million viewers – everyone should own a copy

---

1 Throughout this chapter, "*Semiotext(e)*" (i.e., rendered in italics) refers to the journal, whereas "Semiotext(e)" (i.e., in roman font) refers to the project in general.

2 See Cohen. *The Coming Insurrection* was already the subject of an article in the *New York Times* when a group of approximately 100 people gathered at a Barnes and Noble in New York City for an unscheduled reading to celebrate its translation (see Moniyhan).

of this book – Semiotext(e)'s newest readership was not the Left to whom *L'insurrection qui vient* was addressed, but its counterpart on the Right (for a time, Tea Party manuals dominated the "customers most likely to buy" list on Amazon). While he was not the translator of *L'insurrection qui vient*, Beck is certainly a translator for *The Coming Insurrection*.

Although the book might have more readily found its target audience on the Left had the translation been published under the banner of a radical press like AK Press, PM Press, or Seven Stories, it makes sense that Semiotext(e) published the English translation of *The Coming Insurrection*: the Invisible Committee is allegedly tied to the journal *Tiqqun*, which has its intellectual origins in the "French theory" that Semiotext(e), under the direction of general editor Sylvère Lotringer, had been ferrying across the Atlantic since the seventies. For Semiotext(e), the book represented the opportunity to renew an impulse. As the inaugural volume in the publisher's new "Intervention series," the little blue book signalled a return to the recently abandoned little black book format that Semiotext(e) had been using to publish "Foreign Agents" since the eighties. With a small-print paragraph from the United States Foreign Agents Registration Act repeated in columns across each cover, Semiotext(e) sold long essays by, and interviews with, Jean Baudrillard, Gilles Deleuze, Félix Guattari, and Paul Virillio as subversive tracts that were manufactured to move: cheap and quick to print and designed for easy transport through New York City via subway in the pockets of spiked leather jackets (Lotringer "My 80's"). As "French theory" has since been heavily institutionalized, it made little sense to continue to publish its texts as though they were in themselves subversive – trade paperbacks with introductions and endnotes are the more appropriate format for the academic marketplace – but the work of the Invisible Committee, emerging from French theory, certainly warranted a restart of the small book format.

Lotringer's approach to the introduction of French theory to an American audience was decidedly different from its introduction via other university channels. While contemporary French theorists were entering America via conventional channels like academic conferences, university presses, and chaired professorships, Semiotext(e), as Henry Schwartz and Anne Balsamo put it, "was conceived as an intervention into cultural politics, not merely as an exercise in theoretical reproduction, and far less an attempt to establish academic legitimacy for some sort of below-the-horizon publishing venture" (208–9). In the inaugural introduction of the *Semiotext(e)* journal, an issue entitled "Alternatives in Semiotics," Lotringer notes that, regardless of how established and complete any system, method, or mode of inquiry pretends to be, the fact of any inquiry is that it will project the project that it is inquiring into elsewhere

("Pour une sémiotique matérialiste" 3). Accordingly, the work that was done in semiotics under the Semiotext(e) banner was not simply about locating and describing alternatives found. Based upon an understanding that coherence is breached – and movement inevitable – as soon as an outside element (inquiry, or looking in from without) becomes involved, Semiotext(e) self-consciously moved the alternatives it located in semiotics elsewhere. Semiotext(e) took an abrupt and explicit turn away from semiotics in the late seventies, but its relatively quiet beginnings in the field are carried with it not only in name – Semiotext(e) being a combination of "semiotics" and "text" with the "(e)" signalling its bilingualism – but also in impulse.

Although Semiotext(e) lacks an immediately coherent politics, the project is not apolitical: the collisions and encounters that the project orchestrated, and the conversations that it made possible, brought out politics that might have escaped unnoticed in another layout or sequence. Furthermore, the orchestration and enabling of cross-boundary exchanges was in itself a political act. Along these lines of exchange, the most important lesson embedded in the history of Semiotext(e) is its practice of conversational theory, developed over the course of the late seventies. Taking the 1974–8 period as my focus, I outline – by moving through the succession of journals released, and events organized, under the Semiotext(e) banner during this time – the way that the project developed micropolitically, liberating lines of thought from disciplinary bounds or discursive orders that segregate impulses from one another. When impulses are desegregated what is revealed is that hitherto non-conversant lines often have a lot in common; such lines can, if considered together, push ways of thinking – and doing – in unanticipated and productive directions. What can we learn about the meeting of French theory and American writing through the lens of Semiotext(e), and what does this have to do with the staging of an event?

In this chapter, I analyse the development of Semiotext(e) as a self-conscious translation project. First, I consider how Lotringer imagined alternatives to the dry rigidity of institutionalized structuralism via semiotics, which represented, for him, a sort of psychosocial undercurrent to a structuralism that seemed ready-made for academic institutionalization. Next, I speak to the significance of the "Schizo-Culture" conference by analysing the conference as an event, explaining through it the ways in which translation between France and America can never be immediate. What the Schizo-Culture event demonstrates – with its stubborn and instructive incommensurabilities – is that it takes time to translate between one language/nation/culture and another, and even when bits and pieces make it across, they are always mediated. After relating these lessons of the Schizo-Culture conference, I analyse the run of *Semiotext(e)* journals that directly followed the conference. While certain collected texts will be important to the argument I develop, rather than performing close readings of such texts I pay particular attention to the textual strategies employed by the journal itself – its presentation and layout – in order to foreground the way in which *Semiotext(e)* did theory.

Lotringer recognized rather early on in his publishing project that if mediation was inevitable, the pursuit of theory could never be objective. Putting an interesting spin on this visionary moment in the translation process, Lawrence Venuti considers this the utopian dimension of translation: "the communities fostered by translating are initially potential" and are "weighted ideologically towards the translating culture" ("Translation, Community" 498). Translation involves the imagination and anticipation of a community; it "projects a utopian community that is not yet realized" (498). The mandated objective of Semiotext(e) was not to understand theory; once it got going, the project sought to stage conversations. While this may sound banal, a conversation is not merely a formal period of exchange. Conversation is what occurs "between the two"; it is what becomes *between* Paris and New York. In the case of Semiotext(e), it is how "Schizo-Culture" is projected. Like a cobblestone, conversation can be conceived as a projectile, and, in Lotinger's utopic imagination, Semiotext(e) was a "Project for a Revolution in New York."[3]

## Alternatives in Semiotics

Because Lotringer wrote his dissertation under the direction of Roland Barthes and had prior experience in organizing conferences while studying at the Sorbonne, he was a fitting candidate to bring the new French thought to Columbia University's Department of French. Although Lotringer was hired in New York, he was immediately shipped back to Columbia's Reid Hall campus in Paris to organize a lecture series for exchange students. In Paris, the controversies surrounding structuralism were of an altogether different sort from the ones that were being generated and discussed in the United States. With the publication of Richard Macksey and Eugenio Donato's *The Structuralist Controversy* in 1972, American critics were marvelling at the pomp and circumstance of structuralism's simultaneous arrival and undoing at the Johns Hopkins conference called the Languages of Criticism and the Sciences of Man. The

---

3 *Project for a Revolution in New York* is the title of a novel by Alain Robbe-Grillet and a heading in Lotringer's introduction to the *"Anti-Oedipus"* issue of *Semiotext(e)*, which I analyse below.

published proceedings consecrated the arrival of Barthes, Jacques Derrida, and Jacques Lacan on American soil in 1966, and the title helped to determine the way that the proceedings would be read – as Derrida's coup – for years to come.[4] While, in the early seventies, Anglo-American academics were grappling with what structuralism was and how it might serve in various fields, Lotringer was surrounding himself with thinkers who were working well beyond its limitations. The Reid Hall series featured lectures by Catherine Clément, Gilles Deleuze, Félix Guattari, Denis Hollier, Luce Irigaray, Sarah Kofman, Julia Kristeva, Jacques Lacan (who nudged his way in when he was told Deleuze was to speak), and Christian Metz. Thus, psychoanalysis and its semiotic subversion were certainly in promise, as were Nietzsche and an early merger between psychoanalysis and film. Had Lotringer been at Columbia in New York and not in Paris in the early seventies, Semiotext(e) would have been an entirely different entity.

Titled "Alternatives in Semiotics," the first issue of the journal, published in 1974, was an unextravagant type-and-mimeograph job that provided no indication that formal experimentation would become one of the defining characteristics of the project. The issue included articles by Guattari and Kristeva, and it therefore put on display the French connections made at Reid Hall. More substantially, it found in recent developments in semiotics the potential to carve a way out of the systemic methodologies being crafted under the umbrella of semiology by various strands of structuralism. Under the influence of structuralism, semiology had become quite ordered; it was honed and used as a tool for analysis. What Lotringer and the Semiotext(e) group saw in semiotics – as opposed to structuralism – was the potential to break the tendency towards systematization and to open up a larger field of possibilities.

The essays collected in the "Alternatives in Semiotics" issue provide illustrations of, and arguments for, the system-subverting potential of recent developments in semiotics. Kristeva proposed the subject in process – as a dialectic between the pre-linguistic geno-text and algebraic pheno-text – and identified in this process a primordial zone of discontinuity and flux perpetually thwarted

---

4 The elements of the title for the published proceedings of the Johns Hopkins conference, *The Languages of Criticism and the Sciences of Man: The Structuralist Controversy* (1970), were reversed when the collection was republished in 1972. Beyond giving less prominence to the gender-offensive language – a move consistent with the university's decision to finally begin to admit women into undergraduate programs in 1970 – the reversal sensationalizes and markets the split represented most emphatically in Derrida's offering in the collection, "Structure, Sign and Play in the Discourse of the Human Sciences."

by various rules of communication ("Four Types of Signifying Practices"); Guattari argued for a micropolitics of desire in an asignifying semiotics (as opposed to signifying semiologies) ("Pour une micro-politique du désir)"; Hollier pondered the paradox of deeming Georges Bataille a transgressive subject ("Le sujet de la transgression"); Leon S. Roudiez asked whether the new novelists and the Tel Quel group had succeeded in stemming the transmission of bourgeois ideology by breaking down the narrative form ("In Dubious Battle: Literature vs. Ideology"); and Lotringer and Rajchman teased and laid out the foundations for a materialist semiotics based in the new French thought collected in the issue (Lotringer "La politique des restes"; Rajchman "Semiotics, Epistemology and Materialism"). If structuralism was rapidly circumscribing the potential of semiological study by rendering it overly systematic, recent developments in semiotics troubled this trend by identifying the pulsions, politics, subjects, and matters that refused to settle.

Although the subversive potential of semiotics was explored and celebrated in the issue, it is important to acknowledge that, at this initial juncture, the project was nevertheless part of the drive to institutionalize French theory. Part of the appeal of semiotics was that it came from the fringes of the French university – neither Kristeva (part of the Tel Quel group) nor Guattari (an activist and schizoanalyst) had academic positions – but the first issue of *Semiotext(e)* carried the distinction of Columbia University affiliation and support. Not only were four of the seven essays in the issue written by Columbia-affiliated academics (an introduction and article by Lotringer; one from Rajchman, then a graduate student at Columbia; and another from Roudiez, then head of the Department of French), but the journal, of course, came into being out of the Reid Hall lecture series made possible by Columbia's appointment of Lotringer to its Paris campus. As announced in a brief mission statement on the copyright page, the journal was "affiliated with Columbia University."[5] Although semiotics was appealing because it was being operationalized on the fringes of the university in France, as translated by Semiotext(e) for the "Alternatives in Semiotics" issue, semiotics appeared as a subject vying for institutionalization. Although affiliation with Columbia University was dropped, the content for the next three issues ("The Two Saussures" [1974], "Saussure's Anagrams" [1975],

---

5  The full statement of purpose for *Semiotext(e)*'s first issue, entitled *Alternatives in Semiotics*, reads as follows: "*Semiotext(e)* is the organ of a theoretical group exploring alternatives in semiotics. It is affiliated with Columbia University. Its official languages are English and French" (ii).

and "Ego Traps" [1975]) was comparable to the first: original translations and critical analyses of French texts.

## The Schizo-Culture Event: On Madness and Prisons

Picture this philosophical loaf: knead together a little radical psychoanalysis and structuralism, add dollops of Marxism and avant-garde art theory, leaven with violent political activism, then bake to a hard crust in an oven of Freudian dialectics. Now imagine all this gastro-intellectualism taking place in France. Well, believe it or not, the dish you have just visualized is an incredibly popular movement in France that you may have read about called Semiotics. But you don't have to cross the Atlantic to sample this particular brand of French Toast. Some of its most prestigious chefs will be here for "A Colloquium on Schizo-Culture," a three-day slugfest beginning November 13 at Columbia University.

Semiologians Jean-François Lyotard, Gilles Deleuze, Félix Guattari (the R.D. Laing of Gaul) and Michel Foucault will meet head-on with novelist William Burroughs, feminist Ti-Grace Atkinson, musical Dadaist John Cage, and representatives from gay liberation, Ontological Hysterical Theatre, radical therapy organizations, Mental Patients' Liberation, and various prison authorities in assorted workshops and panels. The affair will culminate with a Schizo party on November 16 starring Patti Smith.

Smith and Van Der Horst, *Village Voice*, November 1975

It is difficult to imagine how Lotringer could characterize the Schizo-Culture conference "a miss." The roster that the *Village Voice* notice announced was formidable; even if the Anglo-American world knew nothing at all about the French intellectuals named in the announcement, the "local" talent would have been a draw. William S. Burroughs, whose writings had filled the newspapers of the American underground, had been abroad (in Tangiers, Paris, and London) during the time that his writings served as an integral locus of expression for the movement. He had not yet performed in the United States. Although Patti Smith would release her legendary debut album, *Horses* (whose marathon title track was based on Burroughs's *Wild Boys*), only later in the year, her fame was, by this point, well established; her spoken word performances were turning into the formative snarl of punk rock, setting CBGBs ablaze.

Based largely on New York's Lower East Side, the just-then burgeoning "downtown movement" was fascinated with movements and madness. The inhabitants of the area, many graduates of the fine arts, were studied in avant-garde music and theatre and immersed in the gay and women's liberation movements that developed on New York streets and in the same New York undergrounds that maintained Burroughs's presence in the city while he was overseas. Even if few

New Yorkers were familiar with the French visitors, there were sufficient buzz-words in "structuralism" and "psychoanalysis" to draw in a number of American academics and graduate students who frequented both campus seminars and the downtown scene. As for the transcontinental combination, hindsight certainly renders resonance more readily discernible today, but the markers of overlap were already announced in the *Village Voice*: if semiotics and structuralism were a stretch, that the basis of these French-specific markers had something to do with avant-garde art, madness, and political activism certainly went a long way towards bridging the distance that separated New York from Paris. On the basis of the *Village Voice*'s announcement, along with further promotion for, and con-versation about, the event on Bob Fass's radio show on WBAI,[6] the Schizo-Culture conference drew in 2,000 spectators, a staggeringly successful turnout, especially when compared to the 1966 Johns Hopkins conference, which was considered a sensation with an audience of 150 academics.

Although the constituencies being crossed were by no means incommensu-rable (they *did* resonate), the translation of thought – the movement of culture across substantial barriers (linguistic, geopolitical) – is not immediate. It took a while for structuralism to gain a foothold in the Anglo-American academy, and it is only in hindsight that Jacques Derrida's "Structure, Sign and Play" single-handedly rendered the Johns Hopkins conference a "controversy," marking the birth of post-structuralism at the very moment that structuralism sought entry. The translation of primary texts takes time, as does the assembly of a body of criticism around primary texts and figures. These secondary texts are discourses of legitimation that serve to admit foreign thought into univer-sity presses and journals. Although the encounters Lotringer orchestrated at the conference made sense, the collision of such a diverse set of thinkers, ac-tivists, and artists is not conducive to the production of immediate conver-sation, nor is immediate conversation necessarily desirable, as it could be tantamount to a collapse of differences rather than their productive (and some-times violent) play.

More fundamental than the necessity of delay is the fact that translation is not immediate because it is *mediated*. As was the case with both structuralism

---

6  Although Lotringer states that Jean-Jacques Lebel encouraged people to attend the confer-ence on Bob Fass's radio show and that he staged happenings at the conference ("Doing Theory" 140–1), Lebel denies both of these statements, pointing out that the last happenings he staged were in 1968, and he appeared on Bob Fass's radio show to discuss how political and artistic activists, philosophers, militants, and intellectuals prepared for '68; Lebel did nothing to publicize the Schizo-Culture conference (Lebel, conversation with the author).

and the internationally circulating politics that constituted a global "move-ment" at the turn of the seventies, local inflections are not only lost but re-placed upon mediation. French structuralism in the sixties was produced out of a decades-old tradition of phenomenological thinking, the demise of institu-tional Marxism (particularly as preached by the Parti communiste français), and a crisis in the French university system, whereas, on the other side of the Atlantic, structuralism was very quickly adopted as a possible solution to the crisis in Anglo-American literary criticism within a troubled university. When thought travels, as both Bourdieu (in his work on fields of cultural production) and Said (in his work on travelling theory) make clear, the terms for its contex-tualization are in large part set by the adoptive field.[7]

It is difficult to read the Schizo-Culture conference along field-specific lines because Semiotext(e) had context neither in the university nor on its outside in 1975, rendering the process of locating an adoptive field (even in the vaguest terms) rather futile. Although Lotringer, generally speaking, had been hired to bring semiotics to Columbia, the Schizo-Culture conference did not mark the foundation of a new research centre (like the Johns Hopkins Humanities Center), and it was not backed by a major granting institution (like the Ford Foundation).[8] Although Lotringer was employed by Columbia, the brand of French thought that he ended up importing was a far cry from the textual criti-cism practised by Lotringer's dissertation supervisor, Barthes, and it did not fit

---

7  See, in particular, Bourdieu, "The Field of Cultural Production" and Said, "Travelling Theory."

8  The conference was not funded by a grant or university; the shape the conference took was influenced by a set of chance circumstances. The original impulse for the conference was Guattari's desire to visit the United States, where Lotringer was returning in the fall of 1975 after having spent his first three years with Columbia in Paris. From there, Guattari convinced Deleuze to accompany him (even though Deleuze was averse to travel, given his deteriorating health: it would be his only trip to the United States). Lyotard was already in the United States, having been invited by people associated with the journal *Telos* to give a talk in California on his recent book *Économie libidinale*. Lotringer attended this talk and, at the reception that followed, invited Lyotard to New York. Foucault had just finished a lectureship in Brazil and agreed to a stopover in New York, which would provide him with the opportunity to consult a Jesuit manual on the instruction of children at the New York Public Library (part of his ongoing work on *The History of Sexuality*). Laing was slated to speak in Boston, and, when Lotringer contacted him about the opportunity to meet Foucault, he eagerly accepted the offer. More comfortable than Lotringer in the United States, Rajch-man invited Joel Kovel and Ti-Grace Atkinson, introducing American anti-psychiatry and feminism to the mix. In 1975, Lotringer was already working with John Cage to publish his conversations with Daniel Charles, *Pour les oiseaux,* as the first Semiotext(e) book; Lotringer recalls that the first time he read Cage he thought he was reading Deleuze and Guattari, and therefore thought it appropriate to bring them together at the event. He also

with the profile that Columbia had in mind when they hired him. Lotringer used his office for the Semiotext(e) project, but, with the exception of the first issue of the journal, stated affiliation of Semiotext(e) with Columbia was not allowed: none of Semiotext(e)'s events and publications would ever receive any type of support, funding or otherwise, from the university. Lotringer notes that the administration would not encourage or endorse scholarship that in any way sympathized with, resembled, or rekindled the impulses that had rendered Columbia a volatile and unstable university during the '68 years.[9] In any case, he preferred this arrangement because, in his view, affiliation with the academy carried with it injunctions, instituting strict limits on the movement of discourse and the shapes that discourse might take on in the process of moving ("Agent de l'étranger (foreign agent)" 217). Academic affiliation, in other words, had a tendency to circumscribe the potential of travelling theory.

Beyond differing on the fact of affiliation, the Baltimore and New York conferences were marked by very different approaches to their stated subject matter (Johns Hopkins's "Structuralism" and Schizo-Culture's "Madness and Prisons"). The Johns Hopkins conference was organized in order to import a paradigm. As Macksey and Donato put it, they organized the conference "to explore the impact of contemporary 'structuralist' thought on critical methods and humanistic sciences" and "to stimulate innovations both in the received scholarship and in the training of scholars" (xv–xvi). In 1966, structuralism appeared to carry a fair bit of academic capital in France, a valuation that made it particularly intriguing to the Anglo-American field of literary studies. The Schizo-Culture conference, on the other hand, was organized with the objective of building a bridge between institutions of knowledge (the university and psychiatry in particular) and other communities dealing in deliria (writers, musicians, dramatists, mental patients); it was about collapsing vertical relations between science and object, thinker and artist, theorist and practitioner, and so on, in order to encourage dialogue among conventionally segregated constituencies. As event co-organizer John Rajchman puts it at the end of the *Village Voice* announcement, the event was organized to "allow people who have been

---

saw resonance in the work of Burroughs and Foucault, and he got in touch with Burroughs, who had just returned to the United States after a decade and a half spent in Tangiers, Paris, and London. After his long absence, Burroughs was anxious to develop an audience for his readings in the United States (Lotringer, conversation with the author).

9  Lotringer, conversation with the author.

in touch with various kinds of madness to get in touch with each other. Papers will be presented. And I expect there will be a lot of yelling" (Smith and Van Der Horst 26). Whereas the Johns Hopkins conference related to its subject (structuralism) as a knowledge to be learned, discussed, and, in many cases, paradigmatically applied, for the Schizo-Culture conference, various kinds of *madness* represented instances of, or strategies to, escape from confinement in various kinds of *prisons* – and the academy was one such prison – that organized the public and tempered its impulses.

The chaos that characterized the Schizo-Culture proceedings was in large part due to the difficulty of translating between the individuals and groups presenting and present at the conference. Half a dozen translators attended in order to translate presentations from French to English in real time, but the three that were present for Lyotard's talk, for example, couldn't agree on his meaning.[10] Instead of employing translators for his talk, Deleuze decided to talk slowly and draw diagrams of rhizomes (roots and crab-grass) on the chalkboard, with apparent success. The question of translation, however, runs deeper than the transmission of thought from one language to another: success in conversation requires the location of common ground. Lotringer provided an approximate ground in madness and prisons, terms that meant very different things for those that were present. Further differences and difficulties arise from one of Lotringer's ambitions: to join French thinkers with what remained of the American Left ("Agents de l'étranger" 81). On both sides of the Atlantic, at that very moment, the Left was contending with the end of the sixties in its own way (the sixties, after all, officially ended in America a few months before – on 30 April – with the end of the Vietnam War).

If Americans – particularly the radical culturo-political contingents in New York – "anticipated [the French] without, all the while, knowing who they were" (Lotinger "Agent de l'étranger" 215, my translation), the French participants at the New York conference were only provisionally fluent in the languages and histories of the American underground. While some books by Beat authors and high-profile movement writers such as Eldridge Cleaver and George Jackson were available in translation, most movement writing would have been encountered in the form of pamphlets and Underground Press Syndicate-affiliated magazines like *Actuel* (which carried occasional features

---

10  See Arthur Danto's comments in Charles Bernstein at al.

about, and interviews with, Sartre, Foucault, Lefebvre, Deleuze, and Guattari alongside Weatherman, Valerie Solanis, William S. Burroughs, and the comics of Robert Crumb and Spain Rodriguez).[11] While pamphlets and underground news made the American movement available in France – sometimes even doing the very intriguing work of placing American radicalisms alongside French thinkers[12] – in them, the various facets of the American movement were broken down into digestible bits that obliterated their nuances and divorced them from their contexts.

As noted in chapter 2, Guattari in particular had followed the American movement with some interest; in an early paper on groupuscules, he cited the Weatherman's use of affinity group organization, and he mentioned the American gay and women's liberation movements when defending a special issue of the journal *Recherches*, "Three Billion Perverts" (an "encyclopedia of homosexualities" that was facing obscenity charges in France). Mere citation of the American situation, however, did not denote depth in understanding the mechanics of the various movements. While Guattari's analysis of Weatherman's splitting into alternative families when the organization went underground is accurate and developed along analogous lines to the group's own theorizations,[13] his gloss on the American gay and women's liberation movements is, in the end, somewhat facile and skewed (which is understandable, because the references made in passing were just that, reference for the sake of situating, identifying, and, in this case, defending a correspondent and burgeoning movement in France: the Front homosexuel d'action révolutionnaire).When it came right down to it, however, Guattari was not very well versed in the women's liberation movement in particular, so his passing lip service to the movement at the Schizo-Culture conference, accompanied by his decision to let a band set up in the background during his talk – which would effectively drown out and potentially cancel the Ti-Grace Atkinson talk that was to follow – led to his being booed off the stage by Atkinson's supporters. Guattari was revealed in

---

11  Like Guattari, *Actuel* did not understand the American women's liberation movement, illustrating its coverage of the movement in general, and its translation of Solanis's "SCUM Manifesto" in particular, with cartoons, courtesy of Robert Crumb, of naked women storming through the streets and beating up cops.

12  This being a history of French theory in *America*, I have opted not to analyse the contents of *Actuel* in this book; this is certainly an interesting, important, and rich space for future research that would contribute to further understanding of the French theory-American counter/radical culture assemblage.

13  See "Affinity Groups."

this instance to be a thinker who was out of touch with the very women whom he claimed to support and understand.[14]

It was not always a lack of correspondence and understanding that led to the eruption of conflicts at the New York conference. The chaos that ensued during Foucault's presentations, for example, can be attributed to his tangible involvement with the American movement. During the question period following his presentation, Foucault was accused of being an agent for the CIA by a provocateur who went on in great detail about the affiliations that propped up the GIP at the beginning of the seventies. Lotringer surmises that the provocateur was involved with Lyndon LaRouche's labour committee (Lotringer *Foucault Live* 475; Guattari "Molecular Revolutions" 309 n.1). Whether the LaRouche committee was responsible for the provocation or not, Foucault had already been to New York, and had mobilized in Paris, on behalf of the American prison movement. This was a movement against which the state was organized, and the use of provocateurs during this period was particularly popular.[15] If the purpose of the conference was to conjoin French thought with remnants from the American sixties, groups abounded that had an interest in foiling such an initiative.

After being accused of being an agent for the other side on the first day of the conference, Foucault was mobbed by reporters asking whether the allegations were true, and he spent much of the evening between his presentation and

---

14 Lotringer, conversation with the author. In print form, the break in Guattari's talk is marked by ellipses. See Guattari, "Molecular Revolutions" 276. Chris Kraus's criticism of the white male European desire to instigate change while talking among themselves – in reference to Deleuze, Guattari, Negri, and their various roundtables – is pertinent here. See Kraus, *I Love Dick* 226–7.

15 For accounts of the FBI's COINTELPRO program, the highest profile and most widespread operation that used these tactics, see Blackstock, and Churchill and Wall. The provocation of Foucault is worth investigating further. A Freedom of Information Act request for the FBI's files on the French thinker garnered the release of only five of sixteen pages, all marking Foucault's requests and the granting of visa action requests for travel to the United States over the course of the 1970s. The exclusions are made under section 552, subsections (b) (6) and (b)(7)(C), denoting, in the first case, that they are personal, medical, or similar files whose disclosure "would constitute a clearly unwarranted invasion of privacy" and, in the second, that withheld pages related to "records or information compiled for law enforcement purposes," whose disclosure would also, in this case, constitute an invasion of privacy. Four of the redacted pages were released by U.S. Citizenship and Immigration Services, and were the visa action requests themselves. Foucault's first trip to the United States required a waiver for entry due to his brief membership in the PCF, which provoked a thorough background check. Documents relating to Foucault's 1972 visit – when he remained involved with the GIP – were not released by the FBI or U.S. Citizen and Immigration Services.

the roundtable in concerned solitude, beyond pacification, debating whether he would participate in the roundtable the next day. As far as he was concerned, it did not matter what he said because people would not believe his denials. When confronted during the roundtable the next day, what could not be dispelled in earnest was quickly dispelled with humour: Foucault agreed that everyone involved in the conference, including its organizers, was being paid by the CIA (except for the accuser, that is, who was being paid by the KGB). While Foucault's planned rebuttal calmed the room, he was furious, characterizing the conference as "the last countercultural event of the sixties" (Lotringer *Foucault Live* 475; Guattari "Molecular Revolutions" 309 n.1).

If French and American contingents were foreign to each other, Lotringer, in many ways, was foreign to both. It is important to remember that, much like the French philosophers whom Lotringer invited to New York in 1975, the Columbia professor was not immediately comfortable in the United States. His first three years at Columbia were spent on its Paris campus, and, consequently, the fall of 1975, when the Schizo-Culture conference was organized and took place, marked his return to a country that he had, as yet, only momentarily inhabited. It would take a while for Lotringer to find his footing in what was, for him, a foreign land. If his ambition more specifically was to collect the remnants of the sixties – and, in particular, 1968, very much a feature of the Semiotext(e) project – it was because he had missed 1968 in both countries, doing work with Coopération (the French equivalent of the Peace Corps in which he had enlisted in order to avoid military service in France) in Turkey and Australia. The arrival of French theory, in Lotringer's self-conscious hands, was a process of delicate negotiation; he was invested on either side of the Atlantic, and the encounters he orchestrated between artists, intellectuals, musicians, and writers were acts of creation that filled the void that he missed in both. If we recall Venuti's comment about the utopia of translation in the envisioning of a community on the other end of the translation process, we can certainly see how Lotringer's vision was at least in part a product of his absence from particular places at this juncture in his life.

Controversies and miscalculations aside, it is certainly also worthwhile to consider the chaos that characterized the proceedings to be, at least in part, the product of the conference taking its subject to heart. It is worth arguing, in other words, that "madness" not only determined the shape of the event (the selection of its participants) but it also animated its proceedings, rendering them mad. As Foucault demonstrated in his history of madness, although madness has a historical tendency to be co-opted and defined by institutional interests, it has a history of its own, it speaks for itself; the problem of "madness" is that its audience would rather stifle and contain it than listen. Lotringer characterizes his approach to theory – and the way in which Schizo-Culture enacted the prison-breaking madness it collected – as follows: "The point of a theory … isn't to be something (someone's intellectual property) or belong somewhere (France, Germany, America), *but to become everything it is capable of*" ("Doing Theory" 127, emphasis in original). It is because the constituencies brought together not only refused to converse but, at times, violently clashed, that Lotringer calls the event a miss: it did not "become everything it was capable of." Assessing the event as such, however, ignores the manner in which the event is always outside of itself: it is constituted of a multiplicity of external elements coming together, and it is constituent of the directions that its collected elements might go in light of new encounters.

The Schizo-Culture conference on madness and prisons provided no determinate outcome, only new possibilities. It was an event not because it brought together, once and for all, the definitive constellation in which French theory belonged (and therefore holds the key that is lacking in the edited collections that brought theory in under the banner of post-structuralism); it was an event because it refused the very thing that the Johns Hopkins conference encouraged: to be tangible, to be the advent of something, the arrival or *origin* of "French theory" or "semiotics" (as distinct from "structuralism," "deconstruction," and "post-structuralism") in America. The event, rather, was a flash of productive potential sparked by the meeting of diverse elements. An important point of contrast between the Johns Hopkins and Semiotext(e) events is the lack of collected proceedings, until only recently, for the latter. Although Semiotext(e) put out a "Schizo-Culture" issue in 1978, the contents did not consist of the proceedings but re-enacted the conference by way of the possibilities afforded by print. Some of the proceedings for the conference were scattered about here and there, but, even when essays and roundtables were printed, the contents were suspect.[16] Semiotext(e) did not seek to consecrate

---

16  While Lyotard's "On the Strength of the Weak," Burroughs's "The Limits of Control," and Giorno's "Grasping at Emptiness" are representative of proceedings collected in the *Schizo-Culture* issue, Guattari's "Molecular Revolutions" and "Desire Is Power, Power Is Desire" are collected in *Chaosophy*, and Foucault's "Schizo-Culture: Infantile Sexuality" and the roundtable "Schizo-Culture: On Prisons and Psychiatry" are collected in *Foucault Live*. The circumstances around the publication of the roundtable, however, are particularly telling: when Lotringer asked Laing whether he could publish the transcript in the *Schizo-Culture* issue of the journal, Laing refused. In the process, Lotringer disclosed that the roundtable proceedings were being not only edited but rewritten at liberty for the occasion, and that Laing, who was disappointed with all of his contributions to the roundtable (Laing, Letter to Sylvère Lotringer), should feel free to follow suit (Lotringer, Letters to R.D. Laing, 18 May 1977 and 1 June 1978).

the conference's proceedings by repeating them in print, because the point of the project was always to forge connections with an outside. In other words, it is not what happened at the event that is important, but what the event made – and continues to make – possible.[17] Taking Lotringer's assessment of the conference as a miss at face value, François Cusset concludes, "One can always imagine the encounters that might have taken place between Foucault, Lyotard, or Deleuze and the Americans present" (68). This is exactly what the Semiotext(e) project itself continued to do in the aftermath of the "failed" conference: it brought French and American elements together and forced them to converse.

~~~

INTERLUDE: ON THE ROAD WITH GILLES DELEUZE AND FÉLIX GUATTARI

One of the directions taken by Deleuze and Guattari directly following the conference was a road trip west with Jean-Jacques Lebel, beginning in Lowell, Massachusetts, and ending in southern California.[18] In Lowell, the group caught up with Bob Dylan's Rolling Thunder Review, and Lebel introduced the French philosophers to the American singer and to Allen Ginsberg (Ginsberg was opening

---

17  A similar argument could be made about some of the first issues produced by the group. The Schizo-Culture conference would mark Semiotext(e)'s most discernible turn in 1975, but it was not the first conference that the group sponsored. Inspired by Lotringer's work on Saussure's anagrams in Genevan archives, Lotringer organized a conference, "The Two Saussures," in spring 1974. The papers would be collected in the following two issues of *Semiotext(e)*. Presented by some of the earliest interrogators of structuralism in America – Peter Caws, Michael Riffaterre, Wlad Godzich – the volume begins with papers that introduce Saussure's course before moving onto his anagrams. At the centre of the issue, Lotringer reproduces some of the anagram work that he collected from Saussure's archives. The anagrams act as a bridge between the two halves of the journal issue, entitled "Saussure's Course" and "Saussure's Curse," respectively. In his introduction to the issue, Jean Starobinski calls the conference a "confrontation," stating that, if there are two Saussures, there is a difference to note, "and Saussure is the first to teach us that differences are productive" ("et Saussure est le premier à nous enseigner que les différences sont productives") (5, my translation).

18  Although Deleuze was scheduled to speak at the University of California, San Diego on the invitation of Fredric Jameson, the group made it only as far as San Francisco, more interested in taking in gay film in the Castro district than fulfilling their remaining academic engagements funded by France Culture (Denis Hollier, conversation with the author, and Fredric Jameson, conversation with the author).

Dylan's shows at the time with his singing of mantras); in Berkeley, the French philosophers took in a Patti Smith concert; and in San Francisco they met Michael McLure and Lawrence Ferlinghetti at City Lights Bookstore before staying at Ferlinghetti's Bixby Canyon cabin in Big Sur. The trip, then, began at Kerouac's burial site and ended at the site where he wrote two of his books. A photograph that Lebel took of Deleuze sitting cross-legged on the beach at Big Sur adorns the cover of the Semiotext(e) collection *Desert Islands and Other Texts*.

Although mention of the American writers in Deleuze and Guattari's texts is limited, references to Cage, Burroughs, Ginsberg, Kerouac, and other American writers, artists, and activists were commonplace in Guattari's conversations with Lebel, as the latter notes, and the work of contemporary American writers – Kerouac in particular – was often featured in Deleuze's weekly seminars at Vincennes and St. Denis. American writing is given a prominent place in the work of Deleuze and Guattari in the immediate aftermath of their 1975 excursion to the United States. As noted in chapter 2, in the "Rhizome" chapter that opens *A Thousand Plateaus* (published on its own in 1976, four years before the publication of the completed project), Deleuze and Guattari argue that "America is a special case," noting the way that its literatures, "beatnicks, the underground, bands and gangs," are not about a search for roots; they follow "the route of the American rhizome" (19). Citing Kerouac and Patti Smith (who "sings the bible of the American dentist: don't go for the root, follow the canal" [19]) alongside Miller, Fitzgerald, and Whitman, they note that the American propensity is to seek an outside, pushing through the frontier. These tendencies make America a special, rhizomatic case. A year later, in his collaboration with Claire Parnet, Deleuze praises Anglo-American literature for its featuring of "ruptures," "lines of flight," and its treatment of frontiers as "something to cross" (36–7), and he quotes a Bob Dylan lyric from his 1974 *Writings and Drawings* at length, stating that "[a]s a teacher I should like to be able to give a course as Dylan organizes a song, as astonishing producer rather than author" (Deleuze and Parnet 8). Deleuze contrasts the work of American writers and artists with the structuralist moment in France, which, in contradistinction, "is a system of points and positions, which are supposedly significant instead of proceeding by thrusts and crackings. It warps the lines of flight instead of following them and tracing them, and extending them into a social field" (Deleuze and Parnet 37). Coming in the interim between *Anti-Oedipe* and *Mille plateaux*, the American excursion helped Deleuze and Guattari to develop their thinking about the rhizome, from the drawing of diagrams on Columbia's Teacher's College blackboard during the Schizo-Culture conference to a roadtrip from east to west, pushing through the American frontier with significant encounters along the way. Deleuze's characterization of French structuralism was not all that distinct from the movement of Anglo-American criticism and its appropriation of French thought at the time; the conference and road trip were something different altogether.

The encounters that Lebel staged were intentional, and some would prove enduring, like the friendship between Guattari and Ginsberg, who became more profoundly acquainted when trapped in a storm with Lebel en route to a reception for Burroughs in New York. The city at a standstill, the three of them got stoned and listened to jazz on the radio for hours. Ginsberg and Guattari would remain in contact, Ginsberg seeking Guattari's assistance when splitting up with a violent Orlofsky, and Ginsberg twice participating in Lebel's three-month long "Monument à Félix Guattari" at the Beaubourg museum. In the corner of one of Lebel's letters to Ginsberg is a note from Guattari: "Cher Allan [sic], Tu es une de mes raisons de vivre. Tendresse, Félix." (Lebel, Letter).

In the end, I do not mean to suggest that the New York trip of 1975 was responsible for bringing Deleuze and Guattari in contact with American literature, but, considering the timing and constitution of their essay on the rhizome and Deleuze's conversations with Claire Parnet, the conference and road trip had a discernible impact on their theorization of the rhizome. As Deleuze makes clear at the outset of his book of conversations with Parnet, although he was writing with Guattari at the time, his interactions with the thought and work of many of his closest friends and companions – Foucault, Jean-Pierre Bamberger, and Fanny Deleuze – had a profound impact on the flow of his own thinking. Where Anglo-American literature is concerned, a constant influence – cited in *Dialogues II* for her work on D.H. Lawrence's turtles and therefore Deleuze's thinking about animal-becomings (Deleuze and Parnet 10–11) – was Fanny, who was a translator of Lawrence's texts and a scholar of American literature. References to literary works are scattered throughout Gilles Deleuze's books, not only in *Logic of Sense*, his study on Sacher-Masoch, and *Essays Critical and Clinical*. As he points out, literary works were particularly useful to the study of schizophrenia because the authors of literary work seemed to know more about schizophrenia than did psychiatrists and psychoanalysts (Deleuze and Guattari "On *Anti-Oedipus*" 23). In the context of their theorization of schizophrenia, this makes complete sense, because schizophrenia is inherently productive: it creates. Deleuze and Guattari's 1975 road trip was not a determinate encounter with literature as such but a rhizomatic experience constituted of lines of flight away from scheduled academic engagements. Deleuze and Guattari travelled from the East Coast to the West, and they carried with them the intensive points encountered in between.

While Deleuze and Guattari were fascinated by, and became translators of, American countercultures and political subcultures, this does not mean that their work was more suited for translation into this domain. City Lights was originally commissioned in 1976 to translate and publish Deleuze and Guattari's "Rhizome" and "Balance Program for Desiring Machines" – which, Robert Hurley (who offered to translate the texts when it became apparent that Mark Seem, the preferred translator, would be unavailable) pointed out, would not be included as an appendix in his forthcoming translation of *Anti-Oedipus* for Viking – but Lebel, commissioned to write the introduction, never finished the piece. Lebel's road trip with Deleuze and Guattari in 1975 was cited as the reason that Lebel had been chosen to write the introduction (City Lights Books, letter). Although City Lights staffers found Deleuze and Guattari's work "fascinating" and were shocked that it had not yet been translated (Peters, letter, August 1976), they felt that the translation of their work would be a worthless project without an introduction. In a letter to Lebel, Nancy Peters from City Lights explains that Ferlinghetti felt that their technical academic style was more suited to engaged philosophers and psychologists than City Lights's American countercultural readership (and Ferlinghetti was violently opposed to much of the academic rhetorical style of French writing). It was thus necessary, in the publisher's estimation, that Lebel provide an introduction that would situate the work of Deleuze and Guattari, explaining its significance. Lebel's task as translator was to act as a mediator between the French authors and the American counterculture (Peters, letter, 25 March 1977). Ferlinghetti's prediction that Lebel was too busy with his activist commitments to write the introduction would prove right. That Semiotext(e) would publish "Rhizome" in one of its first little black books (*On the Line*) does not simply demonstrate that Lotringer was less concerned or aware of a mismatch between French theory and the American counterculture, it is instead further indication of Lotringer's utopic thinking: whereas City Lights was a publisher of the American counterculture with an established readership, Semiotext(e) was the publisher that envisioned a new community that would assemble around the meeting French and American thought, politics, and culture. While City Lights considered whether Deleuze and Guattari's work would prove to be an appropriate consumable for its audience, Lotringer – very much in line with Deleuze and Guattari's road trip, or the collaborations produced by Deleuze, Guttari, and Parnet – desired to bring different constituencies into conversation.

∽≎∽

## Conversational Theory: Producing the Common

[T]he common is what is always at stake in any conversation: there where a conversation takes place, there the common expresses itself; there where we are in common, there and only there is a conversation possible. Conversation is the language of the common.

Cesare Casarino, "Surplus Common"

In the introduction to *Hatred of Capitalism*, a volume written to mark the end of the Semiotext(e) project (when, really, it was just a new beginning: the project continues under the umbrella of MIT, its new distributor after a falling out with Autonomedia), Lotringer notes that he conducted a lot of interviews throughout the Semiotext(e) project because he wanted theory to "have a direct impact … [to] be grasped as naturally as you breathe" (Kraus and Lotringer 16). When collaborator Chris Kraus goes on to call Lotringer's approach "conversational theory," Lotringer agrees with the term, adding that, beyond the interviews, pieces were put into conversation by surrounding them with other things until they "became part of something more fluid and couldn't be isolated. Documents, images, quotes, ideas being part of some kind of movement that takes you from one thing to the next, and changes everything about the world" (16). The *Semiotext(e)* journal underwent a profound transformation in the aftermath of the Schizo-Culture conference. If the theory that the project was importing was to have a "direct impact" on anything, it was necessary that it not be contained, isolated from the elements with which contact might be desirable or intriguing. *Semiotext(e)* would not be doing much towards the ends of making connections if its contents continued to consist of essays by and about the new French thought, making foreign ideas – sometimes translated, sometimes not – available to an American audience. If the Schizo-Culture conference was organized in order to encourage conversation across various boundaries, the journal proceeded in its aftermath to break down the barriers that kept otherwise intriguingly resonant elements apart at the three-day event. The transformation of the journal did not occur all at once; it changed gradually over the course of four issues. I break this section down into four subsections, following the trajectory that the post–Schizo-Culture issues of the journal trace through the late seventies. In so doing, I wish to delineate how the potential of the Schizo-Culture conference was projected through the journal, culminating in the "Schizo-Culture" issue in 1978. I follow this process of becoming in this section because it foregrounds a politics of translation: a way of doing theory and of producing a common.

### Signalling Downtown

Whereas the initial issues of the journal were devoted primarily to subversions of Saussurean linguistics, the "Georges Bataille" issue that directly followed the conference marked a departure into another kind of semiotics, one that exceeded the restricted economy of the Saussurean sign: an erotics of signification, the accursed share. Because Bataille's semiotics is already fundamentally about exceeding limits, his work does not require the same type of subversive treatment that the journal had enacted against Saussure (splitting him in two – the Saussure of the course in general linguistics and the Saussure of the anagrams – and taking him apart from there by subjecting him to his own madness). As a result of its devotion to a single thinker, the issue does not do much more than provide a case for taking Bataille seriously, each essay situating him among his kin in a growing philosophical canon (Derrida, Kristeva, Hegel, Heidegger, Nietzsche, Schelling); this is a rather restricted economy. That the conference did not appear to have all that much of an impact on the subsequent Bataille issue is not at all surprising: the issue was planned well in advance of the conference, and it was edited by a board member, Hollier, who did not attend the 1975 convention but who was associated with Semiotext(e) through Reid Hall, where he had given lectures on Bataille.

Although the issue does not carry the characteristics of the more radical departures to come, its cover was an important marker of forthcoming changes. Courtesy of Gil Eisner, a satirical cartoonist who did work for *Newsweek*, the *New York Times*, and the *Washington Post*, the cover boasts a giant guillotine hovering menacingly over Place de la Concorde. The promise of an essay by Derrida ("A Hegelian without Reserves") on the cover – Derrida officially arrived at Yale in 1975 – was a marker of academic capital. For the swelling group of American scholars working on the new French thought, Derrida was not only at the forefront but a step beyond the pack (and by now the most American of the group). However, that the cover boasted the work of Eisner also contributed to its being the first issue to come to the attention of the New York art community, a downtown scene graduated from New York's fine arts programs, many of whom had flocked uptown for the Schizo-Culture conference in 1975. In spite of the relatively academic presentation of the journal – translations of Bataille alongside interpretations provided by certified experts – the Eisner graphic acted as a signifier that the journal belonged downtown.[19]

---

19 Lotringer, conversation with the author. The issue is also notable in that it subtly marks the beginning of a more self-conscious approach to the process of translation. Hollier's introduction to the volume speaks of "franglas" (sic), recognizing the impossibility of a perfect fit when moving Bataille from one language and tradition to another, and opting to maintain and play within the space that imperfect transposition affords ("Présentation?"). Bataille's "Hemingway in Light of Hegel" (an American-German affair translated from Bataille's French to American English) continues this play. In this sense, the journal is beginning to demonstrate a self-consciousness that later collections would pointedly produce.

### Project(ion) for a Revolution in New York

When Lotringer retook the helm for the next issue on *Anti-Oedipus*, Semio-text(e) did not exactly leap headlong into a politics of madness, but it did begin, in earnest, its venture in print into the regions explored at the 1975 conference, particularly by continuing to build bridges of the type that the conference had attempted. With the *"Anti-Oedipus"* issue, Lotringer continued his quest to bring French thought and American art together, believing that they had a lot in common. If the Schizo-Culture conference was a failed attempt at staging conversations (as opposed to the sometimes violent encounters that ensued, suggesting incommensurability), Lotringer used the *Semiotext(e)* journal as a means to continue to build the bridges necessary for French and American constituencies to converse.

Like the cover of the "Georges Bataille" issue that preceded it, the *"Anti-Oedipus"* issue was adorned with a cartoon drawn by Gil Eisner, indicating an attempt to build a bridge between the academy and artists but also a bridging of temporal and spatial gaps more broadly. While the previous issue's image was of the guillotine (a dated, relatively distant image evoking the French Revolution), the *"Anti-Oedipus"* issue is adorned by an image that was much more proximate: a troupe of baton-wielding riot police leading a hurried, ordered march with a paddy-wagon in tow. Second, the image bridges a spatial gap: whereas the guillotine of the Bataille issue is nation-bound, the image of the henchmen on the *"Anti-Oedipus"* cover is as American as it is French. The brimmed helmets, slouched posture, and shadowed demeanour of the riot squad might call to mind the graphics of May '68 in France, but the scene was also familiar in the United States, iconic even, broadcast across the nation from the 1968 Democratic National Convention in Chicago. In this sense, the graphic plays the part of transatlantic bridge, but in a more specific way still: if we are thinking in terms of the project's place in New York, the graphic is also a bridge between Columbia and its outside, the Lower East Side community in particular, where Columbia's Students for a Democratic Society and *RAT Subterranean News* were stationed in 1968, producing the movement that drew the paddy wagons onto campus in April 1968.

The Eisner graphic's work does not end with the cover itself; the Paris-New York/Columbia-outside bridge is repeated when the cover is flipped open. On the inside cover page is a picture of a lone protestor throwing a cobblestone down a street. Although the photograph was most likely taken in France, there are no discernible markers of place. The image, in fact, captures the very act that I used to bridge New York and Paris in chapter 1: it is worth recalling, here, that the action of launching cobblestones in the environ and immediate aftermath of Columbia quoted the uprisings in France (a continuation of the struggle, a refusal to allow state oppression on campus to distract the movement from continuing to mobilize around the larger-than-campus issues that were at play in the respective revolts in the first place).

Though much closer to New York in 1977 than to the French Revolution, it should be noted that the image still comes quite late – almost a decade after 1968 – especially considering that its context is the aftermath of a conference dubbed by Foucault to be the last countercultural event of the sixties. In response to this problem, the caption beneath the photograph compels: "Beneath the beach, the paving stones ..." The Paris '68 slogan is altered, rendered in reverse, with "*pavé*" and "*plage*" switching places: throwing cobblestones, the caption points out, is not the same as it used to be. If the lifting of cobblestones marked an intervention against the march of modernity, a revelation of the smooth sand beneath modernity's rigid roads, the reversed quote suggests that the beach uncovered will always be fleeting; there are always more cobblestones buried beneath. As Lotringer explains in his introduction to the volume, "the events in France have proven that revolution is possible in even a highly industrialized capitalist society. But they shouldn't be hailed as another ready-made model to be followed blindly. For even May '68 can become Oedipal" ("Libido Unbound: The Politics of Schizophrenia" 9). The question, then, remains: if the point is not to repeat Paris (or Columbia), then why did the issue stage the provocative launching on its cover?

A closer look at the positioning of the protester provides the answer to this question. Rather than suggesting a repetition of the clash between protestor and police, as per 1968, something different is at play. That the target of the projectile is beyond the horizon of the image might have signified that the target was on the front cover (the cobblestone being launched at the approaching riot police), but the protestor is turned away from the approaching henchmen, launching his cobblestone *into* the text rather than back at the cover just passed (which it is, in effect, ahead of). The squad and protestor are moving in *the same direction*, future-oriented, pointed into the depths of the text, and the issue(s) to come.

This type of movement has everything to do with the direction that the subtitle of the volume signposts: "From Psychoanalysis to Schizopolitics." If the issue is extending the Schizo-Culture conference, it makes sense that *Anti-Oedipus* is the subject matter: the conference, after all, was the result of Lotringer's friendship with Guattari, sparked by his fascination with *Anti-Oedipe*, which had just been published in 1972, and coinciding with his return to Paris to organize seminars. Guattari, who was not an academic, was a regular lecturer among a revolving stream of speakers at Reid Hall, and Lotringer spent

4.1 Front cover of *Semiotext(e)* "*Anti-Oedipus*" issue, vol. 2, no. 3, 1977.

much of a year of leave in 1973 working with him on *Recherches* and at La Borde.[20] While schizopolitics, a Guattarian invention, was very much a practice that was extra-academic, one might consider André Lefevere's point about the sharing of authority in translation, a process whereby authority is both bestowed and usurped (*Translating Literature* 122–5). In having his work translated into English by a Columbia-affiliated professor, Guattari is given authority and academic legitimacy; likewise, Lotringer usurps authority by saying what he wants to say about anti-institutional (and, ironically, anti-authoritarian) politics in America in other people's names.[21]

---

20   On the relationship between Lotringer and Guattari, see also Kraus, *Torpor* 91–111.

21   As Chris Kraus puts it in her semi-fictional novel *Torpor*, Lotringer, named Jerome in her work, was a "carrier of fame. The famous didn't always have time to network for themselves, they needed someone like Jerome. Respected, well credentialed, he was a courtier who, while bearing messages between cultural celebrities in Berlin, New York, London and Paris, appeared to have a mission of his own" (165–6).

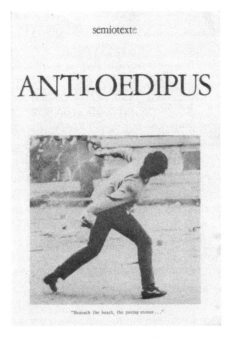

semiotext

# ANTI-OEDIPUS

"Beneath the beach, the paving stones..."

4.2 Inside cover of *Semiotext(e) "Anti-Oedipus"* issue, vol. 2, no. 3, 1977.

In "Libido Unbound: The Politics of Schizophrenia," which serves as an introduction to the volume, Lotringer lays out the terms according to which *Anti-Oedipus* marks a move away from psychoanalysis; it is not only a departure from Freud but also from structuralism and linguistics. While structuralism and linguistics had explicitly advocated a return to Freud via Lacan, they were, more generally and significantly, the same strain of virus: they boasted similar traits and consequences as Oedipus – castration and the unconscious. The two paradigms were apparati for the location and determination of "incontrovertible scientific truths," which produced "pure knowledge reserved strictly for techno-academics" (5). If Lotringer was attempting to build a bridge between continents, it was not for the continued importation of structuralism. Semiotext(e), at this juncture, becomes a project determined to prevent French thought from becoming entrapped within disciplinary prisons that would inhibit the productive potential of its madness.[22]

---

22  While, up until that moment, the statement of purpose listed the divisions of knowledge within which Semiotext(e) was scouring for alternatives, the project, at that point, situated

Lotringer believed that French thought was more suited to, and was even ultimately about, the United States and not its native France. After two short paragraphs of general introduction – explaining what schizopolitics is moving from – Lotringer offers the following heading as a point of entry: "Project for a Revolution in New York" ("Libido Unbound" 5). Whereas Sartre was "the uneasy bedfellow of bureaucratic socialism," a national presence, Deleuze and Guattari, Lotringer proposes, "[turn] somewhat paradoxically towards the United States for another possible face of revolution" (6). "The gamble of *Anti-Oedipus*," Lotringer argues, "is to reformulate revolutionary perspectives from the strong points, and the weak links, of capitalism. No longer moving against the grain, but rather pushing the logic of Kapital further than it ever allowed itself to be led – to its breaking point" (6).[23] In this passage, Lotringer explains not only why schizopolitics is particularly suited to America, but also why the police and protestor on the front and inside cover are running in the same direction: it is not about being against the oppressors pictured on the cover. Instead, there is something to be said about what might be achieved by running with them (or, being just a step ahead, evading apparati of capture). In this we see Deleuze's Nietzsche and the predilection towards active rather than reactive forces, or, to use an American example – as Deleuze and Guattari often do – George Jackson's directive to flee but to grab a weapon in the process.

If Semiotext(e)'s ambition was to build bridges for conversation and not just inroads for a new knowledge, the contents of this issue of the journal, like those of the Bataille issue, ring rather monophonic. Because the journal is devoted to *Anti-Oedipus*, the contents consist mostly of writings by Deleuze and Guattari, written together and apart, as well as early reviews of, and essays about, their work. While the essays provide an important – and rather conversational, as many of the pieces are interviews – foundation in the politics of schizophrenia (as argued by Deleuze and Guattari), the journal is not yet really *doing* the

---

itself outside of these divisions, assuming a critical distance from the university altogether: the project became the "self-supporting journal of a group analyzing the power mechanisms which produce and maintain the present divisions of knowledge (Psychoanalysis, Linguistics, Literature, Philosophy and Semiotics)" (Lotringer, "*Anti-Oedipus*" 2). That semiotics is included in this list is significant, as it was the very signifier that distinguished *Semiotext(e)* from other ventures into the recent work of French thinkers. This line of inquiry, beginning with the "*Anti-Oedipus*" issue, is as suspect as the other domains listed in the project statement.

23  In "Enurgumen Capitalism" Jean-François Lyotard argues that "what [*Anti-Oedipus*] subverts most profoundly" – above and beyond psychoanalysis – "is what it doesn't *criticize*: Marxism" (11).

politics that it is carrying over. If the journal was trying to push beyond ego traps, it was not going to achieve the feat by publishing issues on Bataille and Deleuze and Guattari.

## *What Happens between the Two: A New York Reel*

It was the next issue, "Nietzsche's Return," which began to break through the wall of exclusivity that the conference had so explicitly challenged. Rather than just including essays by French thinkers along with responses to their work by a select number of American scholars, the issue includes a conversation between John Cage and Daniel Charles, a short series of paragraphs that interpret Nietzsche as "The Dancing Philosopher" by New York dancer-choreographer-writer Kenneth King, and work by New York artists Selena Whitefeather, Jose Urbach, and Marim Avillez. All of the pieces engage Nietzsche: King literally makes Nietzsche dance, choreographing him into a "Dionysian frenzy" where "[d]ancing is pure *becoming*" (22, emphasis in original); Whitefeather diagrams the becoming of paramecia; Urbach contributes a drawing of Nietzsche's face, mustache protruding, in the top-right corner of every odd-numbered page so that when the book is flipped, Nietzsche's head goes spinning; and Avillez contributes a comic strip depicting Nietzsche's incestuous relationship with his sister, all of the dialogue provided from Nietzsche's *My Sister and I*, written while Nietzsche was confined to a nursing home in 1890.

A key aspect of the project was the way that it staged conversations, working against the impulse and tendency to fall into ego traps. The Cage/Charles offering is notable and worth pause. The conversation works by breaking down the ego, not only in terms of the way that Cage talks about his use of chance operations (which he uses to determine his performances and poetry) but because the author of Cage's responses to Charles was not always John Cage. As Cage points out in a short (split-column) introduction to the conversation proper, tapes of his conversations with Charles "had been damaged or lost or inadvertently erased, so it had sometimes been necessary for Daniel Charles to compose my responses to his questions" (24). Although much of the conversation was unrecognizable to Cage when he read the galleys, he decided that the manuscript should be published as it was, a co-production between Cage and Charles. The distance between Cage and his words is even further compounded in the *Semiotext(e)* printing: although the conversations between Cage and Charles were conducted in English, the book from which the conversation is extracted for reprinting in the journal was originally published in French, and because the tapes and transcripts had since vanished, the work had to be translated back into its original English for publication.

Cage's gesture – allowing the text to be published without editorial changes, setting thoughts free – was a very Nietzschean one. Assessing the significance of Nietzsche's contribution to philosophy in the essay that precedes the Cage/ Charles conversation, Deleuze describes Nietzsche as a philosopher who "has claimed for himself and his readers, present and future, a certain right to *misinterpretation* ("Nomad Thought" 12, emphasis added). As Cage notes at the end of the introduction to the conversation, he felt that ideas should be allowed to "live their own lives. They are certain to change in certain, unpredictable ways whenever someone takes the time to use them" (24). Although Cage and Charles do not mention Nietzsche explicitly in their conversation, Deleuze's preceding piece, "Nomad Thought," a paper delivered at a 1964 conference on the question of "Nietzsche Today," argues that the Nietzschean today is not simply "the scholar preparing a paper on Nietzsche" but anyone who "in the course of an action, of a passion, of an experience, willingly or unwillingly, produces singularly Nietzschean utterances" (13). Hence the title of Deleuze's presentation ("Nomad Thought"): what Nietzsche celebrates is the movement of thought, and never its framing.

If I am arguing that what is notable about *Semiotext(e)* is the way that it stages conversations, then reading the way that New York pieces are placed in the journal is as significant as what those pieces, in themselves, have to say. The question that I am ultimately asking of the journal after all is how are Parisian thought and New York art put in relation to one another? How does Lotringer's project bring out those things that Paris and New York have in common? If the journal was "doing theory," how was the journal put to work? Although the "Nietzsche's Return" issue is predominantly devoted to translations of French essays (by Bataille, Deleuze, Derrida, Foucault, Lyotard) and contributions by members of the editorial board (by Hollier, Lotringer, Rajchman), it is a piece from New York that ties the issue together. The piece in question is Urbach's spinning Nietzsche head, which begins about a third of the way into the book, weaving New York through the volume. Urbach's heads are like graffitied tags along the volume's seam. When flipped, the tags not only make Nietzsche reel in the margins of the text, they also become a New York reel, a projection of New York through the "French Nietzschean" scene.

The point of the Semiotext(e) project was not for American art to become the fodder of French theory in America but to bring out the elements that French theory and American art had in common. As James Leigh says in his introduction to the volume, "Semiotext(e) demands more than a right to *misinterpretation* (Deleuze); it asserts *sovereign multiplicity*" (10, emphasis in original). If the sovereign represents the centre of a regime, at centre of the Semiotext(e) project, according to Leigh's introduction, is multiplicity.

4.3 Front cover of *Semiotext(e)* "Nietzsche's Return issue, vol. 3, no. 1, 1978.

The right to misinterpret becomes the rule when the sovereign centre is inherently multiple. To strip the sovereign of its singularity is to remove the index that determines relations between all points in a regime of signs, allowing them to converse more freely. The index that Semiotext(e) removed was not only that of the philosopher Nietzsche (as the volume's inclusion of the Cage/Charles piece in particular demonstrates, reference to Nietzsche was not required for inclusion), but also the index that would give critic dominion over artist (with his or her expert status and special interpretive powers) or restrict a writing to its nation (not French theory for France, but for America, and not America as itself, but as that which continually pushes past itself, through its frontiers).

While a levelling out is at play in this process, it is not a levelling of differences. As Casarino points out, *conversation* is not the same as sublation (or, the assimilation and stifling of the other, of difference). Conversation is "that language that brings us together as different from rather than identical to one another" 2). As opposed to monologue or even dialogue (which, in spite of the polyphonic possibilities opened up by Bakhtin, remains bogged down by its Platonic connotations and the liberal-democratic discourse that invokes the term to characterize negotiations that proceed by "reconciling differences"), conversation not only acknowledges differences between the sides coming together but also moves according to these unassimilable differences. To include John Cage in a collection of French theory is not to use French concepts to explain Cage, or vice versa. As Deleuze and Parnet put it, conversation is "simply the outline of a becoming"; it is what passes *between the two*, the orchid *and* the wasp, an "a-parallel evolution of two beings that have nothing whatsoever to do with each other" (2–3). Semiotext(e) was French theory *and* New York: encounters were staged between American artists and French theorists that would bring out currents that they already had in common. Rather than outlining the common as an answer to some prefigured question or puzzle, the common is treated as a line of flight, a moment of double-capture, pulling something away from either side in order to move elsewhere.

### Bounces, Signals, Jumps, and Clicks

While the "Nietzsche's Return" issue marked a weaving of New York through French theory – with its inclusion of Cage and American art – Semiotext(e)'s "Schizo-Culture" issue, published later in the year, was a definitive break with the tendency to sublate rather than converse. Shortly after the Schizo-Culture conference took place, the journal's editorial collective – comprising Lotringer alongside graduate students who were getting jobs on other campuses – began to disperse. The "Schizo-Culture" issue marked the recomposition of an editorial collective that would from that point on be fluid, and that comprised downtown artists rather than uptown academics.[24] Although Lotringer was the

---

24 Lotringer's first impression of New York came in the form of shows at CBGBs and the Mudd Club, where the punk, new wave, and no wave movements were taking shape downtown. Beyond the clubs, an arts movement was thriving: painters, writers, and film-makers taking advantage of the relatively low rent in the rundown neighbourhoods of the city's Lower East Side. The collective comprised a number of artists whom Lotringer met upon moving downtown, and film-makers to whom he was teaching Lacan (film-makers interested in the bridge Christian Metz built between psychoanalysis and film with his *Imaginary Signifier*), but who had enrolled in university primarily so that they could use its film equipment. Lotringer thus became involved with a group of downtown artists that was perpetually in flux and that would ultimately become the journal's editorial collective. He shared a studio with Diego Cortez for four years, and it was this relationship that granted Lotringer access to a wide array of downtown artists. Despised as widely as he was admired, Cortez was referred to as the "king of clubs"; he could get access anywhere and was something of

special editor of the issue, the issue released was the result of collective efforts. Rather than having the editor assume a central role in the organization of the issue, each member of the collective was responsible for a series of pages. The volume was also the first to forgo the convention of stapling an introduction to the beginning of an issue: the pieces are allowed to converse without overarching directives. If Leigh characterized the preceding issue as being directed by "sovereign multiplicity," the collectivization of editorial processes ensured that the "Schizo-Culture" issue would be constructed with multiplicity at its centre.

As noted above, the "Schizo-Culture" issue did not reprint the proceedings of the event whose name it carried but instead performed the themes and overlaps that the conference had been organized to raise. Although New York artists appeared in the previous issue, they had been relegated to the margins; they were the exception in a journal that was, as a rule, devoted to French thought. The "Schizo-Culture" issue, on the other hand, was more American than it was French, featuring essays, poetry, and manifestoes by William S. Burroughs, Kathy Acker, John Cage, John Giorno, and Richard Foreman. Nothing distinguished these pieces from those by Deleuze, Foucault, and Lyotard. Columns divided most of the pages (mimicking the popular characterization of schizophrenia as a simple split in personality), meaning that French and American pieces were literally run side by side with a typeface so similar that it was inevitable that one would read across variously arranged barriers in the process

---

a scout whose association with people and events was a marker of their being significant and of the moment. It was through Cortez that Lotringer met Kathy Acker (Cortez collaborated with Acker for her performances at the Kitchen, a performance space that fostered the downtown literary scene). Lotringer and Acker became very close and shared an apartment for a time at the end of the seventies. Acker discusses the influence of their conversations about Deleuze, Guattari, and Foucault in "Devoured by Myths" (10) and *Don Quixote* (54–5), and Chris Kraus weaves Lotringer's and Acker's conversations about theory throughout *After Kathy Acker*. Consider, as well, the appearance of Deleuze and Guattari, unattributed, in Acker's 1978 novel *Blood and Guts in High School*:

EVERY POSITION OF DESIRE, NO MATTER HOW SMALL, IS CAPABLE OF PUTTING TO QUESTION THE ESTABLISHED ORDER OF A SOCIETY; NOT THAT DESIRE IS ASOCIAL; ON THE CONTRARY. BUT IT IS EXPLOSIVE; THERE IS NO DESIRING MACHINE CAPABLE OF BEING ASSEMBLED WITHOUT DEMOLISHING ENTIRE SOCIAL SECTIONS. (125)

This passage comes towards the end of the novel, as Acker tries to escape with Genet, the thief, in an escapade of plagiarism and improvisation, assembling a desiring machine that calls into question the fundamental structures of capitalism.

of reading each piece.[25] As Lotringer writes in a letter to Allen Ginsberg, soliciting a contribution for the issue (and calling American writing the equivalent of post-'68 radical French thought), "By *Schizo*-Culture, we don't mean, of course, the end-product of institutional repression or social controls of all kinds, but the process of becoming, the flow of creative energy unchecked by ego boundaries: body intensity, affirmative, revolutionary disposition" (Lotringer, Letter to Allen Ginsberg).[26] In this sense, the bleeding of columns into one another was a crucial gesture in the layout: the intensities represented in each piece could not be contained, and the layout was responsible for either attempting to frame these unframable pieces or laying them out in the open and allowing them to move more freely among one another. In this way, both editorial procedure and layout were set to work in the issue as "creative energy" released from the compression of the ego.

The point of the journal was not simply to favour madness over normality but to point out that everything was madness and that it was a matter of strategically channelling flows as opposed to staging a simple war against institutions. As Foucault points out at the end of an interview about Bentham's panopticon that opens the issue, although it might be desirable for inmates to take over the observation tower in Bentham's structure, it would make a difference only if this occupation were temporary, as things would not really be all that different if inmates and guards simply switched places ("The Eye of Power" 19). French Nietzscheanism puts the dialectic to rest and puts its stakes into active as opposed to reactive forces. As the issue demonstrates with its inclusion of ads for psychiatric drugs and exposés written by psychiatrists, various agents and enclosures are employed to repress those desires that exceed normal functioning, but these institutionally sanctioned procedures are as mad as those impulses that they seek to repress (we get this from the beginning in the form of the graffitied word "Schizo" that runs over top of stock market readouts on the cover of the issue). It is not a matter of simply switching social stations but of understanding relations so as to be able to move strategically through them.

---

25  Considering the overlap in concerns and strategies, it is worth noting that the "Schizo-Culture" journal was supposed to be launched – or at least made available – at the same time as Burroughs's and Gysin's launch of *The Third Mind* at the Nova convention co-organized by Semiotext(e). The collective, however, was a bit behind schedule in its preparation of the journal.

26  Ginsberg did not provide a piece for the journal but would participate in the Nova convention in late 1978.

It is precisely this type of strategic movement that characterized Lotringer's project. Because theory often tended to obscure the creative flows about which it spoke, Lotringer employed theory conversationally. As artists became drawn to the project in the aftermath of the Schizo-Culture conference, Lotringer moved downtown and took the opportunity to converse with the artists that he believed shared affinities with the French philosophers whom he had been hired to import. The point was not to assimilate New York, to explain it away with theory, but to locate and feature points of overlap and lines of escape. In the absence of an introduction for the "Schizo-Culture" issue, an obscure performer called Police Band – who improvised with violin and voice over top of real-time projections from a police scanner – provides the most fitting description of this strategic project. Explaining by way of reference to his performances – and not to Deleuze and Guattari, whom he seems to be channelling – why he considers the body to be fascist, Police Band states that the body is

> completely organized, and if you abuse it, it beats you. It's incredibly oppressive and then when you start trying to control it, you start looking for others to control … Schizophrenia is a solution, of course, because it allows you to jump back and forth from position to position without any sense of self. Hopefully one position will click. It's like the scanner. I tell you, you should look at this piece of equipment. It just bounces back and forth until it finds something to signal into and it just stops if there's information coming over that wavelength. So, in effect, my act's quite schizophrenic. (65)

The "Schizo-Culture" issue of *Semiotext(e)*, and the Semiotext(e) project in general, was about finding such frequencies. Jumping back and forth from position to position in search of moments that clicked. These were its conversations, its expressions of the common, and it is in this sense that "downtown" New York provided a more fitting home for French theory than Columbia – organized to create critic/controllers – ever could at the time. Rather than being some form of trick orchestrated by the layout of the journal, conversation conveys an important pedagogical lesson about French theory. Semiotext(e) purposively threw aside academic conventions like introductions and footnotes because theory did not belong in the classroom as such; it was there to use, not to study (and it was everywhere).

Semiotext(e) could not continue to reproduce the "Schizo-Culture" issue, whose 2,000 copies sold out within three weeks. The rapid sellout, alongside Semiotext(e)'s staging of the Nova convention in 1978 (which drew in thousands to celebrate Burroughs's career and, with its readings by Acker, Burroughs, Cage, Ginsberg, Giorno, Gysin, Sanders, and "post-punk" performances by the

B-52s, the Jerks with Lydia Lunch, Patti Smith, Teenage Jesus, and Frank Zappa,[27] made the *Village Voice*'s list of top events in the year in review), was an indication that Semiotext(e) had found its, or become a, public. What good was this constellation, however, if closed? The point of the project was to remain a step ahead, as illustrated by the protestor on the inside cover of the *"Anti-Oedipus"* issue: if the rock was not being launched at the oncoming police, but somewhere beyond, into the depths of the texts yet to come, Semiotext(e) was directed towards an outside and could not repeat the "Schizo-Culture" issue by printing its promised sequel. Semiotext(e) would begin the eighties with an issue devoted to the Italian autonomists (like Schizo-Culture, which was staged months after the end of the sixties, the issue was released just after the Italian movement's "leaders" were rounded up by the Italian government, effectively putting an end to the phenomenon), and would continue in different directions from there as the journal was passed through a series of editors and collectives.[28]

Just as Deleuze and Guattari argue that "May '68 did not take place," the same can be said about Schizo-Culture, or, more generally, the American invention called French post-structuralism. Deleuze and Guattari argue that "there is always one part of the event that is irreducible to any social determinism, or to causal chains," and that this irreducibility "is an opening onto the possible," which can never be outdated ("May '68" 233). What this particular arrival of French post-structuralist theory in America has to offer, in contradistinction to the theorists who, with the exception of Derrida, introduced structuralism to America at the Johns Hopkins conference in 1966, is an impulse towards perpetual connections and possibilities and a refusal of circumscription. This is what led Deleuze to comment on "the superiority of Anglo-American literature," an anti-tradition within which he recognized a constant revelation of ruptures, impulses towards flight and becoming, and relationships with various outsides (Deleuze and Parnet 36–7). If Fredric Jameson's Marxist method is to tease out the dialectical impulse towards utopia *within* cultural works, Deleuze

---

27  Keith Richards was a no-show, nabbed in Canada for possession of marijuana.

28  Chris Kraus's semi-fictionalized rendering of Lotringer's curatorial work is worth noting here. In *Torpor*, Kraus describes how Lotringer and his friends had boiled the movement from underground to mainstream down to a calculus, including the ideal number of books to produce independently before switching to a major publisher, leaving obscure material for critics to discover after the initial round of hype, thereby extending one's life in the limelight (166). Considered in this light, Semiotext(e) emerges as a calculated business venture: it is an independent publishing project with an intriguing back catalogue that was picked up by a major university press.

and Guattari's suggestion, one that is shared by their French contemporaries and that also mirrors Burroughs's cut-ups, Acker's plagiarism, Cage's mesostics, and so on, is experimentation and rhizomatics: to forge connections with an outside because "when one writes, the only question is which other machine the literary machine can be plugged into, must be plugged into in order to work" (Deleuze and Guattari *A Thousand Plateaus* 4). Because Lotringer, with Semiotext(e), opted for a similar approach – juxtaposing texts without meta-commentary or editorial notes in order to stage cultural interventions – his project provides us with a unique perspective on the convergence of French theory and American art.

## Conclusion: Foreign Agents and Time Bombs

Although the fact of a text's translation has historically been buried – the name of a translator tucked away in smaller font on a title page, relegated to endnotes, or omitted entirely – translation not only extends the reach of a text by plugging it into new networks, but it gives a text a new life and meaning via these networks. This is why André Lefevere calls translation "rewriting." In this conception of translation, Lefevere includes not only the explicit translation of a text but also the writing of literary criticism and literary history, the editing of texts, and the compilation of anthologies ("Translation and Canon Formation" 138). While Lotringer enlisted translators to do the work of moving French thought into the English language, not unlike the work of the editors of academic books and journals discussing "structuralist controversies" and "post-structuralism," Lotringer's work as the editor of an independent press rewrote French philosophical texts into new networks that changed their meaning.

While networks change meanings, networks themselves change, and that was particularly true of Semiotext(e). As Semiotext(e)'s initial appeal for a materialist semiotics made clear, there are always many more matters at play than structure ever allows. It seems, at first blush, a stretch to argue that Semiotext(e)'s early dabblings in semiotics have a lot to do with Semiotext(e) today (or the subsequent runs of journals and series that came out under the banner over the course of more than forty years), but a significant seed was planted there. Rather than rooting itself into any given scene, Semiotext(e) persisted in pursuing and emphasizing the outgrowths birthed of resonant recombinations. (Indeed, what can we learn about the fact that *The Coming Insurrection* found its audience among a crowd lapping up volumes on how to start their own Tea Party? This is not just a product of Beck-manufactured hysteria, there is resonance between the European Left and the American Right. Semiotext(e) will run with the profits.)

Just as Semiotext(e) took flight from the university, it did not restrict itself to an obsessive love affair with French theory, nor did it fixate upon the Schizo-Culture event. Crucial for the movement of the project was not to remain entrapped within a particular domain, field, or regime. Rather than aiming for fidelity to a circumscribed set of writings, the project lays itself out as a grounds upon which different kinds of writing can mix, and rather than subjecting one side of the equation to directives from the other (French theory to analyse American writing), Semiotext(e) encourages that which occurs *between the two*. As opposed to questions and objections, which restrict movement, Deleuze likens conversation to "the wasp AND the orchid," rendering the "AND" in caps because it is the "and" itself (and not the "wasp" or the "orchid") that designates conversation. Conversation is not about something that is in one or the other, Deleuze explains, "even if it ha[s] to be exchanged, be mingled, but something which is between the two, outside the two, and which flows in another direction" (Deleuze and Parnet 7). It is an "a-parallel evolution" (7), which is to say that it is not an averaging out but a synthesis that drives between the elements connected as an absolute force or speed; it is absolute movement. Semiotext(e) was neither "French theory," as it was in France (French theory was an American invention), nor was it "downtown" New York (also an American invention, a retroactive designator for an explosion of cultural production in New York's Lower East Side): Semiotext(e) was what happened between the two.

But this "between the two" should not only be considered spatially – each issue of *Semiotext(e)* as the manifestation of the conversation between French theory and American writing – because there is an important temporal dimension to conversation. I do not simply mean to redraw attention to the difficulties that arose when trying to translate French presentations into English on the fly at the Schizo-Culture conference, but also to those things that occurred between Semiotext(e)'s events and its issues. For this reason, in between my discussion of the Schizo-Culture conference and the post-conference journal issues I inserted an interlude, recounting Deleuze and Guattari's post-conference road trip with Jean-Jacques Lebel. Semiotext(e) is an instructive set of constellations, each issue and event bringing intensive points together, but there are also lines of flight. The road trip westward from the conference – through Kerouac, Dylan, Ginsberg, Smith, McLure, Ferlinghetti – is one such line, another constellation (some of the points reappearing in different constellations in Deleuze and Parnet's *Dialogues II* and Deleuze and Guattari's "Rhizome"). There is a becoming-American writing of French theory and a becoming-French theory of American writing: Burroughs, Cage, Dylan, and Smith help Deleuze and Guattari to articulate their concept of the rhizome, becoming a part of it over the course of the eighties, and "theory" becomes increasingly popular downtown, inflecting downtown writing.[29]

And yet we should not restrict consideration of the temporal dimension of this conversation to exchanges that occur between Semiotext(e)'s events and issues because that would be to say that past conversations are closed, their final words already spoken. Consider Lotringer's reference to Semiotext(e)'s Foreign Agents series – a series of little black books by French theorists that were released over the course of the '80s and '90s – as "cumulative time bombs" because it often took as long as a decade for these names to catch (Deleuze and Guattari being a prime example) after he introduced them, in translation, to a North American audience ("My 80's"). The same can be said of the entire Semiotext(e) project. While the communities that Lotringer imagined did not materialize at the Schizo Culture event, the juxtapositions and constellations inscribed in the journals remain suspended. How might we make use, today, of the suggestive relations that Lotringer has forged? How, for that matter, might we push past these suggestions, and invent new association lines, mixed in with our own understanding of "failed" ones? Translation is not only the work of the translator, but it is also the work of the editor (and event curator), and it is the work of literary critics and historians. What is the potential of French theory? This will be an ongoing conversation.

---

29  For accounts and theory's inflection of New York's downtown literary scene in the 1980s, see, Stosuy 94, 98, and Siegle 138–9.

# Conclusion:
# Disseminating Foreign Principles

It should not be difficult, in the contemporary geopolitical and economic climate, to think about the translative work that is generated by association. In October 2017, Donald Trump's campaign manager, Paul Manafort, and fellow campaign official Rick Gates were indicted as part of Robert Mueller's investigation into Russian interference in the 2016 American election. Amidst charges including tax fraud and conspiracy, Manafort and Gates stand accused of acting as agents for a foreign interest without registering with the Department of Justice, as per the Foreign Agents Registration Act (FARA). Largely ignored over the course of its eighty-year history, FARA requires the labelling of political propaganda being circulated in the United States. To be a foreign agent is to act as an agent for the "disseminat[ion]" of "foreign principles" (Foreign Agents Registration Act). Manafort and Gates are connected, via lobbying firms, with the campaign of the former, pro-Russian president of Ukraine, Viktor Yanukovych.[1] The indictments are part of an investigation that is meant to trace the associations by which foreign interests may have been introduced into the American political landscape. The impetus behind the Russia probe is that associations can translate the outcome of an election, or the tenor of a presidency. While the probe has made headlines, government policy has long been the property of lobbyists and campaign donors.[2]

---

1 According to the indictment, they planted talking points in the conservative media, recruiting bloggers and suggesting tweets in the lead-up to the 2012 Ukranian parliamentary elections. See Savage; Gray.
2 See Long; Janetsky. Consider, as well, the American Legislative Exchange Council (ALEC), a pay-to-play forum whereby representatives from the private sector work with conservative state legislators to draft legislation. Annually, about 1,000 ALEC-crafted bills are introduced in state legislatures across the country, and about two hundred become law. See Greeley.

Semiotext(e) disclosed the fact that it was disseminating foreign principles on the front covers of the little black books that it employed to distribute theory in the 1980s and 1990s: the covers were dressed in fine print from FARA. Irrespective of whether or not Semiotext(e), Lotringer, or any of the theorists ferried were officially registered with FARA, the covers registered that the publication of these texts amounted to the dissemination of a kind of political propaganda that might, as per FARA, exert undue influence on the American government, or the American public. Significantly, while Semiotext(e) was acting as a distributor of these foreign philosophers, as per the series title, it was the philosophers themselves who were acting as "foreign agents." French theorists have been disseminating foreign principles in America since the mid-1960s. Via the roster of agents compiled by Semiotext(e), "theory" became part of New York's downtown scene. More dramatically, in the university, "post-structuralism" instigated decades-long wars.

While translation generally implies the study of temporal and spatial disjuncture – making note of the lag between distribution and uptake, Lotringer labelled his little black books time bombs – my interest in this book was to trace the associations, and to track the circulation of influence, implied by a much more interconnected landscape. A large part of my argument has hinged on the fact of globalization, and particularly global revolt, as an important context for these '68 era texts, interventions, and publishing projects. While discussion of French theory in the context of May '68 is by no means revelatory, May '68 is itself a shorthand that reduces decades of politics to a month of mayhem, and a complex network of not just inter-state, but extra-state geopolitical relations – networked by the postwar development and use of new communications technologies – to a showdown between a student-worker alliance and Charles de Gaulle. While opposition between the student-worker alliance and the French state is indispensible to understanding a number of the issues that were at play in an indelible and crucial local context, that context is likewise inseparable from a number of other international struggles, including – following Daniel Cohn-Bendit and the March 22nd movement – opposition to the Vietnam War and inspiration from the Berkeley Free Speech Movement and the revolt at Columbia University.

When we follow these association lines, what we find is that French theorists were agents of foreign principles before they even crossed the ocean. As Deleuze and Guattari say, each of us is many. Icons they may be, but the ideas disseminated by French philosophers are not proper to them. In them we see Martin Luther King Jr, Columbia, UAW/MF, affinity groups, Weatherman, George Jackson, national liberation, gay liberation, women's liberation, the underground press – the list goes on. The rhizome is a network of complexly enfolded philosophical concepts and underground movements. By thinking about translation associatively – by thinking not only of rhizomes, but also of folds, events, transcreation, relays, and conversation – we overcome our tendency to think iconically (and, in the case of French theory, we begin to collect the foreign principles, incommensurable with the principles and policies of established governments of the day, that circulated during the global '68 years).

In the end, we will never be done with the translation of theory. The notion of untranslatability developed and deployed by Barbara Cassin, Emily Apter, and Jacques Lezra does not speak to the impossibility of translation, but to a proliferation of speech due to the incommensurability of a lexicon with the tenor of a concept. To borrow Cassin's dictum on the untranslatable, theory will "never sto[p] being (not) translated" ("Translating the Untranslatable").[3] As we continue to probe theory, we will perpetually be able to dig to find layers of complexity, including those principles that theory, by association, was working to transmit. And what of our own agency in this untranslatable process? Following Derrida, we must continue to think about how to admit others into philosophical discussion without assimilating or mastering difference. Following Deleuze and Guattari, if we find something useful that can help us plug into an outside, then we should take it and run. Or, as per the lessons of Foucault, we might think strategically about running interference through the system while all the while wearing a mask of objectivity. Such, after all, is the nature of politics. And such is the work of translation.

---

3 While Cassin's growing *Dictionary of Untranslatables* is testament to the fact that this is perhaps true of many philosophical movements and concepts, these thinkers whom we have designated as post-structuralist, indicating a resistance to closed systems, hold their own work to the same standard, meaning that their philosophical work is particularly mutable. Derrida does not only undermine the structural integrity of systems but insists that deconstruction "doesn't consist in a set of theorems, axioms, tools, rules, techniques, [or] methods" ("'As if I Were Dead'" 218). Deleuze and Guattari adopt a "read it in whatever order you want, each of us is many" theory as a toolkit approach to their production of mobile concepts. And Foucault's interests are strategic, not systemic: rather than instituting new knowledges, his goal is to upset ways of knowing. Following Cassin's definition that the untranslatable is that which will "never sto[p] being (not) translated," we might say that, in 1968 – as per chapter 2, in particular – to pursue the untranslatable was to transcreatively pursue liberation in all of its forms.

# Works Cited

"Abortion." *RAT Subterranean News*, 20 Mar.–4 Apr. 1970, p. 13.

Acker, Kathy. *Blood and Guts in High School*. Grove, 1978.

– "Devoured by Myths." Interview by Sylvère Lotringer. *Hannibal Lecter, My Father*, edited by Sylvère Lotringer, Semiotext(e), 1991, pp. 1–25.

– *Don Quixote*. Grove, 1986.

"Affinity Groups." *Weatherman*, edited by Harold Jacobs, Ramparts, 1970, pp. 452–5.

Alexander, Michelle. *The New Jim Crow: Mass Incarceration in the Age of Color-blindness*. New P, 2010.

Allyn, David. *Make Love, Not War: The Sexual Revolution – An Unfettered History*. Routledge, 2001.

Alpert, Jane. *Growing Up Underground*. William Morrow, 1981.

Althusser, Louis. *Lenin and Philosophy and Other Essays*. Translated by Ben Brewster, Monthly Review P, 1971.

Álvirez, Román, and M. Carmen-África Vidal, editors. *Translation, Power, Subversion*. Multilingual Matters, 1996.

American Civil Liberties Union. *War Comes Home: The Excessive Militarization of American Policing*. ACLU Foundation, 2014.

Apter, Emily. *Against World Literature: The Politics of Untranslatability*. Verso, 2013.

– *Continental Drift: From National Characters to Virtual Subjects*. U of Chicago P, 1999.

– *The Translation Zone: A New Comparative Literature*. Princeton UP, 2006.

"Are Doctors Pigs." *RAT Subterranean News*, 5–19 June 1970, p. 12.

Armstrong, Gregory. Preface. *Blood in My Eye*, by George Jackson, Bantam, 1972, pp. xi–xix.

Artières, Philippe. "Archives of a Collective Action." *Michel Foucault: une journée particulière*, edited by Alain Jaubert, Ædelsa, 2004, pp. 44–51.

Artières, Philippe, Laurent Quéro, and Michelle Zancarini-Fournel, editors. *Le Groupe d'information sur les prisons: archives d'une lutte, 1970–1972*. Éditions de L'IMEC, 2003.

Attridge, Derek. *Reading and Responsibility: Deconstruction's Traces*. Edinburgh UP, 2010.

Avorn, Jerry L. et al. *Up against the Ivy Wall: A History of the Columbia Crisis*. Atheneum, 1968.

Bailey, Beth. "Prescribing the Pill: Politics, Culture, and the Sexual Revolution in America's Heartland." *Journal of Social History*, vol. 30, no. 4, 1997, pp. 827–56.

"Bail Fund." *RAT Subterranean News*, 17 Dec. 1970–6 Jan. 1971, pp. 8+.

Baring, Edward. *The Young Derrida and French Philosophy, 1945–1968*. Cambridge UP, 2011.

Barry, Peter. *Beginning Theory: An Introduction to Literary and Cultural Theory*. Manchester UP, 2009.

Barthes, Roland. "The Death of the Author." *Image-Music-Text*. Translated by Stephen Heath, edited by Stephen Heath, Hill and Wang, 1977, pp. 142–8.

Bassnett, Susan. "The Meek or the Mighty: Reappraising the Role of the Translator." *Translation, Power, Subversion*, edited by Román Álvirez and M. Carmen-África Vidal, Multilingual Matters, 1996, pp. 10–24.

Bassnett, Susan, and André Lefevere. *Constructing Cultures: Essays on Literary Translation*. Multilingual Matters, 1998.

Bassnett, Susan, and Harish Trivedi, editors. *Postcolonial Translation: Theory and Practice*. Routledge, 1999.

Bataille, Georges. "Hemingway in Light of Hegel." Translated by Ralph Vitello, "Georges Bataille," special issue of *Semiotext(e)*, vol. 2, no. 2, 1976, pp. 5–14.

Bennett, Jane. *Vibrant Matter: A Political Ecology of Things*. Duke UP, 2010.

Bermann, Sandra, and Michael Wood, editors. *Nation, Language, and the Ethics of Translation*. Princeton UP, 2005.

Bernstein, Charles, Arthur Danto, Richard Foreman, Sylvère Lotringer, and Annette Michelson. "Beyond Sense and Nonsense: Perspectives on the Ontological at 30." *Theatre*, vol. 28, no. 1, 1997, pp. 23–34.

Biebricher, Thomas. "The Practices of Theorists: Habermas and Foucault as Public Intellectuals." *Philosophy and Social Criticism*, vol. 37, no. 6, 2011, pp. 709–34.

Birmingham, John, editor. *Our Time Is Now: Notes from the High School Underground*. Bantam, 1970.

Bizot, Jean-François, editor. *Free Press: Underground and Alternative Publications, 1965–1975*. Universe, 2006.

– *Underground: L'histoire*. Actual/Denoël, 2001.

Blackstock, Nelson. *COINTELPRO: The FBI's Secret War on Political Freedom*. Vintage, 1976.

Bloom, Alexander, and Wini Breines, editors. *"Takin' It to the Streets": A Sixties Reader*. Oxford UP, 2003.

Bloom, Joshua, and Waldo E. Martin, Jr. *Black against Empire: The History and Politics of the Black Panther Party*. U of California P, 2014.

"Blows against the Empire." *RAT Subterannean News*, 3–16 May 1968, p. 4.

Bond, Julian, Norman Dorson, Charles Rembar, and Bobby Seale. *The Trial of Bobby Seale*. Grove, 1970.

Bosteels, Bruno. "Post-Maoism: Badiou and Politics." *Positions*, vol. 13, no. 3, 2005, pp. 575–634.

Bouchard, Donald F., editor. *Language, Counter-Memory Practice: Selected Essays and Interviews by Michel Foucault*. Ithaca, NY: Cornell UP, 1977.

Bourdieu, Pierre. "The Field of Cultural Production, or the Economic World Reversed," *The Field of Cultural Production*. Translated by Richard Nice, edited by Randal Johnson, Columbia UP, 1993, pp. 29–73.

Bourg, Julian. *From Revolution to Ethics: May '68 and Contemporary French Thought*. McGill-Queen's UP, 2007.

Bourges, Hervé. *The Student Revolt: The Activists Speak*. Translated by B.R. Brewster, Panther, 1968.

Bradley, Stefan M. "'Gym Crow Must Go!' Black Student Activism at Columbia University, 1967–1968." *Journal of African American History*, vol. 88, no. 2, 2003, pp. 163–81.

– *Harlem vs. Columbia University: Black Student Power in the Late 1960s*. U of Illinois P, 2009.

Breckman, Warren. "Times of Theory: On Writing the History of French Theory." *Journal of the History of Ideas*, vol. 71, no. 3, 2010, pp. 339–61.

Brich, Cecile. "The Groupe d'information sur les prisons: The Voice of Prisoners? Or Foucault's?" *Foucault Studies*, no. 5, 2008, pp. 26–47.

Brodzki, Bella. *Can These Bones Live? Translation, Survival, and Cultural Memory*. Stanford UP, 2007.

Bromwich, Jonah Engel, and Benjamin Mueller. "Ban on Book about Mass Incarceration Lifted in New Jersey Prisons after A.C.L.U. Protest." *New York Times*, 8 Jan. 2018, https://www.nytimes.com/2018/01/08/nyregion/new-jim-crow-nj-jails .html?_r=0. Accessed 10 Jan. 2018.

Brown, Elaine. "The Significance of the Newspaper of the Black Panther Party." *The Black Panther Intercommunal News Service, 1967–1980*, edited by David Hilliard, Atria, 2007, pp. ix–xi.

– *A Taste of Power: A Black Woman's Story*. Anchor, 1994.

Brown, Timothy Scott. *West Germany and the Global Sixties: The Antiauthoritarian Revolt, 1962–1978*. Cambridge UP, 2013.

Burroughs, William S. *Electronic Revolution*. CreateSpace, 2016.

- "The Limits of Control." "Schizo-Culture I," special issue of *Semiotext(e)*, vol. 3, no. 2, 1978, pp. 38–42.
- *Nova Express: The Restored Text*. Grove, 2014.
- "The Revised Boyscout Manual: Excerpt." *RE/Search 4/5*, by William S. Burroughs, Brion Gysin, and Throbbing Gristle, edited by V. Vale and Andrea Juno, RE/SEARCH Publications, 1982, pp. 5–11.
- "Storm the Reality Studios." *The Underground Reader*, edited by Mel Howard and Thomas King Forçade, Plume, 1972, pp. 32–5.
- *The Ticket That Exploded: The Restored Text*. Grove, 2014.
- "William Burroughs Interview." Interview by Jeff Shero. *RAT Subterranean News*, 4–17 Oct. 1968, pp. 1+, 18–31 Oct. 1968, pp. 12+.
Burroughs, William S., and Brion Gysin. *The Third Mind*. Viking, 1978.
Cage, John, and Daniel Charles. "For the Birds." Translated by Daniel Moshenberg, "Nietzsche's Return," special issue of *Semiotext(e)* , vol. 3, no. 1, 1978, pp. 24–35.
Camp, Jordan T. *Incarcerating the Crisis: Freedom Struggles and the Rise of the Neoliberal State*. U of California P, 2016.
Carmichael, Stokely, and Charles V. Hamilton. *Black Power: The Politics of Liberation in America*. Vintage, 1967.
Casarino, Cesare. "Surplus Common: A Preface." *In Praise of the Common: A Conversation on Philosophy and Politics*, by Cesare Casarino and Antonio Negri, U of Minnesota P, 2008, pp. 1–39.
Cassin, Barbara, editor. *Dictionary of Untranslatables: A Philosophical Lexicon*. Translated by Steven Rendall, Christian Hubert, Jeffrey Mehlman, Nathanael Stein, and Michael Syrotinski, translation edited by Emily Apter, Jacques Lezra, and Michael Wood, Princeton UP, 2014.
- "Translating the Untranslatable: An Interview with Barbara Cassin." Interview by Rebecca L. Walkowitz, *Public Books*, 15 June 2014, http://www.publicbooks.org/translating-the-untranslatable-an-interview-with-barbara-cassin/. Accessed 11 Feb. 2017.
Caws, Peter. "On Self-Reference: Comments on Derrida." *Language and Human Nature: A French-American Philosophers' Dialogue*, edited by Paul Kurtz, Warren H. Green, Inc., pp. 219–21.
Chow, Rey. *The Age of the World Target: Self-Reflexivity in War, Theory, and Comparative Work*. Duke UP, 2006.
Christofferson, Michael Scott. *French Intellectuals against the Left: The Antitotalitarian Moment of the 1970s*. Berghahn Books, 2004.
Churchill, Ward, and Jim Vander Wall. *The COINTELPRO Papers: Documents from the FBI's Secret Wars against Dissent in the United States*. South End Press, 2002.
City Lights Books. Letter to Robert Hurley. 23 Aug. 1976. City Lights Books Records: Additions, 1947– (bulk 1970–1994). University of California, Berkeley, Special Collections, box 21, folder 15.

Clay, Steven, and Rodney Phillips. *A Secret Location on the Lower East Side: Adventures in Writing 1960–1980*. Granary, 1998.

Cleaver, Eldridge. "Affadavit #2: Shoot-Out in Oakland." *Eldridge Cleaver: Post-Prison Writings and Speeches*, edited by Robert Scheer, Random House, 1969, pp. 80–94.

Cleaver, Kathleen Neal. "Women, Power, and Revolution." *Liberation, Imagination, and the Black Panther Party: A New Look at the Panthers and Their Legacy*, edited by Kathleen Cleaver and George Katsiaficas, Routledge, 2001, pp. 123–7.

Cohen, Noam. "A Book Attacking Capitalism Gets Sales Help from a Fox Host." *New York Times*, 14 Mar. 2010, https://www.nytimes.com/2010/03/15/business/media/15tract.html?_r=1. Accessed 5 June 2017.

Cohn-Bendit, Daniel. "Danny the Red: Prohibiting Is Forbidden." Interview. *RAT Subterranean News*, 19 July–1 Aug. 1968, pp. 10+.

Cohn-Bendit, Daniel, and Gabriel Cohn-Bendit. *Obsolete Communism: The Left-Wing Alternative*. Translated by Arnold Pomerans, McGraw-Hill, 1968.

Collins, Patricia Hill, editor. *Black Feminist Thought: Knowledge, Consciousness, and the Politics of Empowerment*. Routledge, 2008.

"Columbia Liberation School." *RAT Subterranean News*, 1–14 June 1968, p. 3.

Comiskey, Andrea. "The Campus Cinematheque: Film Culture at U.S. Universities, 1960–1975." *Post Script: Essays in Film and the Humanities*, vol. 30, no. 2, 2011, pp. 36–52.

"Community Takeover." *RAT Subterranean News*, 1–14 June 1968, p. 7.

Cox Commission. *Crisis at Columbia: Report of the Fact-Finding Commission Appointed to Investigate the Disturbances at Columbia University in April and May 1968*. Vintage, 1968.

Crenshaw, Kimberlé. "Mapping the Margins: Intersectionality, Identity Politics, and Violence against Women of Color." *Stanford Law Review*, vol. 43, 1991, pp. 1241–99.

Cusset, François. *French Theory: How Foucault, Derrida, Deleuze, and Co. Transformed the Intellectual Life of the United States*. Translated by Jeff Fort, U of Minnesota P, 2008.

Davis, Angela Y. Introduction. *The Academic Rebellion in the United States: A Marxist Appraisal*, by Bettina Aptheker, Citadel, 1972, pp. 9–18.

– "Notes for Arguments in Court on the Issue of Self-Representation." *If They Come in the Morning*, edited by Angela Davis, pp. 246–55.

– *Women, Race, and Class*. Vintage, 1983.

Debray, Régis. *Revolution in the Revolution*. Translated by Bobbye Ortiz, Verso, 2017.

Défert, Daniel. "Chronologie." *Dits et écrits I, 1954–1969*, by Michel Foucault, edited by Daniel Défert and François Eswald, Gallimard, 1994, pp. 13–64.

Delanda, Manuel. *Assemblage Theory*. Edinburgh UP, 2016.

– *A New Philosophy of Society: Assemblage Theory and Social Complexity*. Continuum, 2006.

Deleuze, Gilles. *Difference and Repetition*. Translated by Paul Patton, Columbia UP, 1994.

– *Essays Critical and Clinical*. Translated by Daniel W. Smith and Michael A. Greco, U of Minnesota P, 1997.

– *The Fold: Leibniz and the Baraoque*. Translated by Tom Conley, Minnesota UP, 1993.

– *Foucault*. Translated by Seán Hand, U of Minnesota P, 1988.

– "Foucault and Prison." *Two Regines of Madness*. Translated by Ames Hodges and Mike Taormina, edited by David Lapoujade, Semiotext(e), 2006, pp. 272–81.

– "H.M's Letters." *Desert Islands and Other Texts*. Translated by Micheal Taormina, edited by David Lapoujade, Semtiotex(e), 2004, pp. 244–6.

– "Letter to Uno: How Félix and I Worked Together." *Two Regimes of Madness*. Translated by Ames Hodges and Mike Taormina, edited by David Lapoujade, Semiotext(e), 2006, pp. 237–40.

– *The Logic of Sense*. Translated by Mark Lester and Charles Stivale, Columbia UP, 1993.

– *Nietzsche and Philosophy*. Translated by Hugh Tomlinson, Columbia UP, 2006.

– "Nomad Thought." Translated by Jacqueline Wallace, "Nietzsche's Return," special issue of *Semiotext(e)* , vol. 2, no. 1, 1978, pp. 12–21.

– "Nomadic Thought." *Desert Islands and Other Texts. 1953–1974*. Translated by Michael Taormina, Semiotext(e), 2004, pp. 252–61.

– "Postscript on Control Societies." *Negotiations*. Translated by Martin Joughin, Columbia UP, 1995, pp. 177–82.

– Preface. *Dialogues II*, by Gilles Deleuze and Claire Parnet. Translated by Hugh Tomlinson and Barbara Habberjam, New York: Columbia UP, 2002, pp. vii–x.

– "'Responses to a Series of Questions.'" Interview by Arnaud Villani. *Collapse III*, edited by Robin MacKay, Urbanomic, 2012, pp. 39–43.

– "Three Group-Related Problems." Preface. *Psychoanalysis and Transversality*, by Félix Guattari. Translated by Ames Hodges, Semiotext(e), 2015, pp. 7–21.

Deleuze, Gilles, and Claire Parnet. *Dialogues II*. Translated by Hugh Tomlinson and Barbara Habberjam, Columbia UP, 2002.

Deleuze, Gilles, and Félix Guattari. *Anti-Oedipus*. Translated by Robert Hurley, Mark Seem, and Helen R. Lane, U of Minnesota P, 1983.

– "May '68 Did Not Take Place." *Two Regimes of Madness, Texts and Interviews 1975–1995*. Translated by Ames Hodges and Mike Taormina, edited by David Lapoujade, Semiotext(e), 2006, pp. 233–6.

– "On *Anti-Oedipus*." Interview by Catherine Backès-Clément. *Negotiations*. Translated by Martin Joughin, Columbia UP, 1995, pp. 13–24.

– *On the Line*. Translated by John Johnston, Semiotext(e), 1983.

– *A Thousand Plateaus*. Translated by Brian Massumi, U of Minnesota P, 1987.

– *What Is Philosophy?* Translated by Hugh Tomlinson and Graham Burchell, Columbia UP, 1994.

de Man, Paul. *Allegories of Reading: Figural Language in Rousseau, Nietzsche, Rilke, and Proust.* Yale UP, 1979.

Demers, Jason. "Taking Deleuze in the Middle, or, Doing Intellectual History by the Letter." *Trans/acting Culture, Writing, and Memory: Essays in Honour of Barbara Godard*, edited by Eva C. Karpinski, Jennifer Henderson, Ian Sowton, and Ray Ellenwood, Wilfrid Laurier UP, 2013, pp. 211–24.

Derrida, Jacques. "'As if I Were Dead': An Interview with Jacques Derrida." Interview by Ruth Robbins and Julian Wolfreys. *Applying: To Derrida*, edited by John Brannigan, Ruth Robbins, and Julian Wolfreys, Palgrave, 1996, pp. 212–27.

– "Des tours de Babel." *Acts of Religion.* Translated by Joseph F. Graham, edited by Gil Andijar, Routledge, 2002, pp. 104–36.

– *Dissemination.* Translated by Barbara Johnson, U of Chicago P, 1981.

– *The Ear of the Other.* Translated by Peggy Kamuf, U of Nebraska P, 1988.

– *Eyes of the University: Right to Philosophy 2.* Translated by Jan Plug et al., Stanford UP, 2004.

– "The Future of the Profession or the University without Condition (Thanks to the "Humanities," What *Could Take Place* Tomorrow)." *Jacques Derrida and the Humanities: A Critical Reader*, edited by Tom Cohen, Cambridge UP, 2001, pp. 24–57.

– "A Hegelianism without Reserves." "Georges Bataille," special issue of *Semiotext(e)*, vol. 2, no. 2, 1976, pp. 25–55.

– "Is There a Philosophical Language?" *Points …: Interviews, 1974–1994.* Translated by Peggy Kamuf, edited by Elizabeth Weber, Stanford UP, 1995, pp. 216–27.

– "Letter to a Japanese Friend." *Derrida and Différance.* Translated by David Wood and Andrew Benjamin, edited by David Wood and Robert Bernasconi, Northwestern UP, 1988, pp. 1–5.

– "Living On: Borderlines." *Parages.* Translated by James Hulbert, edited by John P. Leavey, Stanford UP, 2011, pp. 103–91.

– "A 'Madness' Must Watch over Thinking." *Points …: Interviews, 1974–1994.* Translated by Peggy Kamuf, edited by Elisabeth Weber, Stanford UP, 1995, pp. 339–64.

– *Margins of Philosophy.* Translated by Alan Bass, U of Chicago P, 1982.

– *Memoires for Paul de Man.* Translated by Cecile Lindsay, Jonathan Culler, Eduardo Cadava, and Peggy Kamuf. Rev. ed., Columbia UP, 1989.

– *Politics of Friendship.* Translated by George Collins, Verso, 1997.

– *Positions.* Translated by Alan Bass, U of Chicago P, 1981.

– "The *Retrait* of Metaphor." *Psyche: Inventions of the Other.* Translated by Peggy Kamuf, edited by Peggy Kamuf and Elizabeth Rottenberg, Stanford UP, 2007, pp. 48–80.

– "Structure, Sign and Play in the Discourse of the Human Sciences." *The Structuralist Controversy: The Languages of Criticism and the Sciences of Man*, edited by Richard Macksey and Euginio Donato, Johns Hopkins UP, 1972, pp. 247–72.

– "Tympan." Preface. *Margins of Philosophy*, by Derrida. Translated by Alan Bass, U of Chicago P, 1982, pp. ix–xxix.

– "What Is a 'Relevant' Translation." *Critical Inquiry*. Translated by Lawrence Venutti, vol. 27, 2001, pp. 174–200.

– *The Work of Mourning*. Translated by Pascale-Anne Brault and Michael Naas, U of Chicago P, 2001.

"Des détenus parlent." *Esprit*, no. 6, 1971, pp. 1282–93.

Doggert, Peter. *There's a Riot Going On: Revolutionaries, Rock Stars, and the Rise and Fall of the '60s*. Canongate, 2007.

Dohrn, Bernadine. "WAR: Weather Report." *RAT Subterranean News*, 5–19 June 1970, p. 4.

Dohrn, Bernadine, Bill Ayers, and Jeff Jones, editors. *Sing a Battle Song: The Revolutionary Poetry, Statements, and Communiqués of the Weather Underground, 1970–1974*. Seven Stories, 2006.

Dosse, François. *Gilles Deleuze et Félix Guattari: biographie croisée*. La Découverte, 2007.

– *History of Structuralism*, vol. 2: *The Sign Sets, 1967–Present*. Translated by Deborah Glassman, U of Minnesota P, 1997.

Dreyer, Thorne, Alice Embree, and Richard Croxdale, editors. *Celebrating* The Rag*: Austin's Iconic Underground Newspaper*. Lulu, 2016.

Dutschke, Rudi. "Berlin: A Struggle and a Leader." Interview. Translated by Lee Baxandall, *RAT Subterannean News*, 3–16 May 1968, p. 5.

Eagleton, Terry. *The Function of Criticism: From* The Spectator *to Post-Structuralism*. Verso, 1996.

– *Literary Theory: An Introduction*. U of Minnesota P, 1996.

Eco, Umberto. *The Role of the Reader*. Indiana UP, 1976.

– *A Theory of Semiotics*. Indiana UP, 1979.

Eig, Jonathan. *The Birth of the Pill: How Four Crusaders Reinvented Sex and Launched a Revolution*. Norton, 2014.

Elfenbein, Jessica, Elizabeth Nix, and Thomas Holloway, editors. *Baltimore '68: Riots and Rebirth in an American City*. Temple UP, 2011.

Embree, Alice. "Columbia U: Company Store." *RAT Subterannean News*, 3–16 May 1968, p. 7.

– "The Urban Removal Masquerade." *RAT Subterannean News*, 17–30 May 1968, p. 4.

Eribon, Didier. *Michel Foucault*. Translated by Betsy Wing, Harvard UP, 1991.

Ertel, Emmanuelle. "Derrida on Translation and His (Mis)Reception in America."
    *Trahir*, vol. 2, 2011, pp. 1–16.

Estren, Mark James. *A History of Underground Comics*. Ronin, 1993.

Farber, David. *Chicago '68*. U of Chicago P, 1988.

Farber, Marvin. "On 'Who We Are' as a Philosophical Question: Comments on
    Derrida." *Language and Human Nature: A French-American Philosophers'
    Dialogue*, edited by Paul Kurtz, Warren H. Green, Inc., pp. 215–18.

Feenberg, Andrew, and Jim Freeman. *When Poetry Ruled the Streets: The French May
    Events of 1968*. SUNY P, 2001.

Feldman, Bob. "The King Memorial: Why We Disrupted." *Up against the Wall*,
    22 Apr. 1968, p. 2.

Fenton, David. *Shots: Photographs from the Underground Press*. Liberation News
    Service, 1971.

Ferguson, Kathy. "Becoming Anarchism, Feminism, Indigeneity." *Affinities: A Journal
    of Radical Theory, Culture, and Action*, vol. 5, no. 1, 2011, pp. 96–109.

"The Five Month Run-Around." *RAT Subterannean News*, 3–16 May 1968, p. 9.

Foner, Philip, S., editor. *The Black Panthers Speak*. De Capo Press, 1995.

Forçade, Thomas King. Introduction. *Underground Press Anthology*, edited by
    Thomas King Forçade, Ace Books, 1972, pp. 6–8.

– Introduction. *The Underground Reader*, edited by Mel Howard and Thomas King
    Forçade, Plume, 1972, pp. 1–4.

– editor. *Underground Press Anthology*. Ace Books, 1972.

Foreign Agents Registration Act. Pub.L. 75–583. 52 Stat. 631, 6 Sep. 1938.

Foucault, Michel. *Discipline and Punish: The Birth of the Prison*. Translated by Alan
    Sheridan, Vintage, 1977.

– "The Discourse on Language." *The Archeology of Knowledge*. Translated by A.M.
    Sheridan Smith, Pantheon, 1972, pp. 215–37.

– "The Eye of Power." Interview by Jean-Pierre Barou and Michelle Perrot.
    Translated by Mark Seem, "Schizo-Culture I," special issue of *Semiotext(e)*, vol. 3,
    no. 2, 1978, pp. 6–19.

– *History of Sexuality,* vol. 1, *An Introduction*. Translated by Robert Hurley, Vintage,
    1990.

– "Manifeste du G.I.P." *Dits et écrits I, 1954-1975*. Edited by Daniel Defert, François
    Ewald, and Jacques Lagrange, Gallimard, 2001, pp. 1042–3.

– "Nietzsche, Genealogy, History." *Aesthetics, Method, and Epistemology*. Translated
    by Robert Hurley, edited by James D. Faubion, New Press, 1998, pp. 369–91.

– "On Attica." *Foucault Live: Collected Interviews, 1961–1984*. Translated by John
    Simon, edited by Sylvère Lotringer, Semiotext(e), 1996, pp. 113–21.

– *The Order of Things: An Archeology of the Human Sciences*. Vintage, 1973.

– "Schizo-Culture: Infantile Sexuality." *Foucault Live: Collected Interviews, 1961–1984*. Translated by Lysa Hochroth and John Johnston, edited by Sylvère Lotringer, Semiotext(e), 1996, pp. 154–67.

– "Schizo-Culture: On Prisons and Psychiatry." *Foucault Live: Collected Interviews, 1961–1984*. Translated by Lysa Hochroth and John Johnston, edited by Sylvère Lotringer, Semiotext(e), 1996, pp. 168–80.

– *Society Must Be Defended: Lectures at the Collège de France, 1975–76*. Translated by David Macey, Picador, 2003.

– "Truth Is in the Future." *Foucault Live: Interviews, 1961–1984*. Translated by Lysa Hochroth and John Johnson, edited by Sylvère Lotringer, Semiotext(e), 1996, pp. 298–301.

– "Truth and Power." *Power*. Translated by Robert Hurley, edited by James D. Faubian, New Press, 2000, pp. 111–33.

– "What Is an Author?" *Language, Counter-Memory, Practice: Selected Essays and Interviews*. Translated by Donald F. Bouchard and Sherry Simon, edited by Donald F. Bouchard, Cornell UP, 1977, pp. 113–38.

Foucault, Michel, and Gilles Deleuze. "Intellectuals and Power." *Language, Counter-Memory, Practice: Selected Essays and Interviews*. Translated by Donald F. Bouchard and Sherry Simon, edited by Donald F. Bouchard, Cornell UP, 1977, pp. 205–17.

Fountain, Nigel. *Underground: The London Alternative Press, 1966–74*. Routledge, 1988.

Franklin, Bruce. *From the Movement toward Revolution*. Van Nostrand Reinhold, 1971.

Fraser, Ronald, editor. *1968: A Student Generation in Revolt*. Pantheon, 1988.

"Free Dionne and Joan." *RAT Subterranean News*, 22 May–4 June 1970, p. 4.

Freedom Archives. *Prisons on Fire: George Jackson, Attica, and Black Liberation*. AK Press / Alternative Tentacles, 2002.

Friedan, Betty. *The Feminine Mystique*. Norton, 2013.

– *It Changed My Life: Writings on the Women's Movement*. Harvard UP, 1998.

Friedman, Robert. Introduction. *Up against the Ivy Wall: A History of the Columbia Crisis*, by Jerry L. Avorn and members of the staff of the *Columbia Daily Spectator*, edited by Robert Friedman, Atheneum, 1969, pp. 3–22.

Garcia, Alma M., editor. *Chicana Feminist Thought: The Basic Historical Writings*. Routledge, 1997.

Garvey, Helen, director. *Rebels with a Cause*. Shire Films, 2003.

Genet, Jean. "Angela and Her Brothers." *The Declared Enemy: Texts and Interviews*. Translated by Jeff Fort, edited by Albert Dichy, Stanford UP, 2004, pp. 56–64.

– "Interview with Michèle Manceaux." *The Declared Enemy: Texts and Interviews*. Translated by Jeff Fort, edited by Albert Dichy, Stanford UP, 2004, pp. 42–8.

– Introduction. *Soledad Brother*, by George Jackson. Translated by Richard Howard, Bantam, 1970, pp. 1–8.

– Letter to David Hilliard. No date [1971?]. Stanford University Archives. Letters to David Hilliard and Charles Garry, 1970–2.

– Preface. *L'assassinat de George Jackson*, by Groupe d'informations sur les prisons, Gallimard, 1971, pp. 3–11.

– *Prisoner of Love*. Translated by Barbara Bray, New York Review Books, 2003.

– Untitled letter. *Black Panther Party Intercommunal News Service*. 4 Sep. 1971, p. L.

Gerth, Jeff. "Pigs vs. Panthers." *RAT Subterranean News*, 9–22 Aug. 1968, pp. 3–4.

Gilbert, Ben W., and the staff of the *Washington Post*. *Ten Blocks from the White House: Anatomy of the Washington Riots of 1968*. F.A. Praeger, 1968.

Gilbert, David. *Love and Struggle: My Life in SDS, the Weather Underground, and Beyond*. PM P, 2012.

Gilroy, Paul. *The Black Atlantic: Modernity and Double Consciousness*. Harvard UP, 1993.

Giorno, John. "Grasping at Emptiness." "Schizo-Culture I," special issue of *Semiotext(e)*, vol. 3, no. 2, 1978, pp. 82–94.

GIP (Groupe d'informations sur les prisons). *L'assassinat de George Jackson*. Gallimard, 1971.

– *Cahiers de revendications sortis des prisons lors des récentes révoltes*. n.p., n.d. [c. April 1972].

– *Enquête dans 20 prisons*. Champs Libre, 1971.

– *Le GIP enquête dans une prison-modèle: Fleury-Mérogis*. Champs Libre, 1971.

– *Suicides de prison*. Gallimard, 1972.

Gitlin, Todd. *The Sixties: Years of Hope, Days of Rage*. Bantam, 1989.

"The Glass Cage Must Come Down!" *Black Panther Intercommunal News Service*, 14 Aug. 1971, pp. 10+.

Glessing, Robert J. *The Underground Press in America*. Indiana UP, 1970.

Glissant, Edouard. *Caribbean Discourse*. Translated by J. Michael Dash, UP of Virginia, 1999.

Godard, Barbara. "Deleuze and Translation." *Parallax*, vol. 14, 2000, pp. 56–81.

– "Signs and Events: Deleuze in Translation." *Semiotic Review of Books*, vol. 15, no. 3, 2005, pp. 3–10.

Goodman, Mitchell. *The Movement toward a New America: The Beginnings of a Long Revolution: (A Collage) A What? ...* Alfred A. Knopf, 1970.

Grant, Joanne. *Confrontation on Campus: The Columbia Pattern for the New Protest*. Signet, 1969.

Grauerholz, James. Letter to the Editor. *The Harbinger*, 5 Sep. 2000, http://www.theharbinger.org/xix/000905/editorial.html. Accessed 20 Aug. 2008.

Gray, Rosie. "How the Manafort Indictment Gave Bite to a Toothless Law." *The Atlantic*, 30 Oct. 2017, https://www.theatlantic.com/politics/archive/2017/10/how-the-manafort-indictment-gave-bite-to-a-toothless-law/544448/. Accessed 11 Feb. 2018.

Greeley, Brendan. "ALEC's Secrets Revealed: Corporations Flee." *Bloomberg Businessweek*, 3 May 2012, https://www.bloomberg.com/news/articles/2012-05-03/alecs-secrets-revealed-corporations-flee. Accessed 12 Feb. 2018.

Greenman, Dick. *In a Crisis the Center Falls Out: The Role of Faculty in the Columbia Strike*. Radical Education Project, 1968.

Gregoire, R., and F. Perlman. *Worker-Student Action Committees: France May '68*. Black & Red, 1991.

Gross, Daniel A. "New York Makes It Harder for Inmates to Get Books." *New Yorker*, 9 Jan. 2018, https://www.newyorker.com/books/page-turner/new-york-makes-it-harder-for-inmates-to-get-books. Accessed 11 Jan. 2018.

Guattari, Félix. "The Best Capitalist Drug." Interview by Arno Munster. *Chaosophy*. Translated by Janis Forman, edited by Sylvère Lotringer, Semiotext(e), pp. 209–24.

– "Desire Is Power, Power Is Desire." *Chaosophy: Texts and Interviews, 1972–1977*. Translated by David L. Sweet, Jarred Becker, and Taylor Adkins, edited by Sylvère Lotringer, Semiotext(e), 2009, pp. 282–90.

– "Molecular Revolutions." *Chaosophy: Texts and Interviews, 1972–1977*. Translated by David L. Sweet, Jarred Becker, and Taylor Adkins, edited by Sylvère Lotringer, Semiotext(e), 2009, pp. 275–81.

– "Pour une micro-politique du désir." "Alternatives in Semiotics," special issue of *Semiotext(e)*, vol. 1, no. 1, 1974, pp. 47–62.

– *Psychoanalysis and Transversality: Texts and Interviews, 1955–1971*. Translated by Ames Hodges, Semiotext(e), 2015.

Guy-Sheftal, Beverly. *Words of Fire: An Anthology of African American Feminist Thought*. New P, 1995.

Hall, Stuart. "When Was 'the Post-Colonial'? Thinking at the Limit." *The Post-Colonial Question: Common Skies, Divided Horizons*, edited by Iain Chambers and Lidia Curti, Routledge, 1996, pp. 242–60.

Hannerz, Ulf. "Flows, Boundaries and Hybrids: Keywords in Transnational Anthropology." *Transnational Communities Programme Working Paper Series*, University of Oxford Transnational Communities Programme, 2000, www.transcomm.ox.ac.uk/working%20papers/hannerz.pdf. Accessed 9 June 2017.

Hanrahan, Noelle. "Lethal Censorship." Introduction. *All Things Censored*, by Mumia Abu-Jamal, Seven Stories, 2000, pp. 21–30.

Harris, Olivier. Introduction. *Nova Express: The Restored Text*, edited by Olivier Harris, Grove, 2013, pp. ix–lv.

– Introduction. *The Ticket That Exploded: The Restored Text*, edited by Olivier Harris, Grove, 2014, pp. ix–lv.

Haslam, Jason. *Fitting Sentences: Identity in Nineteenth- and Twentieth-Century Prison Narratives*. U of Toronto P, 2005.

Hayden, Tom. *The Port Huron Statement*. Thunder's Mouth, 2005.

– *The Whole World Was Watching: The Streets of Chicago: 1968*. Panorama West Publishing, 1996.

Heiner, Brady Thomas. "Foucault and the Black Panthers." *City*, vol. 11, no. 3, 2007, pp. 313–56.

Heins, Marjorie, and Leon Gussow. "*La Chinoise* (2 views) or: Who the Hell Does Godard Think He Is and What Does He Think He's Doing." *RAT Subterranean News*, 19–30 Apr. 1968, p. 19.

Helmling, Steven. "Historicizing Derrida." *Postmodern Culture*, vol. 4, no. 3, 1994, DOI: 10.1353/pmc.1994.0041. Accessed 5 May 2016.

Heynan, Nick. "Bending the Bars of Empire from Every Ghetto for Survival: The Black Panther Party's Radical Antihunger Politics of Social Reproduction and Scale." *Annals of the Association of American* Geographers, vol. 99, no. 2, 2009, pp. 406–22.

Hiddleston, Jane. "Jacques Derrida: Colonialism, Philosophy and Autobiography." *Postcolonial Thought in the French Speaking World*, edited by Charles Forsdick and David Murphy, Liverpool UP, 2009, pp. 53–64.

Higgins, Dick. "The Origin of Happening." *American Speech*, vol. 51, nos. 3/4, 1976, pp. 268–71.

Hilliard, David, editor. *The Black Panther Intercommunal News Service, 1967–1980*. Atria, 2007.

Ho Chi Minh. "Declaration of Independence of the Democratic Republic of Viet Nam." *Down with Colonialism!* Verso, 2007, pp. 51–3.

Hoffman, Abbie. *Revolution for the Hell of It*. Thunder's Mouth, 2005.

– *Steal This Book*. Four Walls Eight Windows, 1996.

– "Why We're Going to Chicago." *Telling It Like It Was: The Chicago Riots*, edited by Walter Schneir, Signet, 1969, pp. 11–17.

Hoffman, Marcelo. "Foucault and the 'Lesson' of the Prisoner Support Movement." *New Political Science*, vol. 34, no. 1, 2012, pp. 21–36.

– "Investigations from Marx to Foucault." *Active Intolerance: Michel Foucault, the Prisons Information Group, and the Future of Abolition*, edited by Perry Zurn and Andrew Dilts, Palgrave Macmillan, 2016, pp. 169–85.

Hollier, Denis. "Présentation?" "Georges Bataille," special issue of *Semiotext(e)*, vol. 2, no. 2, 1976, p. 3.

– "Le sujet de la transgression." "Alternatives in Semiotics," special issue of *Semiotext(e)*, vol. 1, no. 1, pp. 75–83.

hooks, bell. *Ain't I a Woman?* South End P, 1981.

– *Feminist Theory: From Margin to Center.* South End P, 1984.

Hopkins, Jerry. *The Hippie Papers: Notes from the Underground Press.* Signet, 1968.

Howard, Mel, and Thomas King Forçade, editors. *The Underground Reader.* Plume, 1972.

Hudson, David L. "Ex-con Fights for Prisoner Rights and Battles Censorship." *American Bar Association Journal*, Oct. 2016, http://www.abajournal.com/ magazine/article/prison_legal_news_wright_profile. Accessed 10 Jan. 2018.

Hull, Akasha, Patricia Bell-Scott, and Barbara Smith, editors. *All the Women Are White, All the Blacks Are Men, but Some of Us Are Brave: Black Women's Studies*, Feminist P, 1993.

Hunter, Ian. "The History of Theory." *Critical Inquiry*, vol. 33, no. 1, 2006, 78–112.

Hurley, Robert. Letter to City Lights Books. July 1976. City Lights Books Records: Additions, 1947– (bulk 1970–94). University of California, Berkeley, Special Collections, box 21, folder 15.

The Invisible Committee. *The Coming Insurrection.* Semiotext(e), 2009.

Jackson, George. "La lutte dans les prisons." *L'assassinat de George Jackson*, edited by GIP, 1971, pp. 13–22.

– "Reflections of George Jackson." *Berkeley Tribe*, 6–22 July 1971, 4+

Jacobs, Harold, editor. *Weatherman.* Ramparts, 1970.

Jabobs, Ron. *The Way the Wind Blew: A History of the Weather Underground.* Verso, 1997.

Jakobson, Roman. "Two Aspects of Language and Two Types of Disturbances." *Selected Writings II*, Mouton, 1971, pp. 239–59.

James, David. "Rock and Roll in Representations of the Invasion of Vietnam." *Representations*, vol. 29, 1990, pp. 78–98.

Jameson, Fredric. *The Political Unconscious: Narrative as a Socially Symbolic Act.* Cornell UP, 1981.

– *The Prison-House of Language: A Critical Account of Structuralism and Russian Formalism.* Princeton UP, 1972.

Janetsky, Megan. "Trump's Top Donors: Where Are They Now?" *OpenSecrets. org: Center for Responsive Politics.* 18 Jan. 2018, https://www.opensecrets.org/ news/2018/01/trump-donors-1-year-later/. Accessed 11 Feb. 2018.

Jennings, Regina. "Why I Joined the Party: An Africana Womanist Reflection." *The Black Panther Party Reconsidered*, edited by Charles E. Jones, Black Classic P, 1998, pp. 257–65.

Jun, N.J. "Deleuze, Derrida, and Anarchism." *Anarchist Studies*, vol. 15, no. 2, 2007, pp. 132–56.

Karlsen, Mads Peter, and Kaspar Villadsen. "Foucault, Maoism, Genealogy: The Influence of Political Militancy in Michel Foucault's Thought." *New Political Science*, vol. 37, no. 1, 2015, pp. 91–117.

"Kathleen." *RAT Subterranean News*, 9–23 Feb. 1970, p. 8.

Katzman, Allan. "Underground Press Syndicate." *East Village Other*, 1–15 July 1966, p. 2.

Keating, Edward M. *Free Huey!* Dell, 1970.

Kempton, Murray. *The Briar Patch: The People of the State of New York v. Lumumba Shakur et al.* E.P. Dutton, 1973.

King, Kenneth. "The Dancing Philosopher." "Nietzsche's Return," special issue of *Semiotext(e)*, vol. 3, no. 1, 1978, p. 22.

King, Martin Luther, Jr. "Beyond Vietnam." *A Call to Conscience: The Landmark Speeches of Dr. Martin Luther King, Jr*, edited by Clayborne Carson and Kris Shepard, Warner Books, 2002, pp. 133–64.

– "Letter from Birmingham Jail." *Testament of Hope: The Essential Writings and Speeches of Martin Luther King, Jr.*, edited by James W. Washington, Harper Collins, 1991, pp. 289–302.

– "The Other America." *The Radical King*, edited by Cornell West, Beacon P, 2015, pp. 235–44.

– "Pilgrimage to Nonviolence." *The Radical King*, edited by Cornell West, Beacon P, 2015, pp. 39–53.

Kioni-Sadiki, Déqui, and Matt Meyer, editors. *Look for Me in the Whirlwind: From the Panther 21 to 21st-Century Revolutions*. PM P, 2017.

Klare, Michael. "IDA: Cold War Think Tank." *RAT Subterannean News*, 3–16 May 1968, p. 15.

Kraus, Chris. *After Kathy Acker: A Literary Biography*. Semiotext(e), 2017.

– *I Love Dick*. Semiotext(e), 2006.

– *Torpor*. Semiotext(e), 2006.

Kraus, Chris, and Sylvère Lotringer. "Introduction: The History of Semiotext(e)." *Hatred of Capitalism*, edited by Chris Kraus and Sylvère Lotringer, Semiotext(e), 2001, pp. 13–21.

Kristeva, Julia. "Four Types of Signifying Practices." "Alternatives in Semiotics," special issue of *Semiotext(e)*, vol. 1, no. 1, 1974, pp. 65–74.

Kumasi. "Panther Politics Cause Major Breakthrough in Prison Censorship." *The Black Panther Intercommunal News Service, 1967–1980*, edited by David Hilliard, Atria, 2007, pp. xviii–xx.

Lacan, Jacques. "The Instance of the Letter in the Unconscious, or Reason since Freud." Translated by Bruce Fink. *Ecrits*, W.W. Norton, 2004, pp. 138–68.

Laing, R.D. Letter to Sylvère Lotringer. 23 May 1977. Papers of Ronald David Laing, University of Glasgow Special Collections, box 262, folder 206.

Lane, Mark. *Chicago Eyewitness*. Astor-Honor, 1968.

Latour, Bruno. *Reassembling the Social: An Introduction to Actor-Network Theory*. Oxford UP, 2005.

Leamer, Laurence. *The Paper Revolutionaries: The Rise of the Underground Press*. Simon and Schuster, 1972.

Lebel, Jean-Jacques. "Burroughs: The Beat Hotel Years." *Naked Lunch @ 50: Anniversary Essays*, edited by Oliver Harris and Ian MacFayden, Southern Illinois UP, 2009, pp. 84–90.

– "A French Diary: At the Barricade." *RAT Subterranean News*, 1–14 June 1968, pp. 3+.

– Letter to Allen Ginsberg. 20 Dec. 1989. Allen Ginsberg Papers, Stanford University Department of Special Collections, box 257, folder 6.

– "Notes on Political Street Theatre, Paris, 1968, 1969." *Drama Review*, vol. 13, no. 4, 1969, pp. 111–18.

– "On the Necessity of Violation." *Drama Review*, vol. 13, no.1, 1968, pp. 89–105.

Leblanc-Ernest, Angela D. "'The Most Qualified Person to Handle the Job': Black Panther Party Women, 1966–1972." *The Black Panther Party Reconsidered*, edited by Charles E. Jones, Black Classic P, 1998, pp. 305–34.

Lefebvre, Henri. *The Explosion: Marxism and the French Upheaval*. Translated by Alfred Ehrenfeld, Monthly Review P, 1969.

Lefevere, André. *Translating Literature: Practice and Theory in a Comparative Literature Context*. Modern Language Association, 1992.

– "Translation and Canon Formation: Nine Decades of Drama in the United States." *Translation, Power, Subversion*, edited by Román Álvirez and M. Carmen-África Vidal, Multilingual Matters, 1996, pp. 138–55.

– *Translation, Rewriting, and the Manipulation of Literary Fame*. Routledge, 1992.

Lefevere, André, and Susan Bassnett. "Introduction: Proust's Grandmother and the Thousand and One Nights: The 'Cultural Turn' in Translation Studies." *Translation, History, and Culture*, edited by André Lefevere and Susan Bassnett, Pinter, 1990, pp. 1–13.

Leigh, James. "Free Nietzsche." Introduction. "Nietzsche's Return," special issue of *Semiotext(e)*, vol. 3, no. 1, 1978, pp. 4–6.

Lentricchia, Frank. *After the New Criticism*. U of Chicago P, 1980.

Lepper, Marcel. "'Ce qui restera …, c'est un style.' Eine institutionengeschichtliche Projektskizze (1960–1989)." *Jenseits des Poststrukturalismus? Eine Sondierung*, edited by Marcel Lepper, Steffen Siegel, and Sophie Wennerscheid, Peter Lang, 2005, pp. 51–75.

Lévi-Strauss, Claude. *The Elementary Structures of Kinship*. Translated by James Harle Bell, John Richard von Sturmer, and Rodney Needham, Beacon P, 1969.

Levine, Mark L., George C. McNamee, and Daniel Greenberg. *The Tales of Hoffman*. Bantam, 1970.

Lewis, Philip E. "The Measure of Translation Effects." *Difference in Translation*, edited by Joseph F. Graham, Cornell UP, 1985, pp. 31–62.

Lezra, Jacques. *Untranslating Machines: A Genealogy for the Ends of Global Thought*. Rowman and Littlefield, 2017.

Lionnet, Françoise. *Autobiographical Voices: Race, Gender, Self-Portraiture*. Cornell UP, 1989.

Lionnet, Françoise, and Shu-mei Shih. "The Creolization of Theory." Introduction, *The Creolization of Theory*, edited by Françoise Lionnet and Shu-mei Shih, Duke UP, 2011, pp. 1–33.

– "Introduction: Thinking through the Minor, Transnationally." *Minor Transnationalism*, by Françoise Lionnet and Shu-mei Shih, Duke UP, 2005, pp. 1–23.

Lipsitz, George. "Who'll Stop the Rain? Youth Culture, Rock 'n' Roll, and Social Crises." *The Sixties: From Memory to History*, edited by David Farber, U of North Carolina P, 1994, pp. 206–34.

Long, Heather. "Private Prison Stocks Up 100% since Trump's Win." *CNN Money*, 24 Feb. 2017, http://money.cnn.com/2017/02/24/investing/private-prison-stocks-soar-trump/index.html. Accessed 11 Feb. 2018.

Lotringer, Sylvère. "Agent de l'étranger (foreign agent)." Interview with Rainer Ganahl, *Imported: A Reading Seminar*, edited by Rainer Ganahl, Semiotext(e), 1998, pp. 211–20.

– "Agents de l'étranger: *Semiotext(e)* à la découverte de son Amérique." *La revue des revues: histoire et actualité des revues*, no. 34, 2003, pp. 77–97.

– editor. "Alternatives in Semiotics," special issue of *Semiotext(e)*, vol. 1, no. 1, 1974.

– editor. "*Anti-Oedipus:* From Psychoanalysis to Schizopolitics," special issue of *Semiotext(e)*, vol. 2, no. 3, 1977.

– "Doing Theory." *French Theory in America*, edited by Sande Cohen and Sylvère Lotringer, Routledge, 2001, pp. 125–62.

– editor. *Foucault Live: Collected Interviews, 1961–1984*. Semiotext(e), 1996.

– "La politique des restes." "Alternatives in Semiotics," special issue of *Semiotext(e)*, vol. 1, no. 1, 1974, pp. 29–43.

– Letter to Allen Ginsberg. 3 Dec. 1977. Allen Ginsberg Papers, Department of Special Collections, Stanford University, box 140, folder 7.

– Letter to R.D. Laing. 18 May 1977. Papers of Ronald David Laing, University of Glasgow Special Collections, box 262, folder 207.

– Letter to R.D. Laing. 1 June 1978. Papers of Ronald David Laing, University of Glasgow Special Collections, box 262, folder 208.

– "Libido Unbound: The Politics of Schizophrenia." "*Anti-Oedipus*: From Schizo-analysis to Schizopolitics," special issue of *Semiotext(e)*, vol. 2, no. 3, 1977, pp. 5–10.

– "My 80's: Better Than Life." *Semiotext(e)*. 2003, http://semiotexte.com/?p=121. Accessed 5 June 2017.

–   "Pour une sémiotique matérialiste." "Alternatives in Semiotics," special issue of *Semiotext(e)*, vol. 1, no. 1, 1974, pp. 3–8.

Lyotard, Jean-François. "Enurgumen Capitalism." Translated by James Leigh. "*Anti-Oedipus*: From Schizoanalysis to Schizopolitics," special issue of *Semiotext(e)*, vol. 2, no. 3, 1977, pp. 11–26.

–   "On the Strength of the Weak." Translated by Roger McKeon, "Schizo-Culture I," special issue of *Semiotext(e)*, vol. 3., no. 2, 1978, pp. 204–14.

Macey, David. *The Lives of Michel Foucault: A Biography*. Pantheon, 1993.

Macksey, Richard, and Eugenio Donato. Preface. *The Structuralist Controversy: The Languages of Criticism and the Sciences of Man*, edited by Richard Macksey and Eugenio Donato, Johns Hopkins UP, 1972, pp. xv–xix.

Malcolm X. "Message to the Grassroots." *Malcolm X Speaks: Selected Speeches and Statements*, edited by George Breitman, Merit Publishers, 1965.

Mao, Zedong. "Oppose Book Worship." *Selected Works of Mao Tse-tung,* vol. 6, Kranti Publications, 1990, pp. 28–36.

–   "Preface and Postscript to Rural Surveys" *Selected Works of Mao Tse-tung,* vol. 3, Foreign Language P, 1965, pp. 11–16.

Martin, Bradford S. *The Theatre Is in the Streets: Politics and Public Performance in 60s America*. U of Massachusetts P, 2004.

Matthews, Trayce. "'No One Ever Asks What a Man's Role in the Revolution Is': Gender and the Politics of the Black Panther Party, 1966–1971." *The Black Panther Party Reconsidered*, edited by Charles E. Jones, Black Classic P, 1998, pp. 267–304.

May, Todd. *The Political Philosophy of Poststructuralist Anarchism*. Penn State UP, 1995.

McCarthy, Sen. Eugene J. Introduction. *The Battle for Morningside Heights: Why Students Rebel*, by Roger Kahn, William Morrow, 1970, pp. 11–13.

McLuhan, Marshall. *The Medium Is the Massage*. Penguin, 1967.

–   *War and Peace in the Global Village*. Bantam, 1968.

McMillan, John. *Smoking Typewriters: The Sixties Underground and the Rise of Alternative Media in America*. Oxford UP, 2011.

Metz, Christian. *The Imaginary Signifier: Psychoanalysis and the Cinema*. Translated by Celia Britton, Annwyl Williams, Ben Brewster, and Alfred Guzzetti, Indiana UP, 1986.

Miles, Barry. *William Burroughs: El Hombre Invisible*. Hyperion, 1992.

Miller, J. Abbott. "Quentin Fiore: Massaging the Message." *Eye Magazine*, Autumn 1993, http://www.eyemagazine.com/feature/article/quentin-fiore-massaging-the-message. Accessed 7 Nov. 2017.

Miller, James. *Democracy Is in the Streets: From Port Huron to the Siege of Chicago*. Harvard UP, 1994.

–   *Flowers in the Dustbin: The Rise of Rock and Roll, 1947–1977*. Fireside, 1999.

Millman, Paul. "Aftermath(ematics)." *RAT Subterranean News*, 17–30 May 1968, pp. 5+.

"Modern Midwifery." *Women's LibeRATion*, 11–25 Sep. 1970, p. 23.

Moore, Jon. "The Bust Comes." *RAT Subterranean News*, 3–16 May 1968, p. 10.

Moraga Cherríe, and Gloria Anzaldúa, editors. *This Bridge Called My Back: Writings by Radical Women of Color*. SUNY P, 2015.

Morea, Ben. "Ben Morea: An Interview." Interview by Iain McIntyre. *Up Against the Wall Motherfucker! An Anthology of Rants, Posters, and More*, edited by Homebrew Press, Homebrew Publications, 2007, pp. 15–23.

Morgan, Robin. "Goodbye to All That." *RAT Subterranean News*, 9–23 Feb. 1970, pp. 6–7.

– "The Women's Revolution." Introduction. *Sisterhood Is Powerful: An Anthology of Writings from the Women's Liberation Movement*, edited by Robin Morgan, Vintage, 1970, pp. xiii–xl.

– *The Word of a Woman: Feminist Dispatches 1968–1992*. Norton, 1992.

"Morningside Confidential." *RAT Subterannean News*, 3–16 May 1968, p. 8.

Moynihan, Colin. "Liberating Lipsticks and Lattes." *New York Times*, 15 June 2009, https://www.nytimes.com/2009/06/16/books/16situation.html. Accessed 5 June 2017.

New York Area Venceremos Brigade. "Women in Cuba." *RAT Subterranean News*, 20 Mar.–4 Apr. 1970, p. 12.

– "Women in Cuba ..." *RAT Subterranean News*, 4–18 Apr. 1970, p. 16.

Newman, Saul. "War on the State: Stirner and Deleuze's Anarchism." *Anarchist Library*, 18 Feb. 2009, http://theanarchistlibrary.org/library/saul-newman-war-on-the-state-stirner-and-deleuze-s-anarchism. Accessed 6 Nov. 2017.

Newton, Huey P. *Revolutionary Suicide*. Harcourt Brace Jovanovich, 1973.

Nietzsche, Friedrich. "From *On Truth and Lie in an Extra-Moral Sense*." *The Portable Nietzsche*, edited by Walter Kaufmann, Penguin, 1977, pp. 42–7.

– *The Twilight of the Idols*. Translated by Duncan Large, Oxford UP, 1998.

Niranajana, Tejaswini. *Siting Translation: History, Post-structuralism, and the Colonial Context*. U of California P, 1992.

Orchard, Vivienne. *Jacques Derrida and the Institution of French Philosophy*. Legenda, 2011.

Osayande, Ewuare X. "Word to the Wise: Unpacking the White Privilege of Tim Wise." *AfricaSpeaks.com*, 2010, http://www.africaspeaks.com/reasoning/index.php?topic=7428.0;wap2. Accessed 2 Jan. 2018.

"Out of the Closets into the Streets." *RAT Subterranean News*, 20 Mar.–4 Apr. 1970, p. 10.

Panther 21. "To: Judge Murtagh, From: The Panther 21." *RAT Subterranean News*, 7–21 Mar. 1971, pp. 12+.

Parenti, Christian. *Lockdown America: Police and Prisons in the Age of Crisis.* Verso, 2008.

Patton, Paul. *Deleuzian Concepts: Philosophy, Colonization, Politics.* Stanford UP, 2010.

Paul, Jon, and Charlotte, editors. *Fire! Reports from the Underground Press.* E.P. Dutton, 1970.

Pawlik, Joanna. "Surrealism, Beat Literature and the San Francisco Renaissance." *Literature Compass*, vol. 10, no. 2, 2013, pp. 97–110.

Peck, Abe. *Uncovering the Sixties: The Life and Times of the Underground Press.* Pantheon, 1985.

Peeters, Benoît. *Derrida: A Biography.* Translated by Andrew Brown, Polity, 2010.

Peters, Nancy. Letter to Jean-Jacques Lebel. Aug. 1976. City Lights Books Records: Additions, 1947– (bulk 1970–1994). University of California, Berkeley, Special Collections, box 21, folder 15.

– Letter to Jean-Jacques Lebel. 25 Mar. 1977. City Lights Books Records: Additions, 1947– (bulk 1970–1994). University of California, Berkeley, Special Collections, box 21, folder 15.

Piersol, Wesley C. "Comments on Derrida." *Language and Human Nature: A French-American Philosophers' Dialogue*, edited by Paul Kurtz, Warren H. Green, pp. 222–4.

Police Band. "Antidisestablishment Totalitarianism." Interview with Sylvère Lotringer. "Schizo-Culture I," special issue of *Semiotext(e)*, vol. 3, no. 2, 1978, pp. 64–5.

Popkin, Richard. "Comments on Professor Derrida's Paper." *Language and Human Nature: A French-American Philosophers' Dialogue*, edited by Paul Kurtz, Warren H. Green, pp. 207–14.

Puchner, Martin. *Poetry of the Revolution: Marx Manifestoes and the Avant-Gardes.* Princeton UP, 2005.

Rajchman, John. "Semiotics, Epistemology and Materialism." "Alternatives in Semiotics," special issue of *Semiotext(e)*, vol. 1, no. 1, 1974, pp. 11–27.

The Rat Women. "Women Take Over Rat." *RAT Subterranean News*, 9–23 Feb. 1970, p. 2.

A Rat Worker. "From a Rat." *RAT Subterranean News*, 22 May–4 June 1970, p. 2.

"Revolutionaries Are Unfit Mothers." *RAT Subterranean News*, 20 Mar.–4 Apr. 1970, p. 21.

Richards, William. *Revolt and Reform in Architecture's Academy: Urban Renewal, Race, and the Rise of Design in the Public Interest.* Routledge, 2017.

Risen, Clay. *A Nation on Fire: America in the Wake of the King Assassination.* Wiley, 2009.

Robinson, Andrew. "Why Deleuze (Still) Matters: States, War-Machines and Radical Transformation." *Ceasefire*, 10 Sep. 2010, https://ceasefiremagazine.co.uk/in-theory-deleuze-war-machine/. Accessed 23 Dec. 2017.

Rosenkranz, Patrick. *Rebel Visions: The Underground Comix Revolution, 1963–1975.* Fantagraphics, 2002.

Ross, Kristin. *May '68 and Its Afterlives.* U of Chicago P, 2002.

Roth, Benita. *Separate Roads to Feminism: Black, Chicana, and White Feminist Movements in America's Second Wave.* Cambridge UP, 2003.

Roudiez, Leon S. "In Dubious Battle: Literature vs. Ideology." "Alternatives in Semiotics," special issue of *Semiotext(e)*, vol. 1, no. 1, pp. 87–95.

Rubin, Jerry. *Do It! Scenarios of the Revolution.* Simon and Schuster, 1968.

Rudd, Mark. *Underground: My Life with SDS and the Weathermen.* HarperCollins, 2010.

Ryan, Sheila. "Refugee Revolution." *RAT Subterranean News*, 6–23 Feb. 1970, pp. 18+.

Said, Edward W. "Travelling Theory." *The World, the Text, and the Critic.* Harvard UP, 1983, pp. 226–47.

Salle, Grégory. "Statactivism against the Penal Machinery in the Aftermath of '1968': The Case of the French Groupe d'information sur les prisons." *PArtecipazione e COnflitto: The Open Journal of Sociopolitical Studies*, vol. 7, no. 2, 2014, pp. 221–36.

Sartre, Jean-Paul. "Replies to Structuralism: An Interview with Jean-Paul Sartre." Translated by Robert D'Amico, *Telos*, 1971, pp. 110–17.

Saussure, Ferdinand de. *Course in General Linguistics.* Translated by Roy Harris, Open Court, 1986.

Savage, Charlie. "What It Means: The Indictment of Manafort and Gates." *New York Times*, 30 Oct. 2017, https://www.nytimes.com/2017/10/30/us/politics/special-counsel-indictments.html. Accessed 11 Feb. 2018.

Schnapp, Alain, and Pierre Vidal-Naquet. *The French Student Uprising, November 1967– June 1968: An Analytical Record.* Translated by Maria Jolas, Beacon P, 1971.

Schneir, Walter, editor. *Telling It Like It Was: The Chicago Riots.* Signet, 1969.

Schrift, Alan. "'Is There Such a Thing as 'French Philosophy'? Or Why Do We Read the French So Badly?" *After the Deluge: New Perspectives on the Intellectual and Cultural History of Postwar France*, edited by Julian Bourg, Lexington Books, 2004, pp. 21–47.

Schultz, John. *No One Was Killed: The Democratic National Convention, August 1968.* U of Chicago P, 2009.

Seale, Patrick, and Maurren McConville. *Red Flag / Black Flag: French Revolution 1968.* G.P. Putnam's Sons, 1968.

Shakur, Afeni. "Afeni Shakur of the Panther 21." Interview with Jane Alpert. *RAT Subterranean News*, 6–23 Feb. 1970, pp. 1+.

Shank, Theodore, and Wyley L. Powell. "The Theatre of the Cultural Revolution." *Yale French Studies*, no. 46, 1971, pp. 167–85.

Shelley, Martha. "Making the Revolution." *RAT Subterannean News*, 17 Apr. 1970, p. 24.

Shero, Jeff. "Blockade and Siege." *RAT Subterannean News*, 3–16 May 1968, pp. 3+.

"Shucking with the Times." *RAT Subterannean News*, 3–16 May 1968, p. 6.

Sibertin-Blanc, Guillaume. "The War Machine, the Formula and the Hypothesis: Deleuze and Guattari as Readers of Clausewitz." *Theory and Event*. Translated by Daniel Richter, vol. 13, no. 2, 2010. *Project Muse*, 10.1353/tae.2010.0012. Accessed 23 Dec. 2017.

Siegle, Robert. "Writing Downtown." *The Downtown Book: The New York Art Scene, 1974–1984*, edited by Marvin J. Taylor, Princeton UP, 2006, pp. 131–53.

Simon, Alfred, and William F. Panici. "The Theatre in May." *Yale French Studies*, no. 46, 1971, pp. 139–48.

Simon, Sherry. *Gender in Translation: Cultural Identity and the Politics of Transmission*. Routledge, 1996.

Situationist International and Students at the University of Strassbourg. *On the Poverty of Student Life Considered in Its Economic, Political, Psychological, Sexual, and Particularly Intellectual Aspects with a Modest Proposal for Its Remedy*. Black & Red, 2000.

Sloman, Larry. *Steal This Dream: Abbie Hoffman and the Countercultural Revolution in America*. Doubleday, 1998.

Smith, Howard, and Brian Van Der Horst. "Schizo Culture." *Village Voice*, 10 Nov. 1975, p. 26.

Smith, Neil. *The New Urban Frontier: Gentrification and the Revanchist City*. Routledge, 1996.

Solanis, Valerie. "Scum Manifesto." *Actuel*, no. 4, 1971, pp. 12–17.

Stansill, Peter, and David Zane Mairowitz, editors. *BAMN (By Any Means Necessary): Outlaw Manifestoes and Ephemera, 1965–70*. Penguin, 1971.

Starobinski, Jean. "Pour introduire au colloque." "Les deux Saussures," special issue of *Recherches*, no. 16, 1974, pp. 5–6.

"Statements of Injured Students." *RAT Subterannean News*, 3–16 May 1968, pp. 12+.

Stein, David Lewis. *Living the Revolution: The Yippies in Chicago*. Bobbs-Merrill, 1969.

Stewart, Sean, editor. *On the Ground: An Illustrated Anecdotal History of the Sixties Underground Press in the U.S.* PM P, 2011.

Stiles, Kristine. "Jean-Jacques Lebel's Phoenix and Ash." Introduction. *Jean Jacques Lebel: Works from 1960–1965*, Mayor Gallery, 2003, pp. 3–15.

Stosuy, Brandon, editor. *Up Is Up but So Is Down: New York's Downtown Literary Scene, 1974–1992*. New York UP, 2006.

Stronger, Anna Louise. "Are Women Seizing Power in China." *RAT Subterranean News*, 9–23 Feb. 1970, pp. 28+.

Syrotinski, Michael. *Deconstruction and the Postcolonial: At the Limits of Theory.* Liverpool UP, 2007.

"Tear Down the Walls!" *RAT Subterranean News*, 17 Dec. 1970–6 Jan. 1971, pp. 9+.

Thiher, Gary. "He Not Busy Being Born Is Busy Dying." *RAT Subterranean News*, 7–21 Mar. 1970, p. 2.

Thompson, Becky. "Multiracial Feminism: Recasting the Chronology of Second Wave Feminism." *No Permanent Waves: Recasting Histories of U.S. Feminism*, edited by Nancy A. Hewitt, Rutgers UP, pp. 39–60.

Up Against the Wall Motherfucker. "Affinity Groups." *RAT Subterranean News*, 9–22 Aug. 1968, p. 11.

Valk, Anne M. *Radical Sisters: Second-Wave Feminism and Black Liberation in Washington, D.C.* U of Illinois P, 2010.

Venuti, Lawrence, editor. *Rethinking Translation: Discourse, Subjectivity, Ideology.* Routledge, 1992.

– "Translating Derrida on Translation: Relevance and Disciplinary Resistance." *Yale Journal of Criticism*, vol. 16, no. 2, 2003, pp. 237–62.

– "Translation, Community, Utopia." *The Translation Studies Reader*, edited by Lawrence Venuti, Routledge, 2004, pp. 482–502.

– editor. *The Translation Studies Reader*. Routledge, 2004.

Wachsberger, Ken, Editor. *Insider Histories of the Vietnam Era Underground Press*, Part 1. Michigan State UP, 2011.

– *Insider Histories of the Vietnam Era Underground Press*, Part 2. Michigan State UP, 2012.

Walker, Daniel. *Rights in Conflict: The Violent Confrontation of Demonstrators and Police in the Parks and Streets of Chicago during the Week of the Democratic National Convention of 1968*. Signet, 1968.

"Weather Retort." *RAT Subterranean News*, 5–19 June 1970, p. 5.

Weatherwoman. "Inside the Weather Machine." *RAT Subterranean News*, 9–23 Feb. 1970, pp. 5+.

Welch, Michael. "Counterveillance: How Foucault and the Groupe d'Information sur les Prisons Reversed the Optics." *Theoretical Criminology*, vol. 15, no. 3, 2011, pp. 301–13.

– "Pastoral Power as Penal Resistance: Foucault and the Groupe d'Information sur les Prisons." *Punishment and Society*, vol. 12, no. 1, 2010, pp. 47–63.

West, Cornel. *The American Evasion of Philosophy: A Genealogy of Pragmatism.* U of Wisconsin P, 1989.

White, Edmund. *Genet: A Biography*. Vintage, 1993.

*Who Rules Columbia*. North American Congress on Latin America, 1968.

Wilkerson, Cathy. *Flying Too Close to the Sun: My Life and Times as a Weatherman.* Seven Stories, 2007.

Williams, Raymond. *Marxism and Literature*. Oxford UP, 1977.

"WITCH Documents." *Sisterhood Is Powerful: An Anthology of Writings from the Women's Liberation Movement*, edited by Robin Morgan, Vintage, 1970, pp. 538–53.

Wolf, Jennifer. "Has the Time for Demonstration Passed?" *RAT Subterranean News*, 9–22 Aug. 1968, p. 9.

Wolin, Richard. *The Wind from the East: French Intellectuals, the Cultural Revolution, and the Legacy of the 1960s*. Princeton UP, 2010.

"Women Are the Revolution." *Women's LibeRATion*, 30 Mar.–30 Apr. 1971, pp. 10+.

"Women's Liberation Is a Lesbian Plot." *RAT Subterranean News*, 8–21 May 1970, p. 12.

"Women Unite." *RAT Subterranean News*, 20 Mar.–4 Apr. 1970, p. 16.

Wortham, Simon Morgan. *Counter Institutions: Jacques Derrida and the Question of the Humanities*. Fordham UP, 2006.

"Your National Guard: Riot Control or Nigger Control." *RAT Subterranean News*, 15–28 June 1968, p. 7.

Zurn, Perry. "Publicity and Politics: Foucault, the Prisons Information Group, and the Press." *Radical Philosophy Review*, Online First, 28 May 2014, pp. 1–18.

# Index

# CULTURAL SPACES

Cultural Spaces explores the rapidly changing temporal, spatial, and theoretical boundaries of contemporary cultural studies. Culture has long been understood as the force that defines and delimits societies in fixed spaces. The recent intensification of globalizing processes, however, has meant that it is no longer possible – if it ever was – to imagine the world as a collection of autonomous, monadic spaces, whether these are imagined as localities, nations, regions within nations, or cultures demarcated by region or nation. One of the major challenges of studying contemporary culture is to understand the new relationships of culture to space that are produced today. The aim of this series is to publish bold new analyses and theories of the spaces of culture, as well as investigations of the historical construction of those cultural spaces that have influenced the shape of the contemporary world.

General Editor: Jasmin Habib, University of Waterloo

**Editorial Advisory Board**
Lauren Berlant, University of Chicago
Homi K. Bhabha, Harvard University
Hazel V. Carby, Yale University
Richard Day, Queen's University
Christopher Gittings, University of Western Ontario
Lawrence Grossberg, University of North Carolina
Mark Kingwell, University of Toronto
Heather Murray, University of Toronto
Elspeth Probyn, University of Sydney
Rinaldo Walcott, OISE/University of Toronto

**Books in the Series**

Lightning Source UK Ltd.
Milton Keynes UK
UKHW040111130119
335321UK00008B/438/P